THE VIEW FROM
MOUNT
CALVARY

OTHER WRITINGS BY JOHN PHILLIPS

THE VIEW FROM
MOUNT
CALVARY

24 Portraits of the Cross Throughout Scripture

JOHN PHILLIPS

Kregel
Publications

The View from Mount Calvary: 24 Portraits of the Cross Throughout Scripture

© 2006 by John Phillips

Published by Kregel Publications, a division of Kregel, Inc., P.O. Box 2607, Grand Rapids, MI 49501.

All Scripture quotations are from the King James Version of the Holy Bible.

ISBN 0-8254-3376-2

Printed in the United States of America

06 07 08 09 10 / 5 4 3 2

CONTENTS

Part 5: Portrayal

Part 6: Practical

Part 7: Perennial

Foreword

THE MOST IMPORTANT PERSON IN Scripture is Jesus Christ, our Savior and Lord, and the most important theme about Jesus is His death on the cross for the sins of the world. Without Jesus, the Bible makes no sense; without His atoning death on the cross, the Bible makes no difference. The gospel is gone.

That's why all of us need to walk with the two Emmaus disciples who listened to the Lord teach from Scripture concerning His suffering and glory. Beginning with Moses and all the Prophets, the Lord expounded the Word and made their hearts burn within them. Our Lord's words during that walk had to be the greatest "Bible survey" course ever taught on earth!

But in His grace, the Lord has sent His Spirit to teach His servants the Word and then enable them to teach others. One of His choice servants is my friend John Phillips. I have read his books, and we have preached together in conferences. I have found him to be a man who loves the Savior and magnifies Him as he preaches and teaches the Word.

Not unlike Campbell Morgan and Sidlow Baxter of a previous generation, Dr. Phillips has the rare gift of bringing diverse Scripture passages together so that we see beautiful patterns in Scripture and as a result, better understand "the big picture." Unashamed of the gospel and of the evangelical faith, he boldly proclaims Jesus Christ and magnifies Him as the only Savior of the world. But he goes on to explain what the Cross means to believers in their daily walk with the Lord. Like Paul, he seeks not only to testify to "the gospel of the grace of God" but also to declare "the whole counsel of God."

Reading these pages, I marveled at the depth of insight and the breadth of understanding our Lord has given to His servant. I also gave thanks that Dr. Phillips applies Scripture practically and encourages us to identify with the Cross of Christ and glory in it. This book makes it easier for us both to grow in knowledge as we get to know Christ better and to grow in grace as we love Him more and obey Him.

I highly recommend this book to all who want to draw "near the cross" and be transformed by the Holy Spirit as they receive God's Word and obey it.

—WARREN W. WIERSBE

PREFACE

ALL AGES PAST LOOKED FORWARD to the Cross, for Jesus was the Lamb slain "from the foundation of the world" (Rev. 13:8). And in eternities to come, those yet unborn will look back to the Cross. In the highest heavens they sing, "Worthy is the Lamb that was slain" (Rev. 5:12).

No matter where we are in our biblical reading, we are never very far from the Cross. It looms up before us *prehistorically* as God's answer to human sin, long before the "mystery of iniquity" first raised its head in the universe. It is found *pictorially* in the types and illustrations of the Old Testament. It is set before us *poetically* in the book of Psalms and in Jeremiah's Lamentations. It is presented to us *prophetically* and in awesome detail by many an ancient Hebrew seer. The Gospels are completely overshadowed by Mount Calvary. They show us what the Cross meant to Jesus *personally.* The Epistles apply Calvary truth to us *practically.* The book of Revelation reveals what the Cross means *potentially* for this world where, for now, "sin reigns."

This is essentially a book of devotion. Hopefully, it will help inspire worship by giving us a better understanding of the Cross from eternity to eternity. Ordinary Christians will find thoughts here to deepen their appreciation of the finished work of Christ. Pastors and preachers will find truths here suitable for the Communion service, for Easter, for stirring devotion to Christ.

Come, then, join with me as we lift our eyes to see something at *The View from Mount Calvary*.

This book is designed to take us to Calvary. Joseph Hoskins (1745–1788) puts it like this in the hymn "Behold, Behold the Lamb of God":

> By faith we see Him lifted up, on the cross,
> He drinks for us the bitter cup, on the cross;
> The rocks do rend, the mountains quake,
> While Jesus doth atonement make,
> While Jesus suffers for our sake, on the cross.

PART 1

PREHISTORICAL

Rock of Ages, cleft for me
Let me hide myself in Thee;
Let the water and the blood,
From Thy riven side which flowed,
Be of sin the double cure,
Save from wrath and make me pure.

While I draw this fleeting breath,
When mine eyes shall close in death,
When I soar to worlds unknown,
See Thee on Thy judgment throne;
Rock of Ages, cleft for me
Let me hide myself in Thee.[1]
 —Augustus Toplady (1740–1778)

CHAPTER 1

BEFORE THE FOUNDATION
OF THE WORLD

1. The splendor of the Lord's person (John 17:24)
2. The selection of the Lord's people (Eph. 1:3–5)
3. The scope of the Lord's passion (1 Peter 1:18–20)

THE OPENING SENTENCE OF THE Bible draws our attention to the importance of our planet in the divine scheme of things: "In the beginning God created the heaven *and* the earth" (Gen. 1:1, italics added). Right from the start, our planet is singled out.

The significance of the earth is emphasized by the Holy Spirit through the constant repetition of the word *and* in Genesis 1. This figure of speech (known as a *polysyndeton*) is used to emphasize each and every item mentioned. The *polysyndeton* is a literary device designed to slow us down in our reading and to direct our thoughts more carefully to what is being said. The word *and* occurs about a hundred times in the first chapter of Genesis. Thus, our attention is drawn to the various steps taken by the Creator as He prepared Planet Earth for human habitation.

No details are given in Genesis 1 about the original laying down of the earth's foundations, but it is mentioned numerous times elsewhere (see Matt. 13:35; 25:34; Luke 11:50; John 17:24; Eph. 1:4; Heb. 1:10; 4:3; 9:26; 1 Peter 1:20; Rev. 13:8; 17:8). At some unspecified moment in the past, the Creator put forth His power, and earth's foundations were formed.

The use of the *polysyndeton* continues: "*And* the earth was (became) without form, *and* void; *and* darkness was upon the face of the deep" (Gen. 1:2). The words "without form" translate the Hebrew *tohū vā bohū*. The prophet Isaiah makes direct reference to this Hebrew expression and tells us that the earth was not originally created in such a state (Isa. 45:18). It came to be that way at a later date. The words "empty and void" are believed by many to describe the result of some colossal catastrophe that overtook the planet in prehistoric times.

While the Bible makes reference to various things related to the actual foundation of the world, it is also concerned with three things in the mind of God from *before* the foundation of the world. It is these that we shall consider here.[2] They have to do with God's eternal purposes in redemption, in contrast to His eternal purposes in creation.

1. The splendor of the Lord's person

Father, I will that they also, whom thou hast given me, be with me where I am; that they may behold my glory, which thou hast given me: for thou lovedst me before the foundation of the world. (John 17:24)

This verse takes us back before the beginning of time, matter, and space—back to the vast silences of eternity when the eternal, uncreated, self-existing members of the triune Godhead communed in an atmosphere ablaze with glory, bathed in love, and resplendent in wisdom and in power. The prayer, recorded here, took the Lord's disciples back to scenes beyond their powers of thought, to scenes the Lord Himself remembered well.

The earthly setting was ordinary enough—a dozen men seated

around the tattered remains of a feast in an upper room in Jerusalem. The men were in a state of shock. The Lord had just told them He would be leaving them soon. He was going back home to heaven. Moreover, He knew something they did not know, though He had told them often enough before. The way home would be by way of a Roman cross on Calvary's hill—just down the road.

Even without that knowledge, these men could still hardly concentrate on a word He said. Christ was praying. It was a most significant prayer, a comparatively long prayer. We call it the Lord's high priestly prayer—though as has been said, in John's gospel the Lord's prayers are not so much petitions as conversations between equals.

By this time, the Lord's thoughts were as much over there in heaven as they were down here on earth. He was talking to His Father about His Father's changeless love, a love that had moved Him to bestow upon His Son the glory that had once been His before the foundation of the world.

The men barely comprehended what He was saying. They looked down at the unsightly remains of the meal, still cluttering up the table. They looked over at Him as, with His face raised toward heaven, He was talking with His Father about them. They were used to that kind of thing. They looked at each other, a motley group of very ordinary men. Disbelief was etched on each countenance. Going home? What about them? Why couldn't they go with Him? Had they not given up their homes for Him? They could hardly pay Him any heed as He poured out His soul in earnest conversation with His Father. Thankfully, John, seated next to his Lord, was listening. Later on he would write it all down.

The Lord tells us *where He wants us to be:* ". . . with me," He says, "where I am." He had been with the men where they were. Some of them had known Him for years. Some, like James and John, were related to Him. They had seen His miracles, heard His words. Three of them had seen Him on the Mount of Transfiguration. But they had never seen the unshielded glory that had been His in a past eternity, nor had they seen the land from whence He came. He had left all that behind when He stepped out of that eternity and into time.

He had been born in a cattle shed and had grown up in a despised provincial town. He had visited in the homes of publicans and sinners. His closest companions (no princes of the realm, no gifted orators, no men with earned degrees, no renowned military men) were sneered at by the Jewish establishment who wrote them off as "unlearned and ignorant men" (Acts 4:13). This same establishment dismissed Christ's peerless teaching because He was not the product of their schools. They called Him a "Galilean," and referred to Him as "the carpenter's son." Even the Lord's closest disciples, gazing around that Upper Room, would be hard-pressed to detect any outwardly visible traces of glory about Him. There was an aura of holiness, perhaps, but none of the pomp and splendor of even an earthly prince.

Moreover, opposition from the Sanhedrin had been growing. It was hardly safe anymore for the disciples to appear in public. The disciples doubtless considered Judas a brave man. He was out there somewhere on a philanthropic mission for the Master, seemingly unafraid of Sanhedrin spies and the temple police. Little did they know!

Their brave Judas was safe enough. In his pocket he jingled the thirty silver coins given to him by the Sanhedrin—the price of his soul. He was abroad on errands of Caiaphas not Christ, collecting his quota of men, police, soldiers, and a growing multitude of Jewish riffraff. He would soon lead them all to Gethsemane. At the same time, the Jewish rulers were rounding up a ragtag and bobtail of false witnesses to speed a conviction once the trial of Jesus began. Somewhere down the road soldiers were getting crosses ready. Christ's exodus from this planet was to be both incredibly painful and unbelievably shameful. Soon the Romans, the rabbis, the robbers, and the rabble would be heaping ignominy upon Him.

No wonder Jesus said: "Father, let these men see the other side of all this. Let them be with Me where I am, when once more I don My robes of glory." That is where He wants us to be. And, assuredly, one of these days, there we will be. He arranged it with His Father a long time ago.

John tells us, too, *what He wants us to see:* ". . . that they may behold my glory." Three of the men in that Upper Room had already been given a glimpse of His glory on the Mount of Transfiguration. G. Campbell Morgan took the view that "the transfiguration of Christ was the consummation of His human life, the natural issue of all that had preceded."[3] He wrote, "The life of Jesus was bound to reach this point of transfiguration. It could do no other." He likened the life of Christ to a seed that, to all outward appearances, was devoid of beauty but that, within, held all the colors of the rainbow, awaiting the day when it could blossom forth in breathtaking glory. And he continued, "the transfiguration was effected, not by glory falling upon Him, but by inherent glory flashing forth from within."

There is a glory, however, beyond that seen by Peter, James, and John, the glory that God the Son had with His Father before the foundation of the world. Christ's prayer was that His disciples and all His own, down through the ages, might see *that* glory. It is a glory that dims the lightning, a brightness beyond the brightness of the noonday sun, a glory that dazzles the eyes of the shining seraphim themselves. He thought of the glory He had shared with His Father before the worlds began. It was a glory beyond the brightness of the noonday sun, a glory before which the atomic fires of the sun paled to the feeble flicker of a candle. It was a glory before which the seraphim veiled their faces as they cried His holiness. He wanted these men to see that. He wants us to see that. *That* is the glory that one day we will see.

2. The selection of the Lord's people

> Blessed be the God and Father of our Lord Jesus Christ, . . . he hath chosen us in him before the foundation of the world, that we should be holy and without blame before him in love: having predestinated us unto the adoption of children by Jesus Christ to himself. (Ephesians 1:3–5)

Peter reminds us in his first epistle that election and predestination are both based on God's foreknowledge (1 Peter 1:2). The primary purpose of predestination is to ensure the glorious future destiny

God has in mind for His own, a destiny secured for them before the beginning of time. Paul says much the same thing (Rom. 8:29–30).

The doctrine of election bristles with problems. Simply stated, the major issue is this: Did I choose Him because He chose me or did He choose me because I chose Him? These are questions that may be beyond us for now.

One view is that, in a dateless, timeless past, God chose certain of Adam's race to be the recipients of His grace. In the unfolding ages of time and in due course, those who have been chosen inevitably choose Him. As for the others, the unchosen, they have no choice or chance—a most unsatisfactory proposition. We might well ask, "Why did God choose certain ones? Why did He choose any? Why did He not choose everyone? What kind of a person would it be who, if his house caught on fire, and he had the ability to save all inside, would choose only to save some?"

On the other hand, there is the view that God's choice is conditioned by our choice. A person hears the gospel and, in a certain place and at a certain time as a conscious act of the will, chooses to accept Jesus as Savior and Lord. By virtue of God's foreknowledge, based on our choice of Christ, God makes His choice of us and, indeed, did make it before the foundation of the world. In that case, God's choice is determined by our choice—a proposition that would put us in charge, not God.

Some have taken the view that when God brought other volitional beings into existence He, to that extent, limited His own sovereignty, something He took into account when He decided to act in creation. Not that any such voluntary limiting would in anyway diminish His omniscient wisdom, matchless love, and omnipotent power! For God is always God, as far above the creature, whether human or angelic, as the heavens are high above the earth (Isa. 55:8–13).

The fact remains, however, that before the very foundation of the world, before God stooped down to fashion Adam's clay, before the galaxies burst forth from nothingness, before ever the rustle of an angel's wing disturbed the silence of eternity God chose us!

And He chose us in Christ. And He chose us that we should be holy and without blame. He chose us that forever and ever, beyond all the confines of space and time, we should be before Him in love. And there, indeed, is a mystery beyond all mysteries.

At this point, an illustration might help. Suppose a novice was to play a game of chess with Bobby Fischer, the chess master. The champion has at his disposal countless ways to open and close the game, and all kinds of strategies in between. The novice barely knows how to put the pieces on the board and has only lately learned the kind of moves each piece can make. The pieces are put on the board, and the game begins.

Each player has a measure of sovereignty over the board, and each has the power of choice. Each can make any move he likes, so long as his moves are within the rules of the game.

It takes the chess master a few scant minutes to declare the game over. The novice says, "The game can't be over. There are lots of moves I can still make." The champion says, "Go ahead and make them. The game's over." And, sure enough, in two or three more moves he checkmates the novice.

Now, not once did the chess master interfere with his opponent's power of choice or his right to make the moves he did. The chess master, however, having so much more skill, had greater sovereignty over the board. He did not interfere with his adversary's moves; he simply overruled them.

It is like that in the great chess game of life. We have been endowed with a human will, with a measure of sovereignty over the moves we make. We have freedom to choose and to exercise our will. So, we make our choices, and God makes His. He can checkmate us at will because His sovereignty is so much greater than ours. The wonderful thing is, however, that God really wants us to win. He is eager to show us, day by day, the steps to a holy, happy, and heaven-bound life.

Chosen! Chosen in Him before the foundation of the world! Chosen and predestinated "unto the adoption of children by Jesus Christ to himself" (Eph. 1:4–5). That is what election and predestination are all about. Election is not so much about the salvation of sinners (if at all). It is about the high calling, the magnificent destiny, and the eternal enrichment of God's people. And it all began long, long ago in a past eternity. God has elected and predestinated the saints of the church age to sit with Christ in the heavenlies, above all principalities and powers, thrones and dominions—not only in this world but also in the world to come. Blessed be His name!

All this has already been settled in heaven. God is not restricted by the tenses of time. He is the great I AM (Exod. 3:11–14) and lives in the present tense of time. Jesus, in answering His critics, declared, "Before Abraham was, I am" (John 8:58). He did not say: "Before Abraham was, I was" (although that would have been perfectly true). He said, "Before Abraham was, I am." Since God dwells in the eternal present, it is obvious that the moment He chose us and the moment we chose Him was the very same moment in God's eternal present tense. It was right now. But, from our viewpoint, that moment was "before the foundation of the world" (Eph. 1:4).

3. The scope of the Lord's passion

> Redeemed . . . with the precious blood of Christ, as of a lamb without blemish and without spot: who verily was foreordained before the foundation of the world, but was manifest in these last times for you. (1 Peter 1:18–20)

When God the Father, God the Son, and God the Holy Spirit sat down together in the council chambers of eternity to decide whether or not they should act in creation, one fact was obvious to them. If ever they acted in *creation*, the time would come when they would have to act in *redemption*. And that would mean the Cross. One member of the triune Godhead would need to come to Planet Earth, become a human being, and die for lost humankind. We note *when redemption's plan was conceived*—". . . before the foundation of the world." Calvary was no afterthought with God. It was all thought through before sin ever raised its head in the universe.

We note, too, *what redemption's plan was to cost*—we are "redeemed . . . with the precious blood of Christ." The life that Jesus laid down on the cross of Calvary for our sin was an infinite life, and the blood He shed was of infinite worth. The Holy Spirit Himself calls it "precious blood" (1 Peter 1:19). How great is the guilt and folly of those who shed that blood! How great is the guilt and folly of those who trample on that blood! How great is the worth to God of those who are redeemed by that blood!

We shall never fathom the mystery of it. Before God flung the worlds into space, He took Calvary into account. The three members of the triune Godhead weighed fully, before time began, all the pros and cons, all the pluses and minuses of a creation brought into being at the cost of Calvary. Down came the scales in favor of proceeding with the mighty plan.

We note, too, *whom redemption's plan would concern*—it "was fore-ordained . . . but was manifest in these last times for you." Peter, of course, was an eyewitness of what happened when Christ finally came. Wonder of wonders, we are the focus of it all!

My wife used to have a little music box. When the lid was raised, the contraption played the tune "Raindrops Keep Falling on My Head." You could open the box and see how it all worked. Inside, there was a small brass cylinder. That cylinder had a lot of little spikes sticking up all over it. Along with the cylinder there were a number of prongs. Those prongs produced the various sounds as the rotating spikes struck them.

In a sense, when people looked into that music box, they were looking at the whole tune. It was all pegged out, so to speak. But in order to hear the music and experience it, they would have to wait for the process of time to run its course—for the slow turning of the cylinder, and for all the little spikes to hit all the corresponding prongs. As the cylinder slowly turned, the music was born.

That is how it is with us and with God. God sees the whole plan of redemption. The whole plan, from a past eternity to ages yet unborn, is all pegged out in heaven. We, however, are creatures of time. We have to wait for the slow day-by-day process whereby the timeless purposes of God are worked out in human experience. In the fullness of time, the appropriate spike on God's great cylinder struck the corresponding prong, and the Son of God came down to earth to accomplish our redemption. The cylinder still turns. God's purposes in redemption await events that hinge upon the Lord's coming again (Rom. 8:19–23). But all is well. God's purposes cannot fail. He transcends all time and space.

I was a boy in Britain when World War II broke out. The early days of the war were full of doom and gloom. Our army was drummed out of Europe. German bombers filled the skies, and our survival hung by a thread. The victorious German army threatened us with invasion. Our ships were being sunk faster than they could be replaced. We would listen to the newscasts over the BBC. There seemed no end to the bad news. However, the authorities had one phrase that covered it all. We were told, "Everything is proceeding according to plan." We wondered whose plan it was, and why they didn't get somebody with a better one.

Well, with God all things *are* proceeding according to plan no matter what transpires. Blessed be God, our God!

PART 2

PICTORIAL

Jesus keep me near the Cross:
There a precious fountain,
Free to all, a healing stream,
Flows from Calvary's mountain.

Near the Cross, a trembling soul,
Love and mercy found me;
There the bright and morning
Star sheds its beams around me.

Near the Cross! O Lamb of God,
Bring its scenes before me;
Help me walk from day to day,
With its shadow o'er me.

In the Cross, in the Cross,
Be my glory ever;
Till my raptured soul shall find
Rest beyond the river.[1]
     —Fanny Crosby (1820–1915)

Mount Moriah

Genesis 22:1–24

1. The setting of the great sacrifice (v. 1)
2. The story of the great sacrifice (vv. 2–19)
   a. The place
   b. The plea
   c. The pledge
3. The sequel to the great sacrifice (vv. 20–23)

ANY LIST OF THE TEN MOST important chapters in the Bible should certainly include Genesis 22. Its great value lies in the pictorial foreview it gives us of Calvary.

The New Testament confirms this. We read: "By faith Abraham, when he was tried, offered up Isaac: and he that had received the promises offered up his only begotten son, of whom it was said, that in Isaac shall thy seed be called: accounting that God was able to raise him up, even from the dead; from whence also he received him in a figure" (Heb. 11:17–19). In other words, what happened on Mount Moriah was a divinely painted picture of what would happen eventually on Mount Calvary.

Four words leap out at us from even the most casual reading of the

Abraham story in Hebrew 11:17: "his only begotten son"! The words arrest us and transport us at once to John 3:16, another monumental passage of Scripture.

1. The setting of the great sacrifice

"And it came to pass after these things" (Gen. 22:1) we read. What things? The things in Abraham's life that had produced his grace and growth and the remarkable increase in his knowledge of God, the things that made it possible for him to obey God's call in Genesis 22. Abraham's great faith, which blazed out so gloriously on Mount Moriah, did not appear out of a vacuum. Some eighty years before, God had asked Abraham to give up his father (Gen. 12:1–3). Now, He asked him to give up his son.

The story, as written up in Genesis, tells us how God *discovered* His man. Abraham was a pagan in Ur of the Chaldees. He was wandering through the spiritual darkness of this world, on his way to the endless darkness of the lost. God arrested him and gave him a twofold vision—the vision of a *promised land* down here along with the prospect of becoming a blessing to the nations of the world; and the vision of a *celestial city*, a city with mighty foundations "whose builder and maker is God" (Heb. 11:10), a full description of which is given in Revelation 21:10–22:5.

The story continues with an account of how God *detached* His man. Abraham was to leave his father's house and all his kindred. He was to turn his back on his old way of life and become a pilgrim and a stranger on the earth. Henceforth, he was to live by faith, with his affections set on things above.

Then we see how God *developed* His man. He brought all kinds of experiences into Abraham's life, experiences designed to develop Abraham's faith. Abraham staked his claim to the Promised Land at Bethel but then took an unfortunate excursion into Egypt and ended up a backslider surrounded by perils. Restored to his pilgrim character, he was promised a son by God. Sad to say, however, he tried to produce that promised seed in the energy of the flesh with disastrous results. In a further vision from God, Abraham's territorial claims down here were vastly expanded—they included everything from the Nile to the Euphrates. About this same time, he won a tremendous victory over an invading army from the East.

He was forever giving things up so as to prevent his spiritual life from being impaired. He gave up his life in Babylon, gave up the well-watered plains of Jordan to Lot, gave up the spoils of war, and gave up Hagar and Ishmael. God was developing His man.

Finally, we are told how God *displayed* His man—on Mount Moriah. In effect, God said to Abraham, "I want you, as a human father, to take your only begotten son to a place called Moriah, there to offer him up as a burnt offering. I want you to do this so that the world will be able to comprehend in some measure what it will mean for Me, one day, as a heavenly Father, to take My only begotten Son to a place called Calvary, there to offer Him up for the sins of the world."

We often think what Calvary meant to the Son. What happened on Mount Moriah shows us, in pictorial form, what Calvary meant to the Father.

Genesis 14 begins with the word *and*. We have already seen the significant role the word *and* plays in the story of creation. Here we see that little word at work in the story of redemption. Shortly afterward we read, "*and* Abraham planted a grove in Beersheba, *and* called there on the name of the LORD, the everlasting God. *And* Abraham sojourned in the Philistines' land many days. *And* it came to pass after these things . . ." (Gen. 21:33–22:1).

We are invited to picture Abraham living in the land of the enemy, an enemy occupying territory God had promised to him. God has had Abraham's enemies make peace with him. Abraham's astounding victory over the combined armies of the kings of the East (Gen. 14) had put fear, both of him and his God, into the hearts of all the kingdoms roundabout.

We are invited, also, to see Abraham calling, not just on God—something he had often done before—but on "the name of the LORD, the *everlasting* God" (21:33, italics added). There we have it! The everlasting God! The title that boosted Abraham's faith when he was

facing the greatest trial of his life! It is a title that takes us back beyond
the beginning of time and forward into eternities to come. Abraham's
God was a very great God indeed! "The everlasting God who takes
death in His stride."

The story that follows centers on a place called Moriah. This name
means "foreseen of Jehovah." Everything has been foreseen! The various falls of Satan have all been foreseen. God was not taken by surprise
by Lucifer's fall from the high halls of heaven to what is called "the
heavenlies." It was a fearful fall. It is rendered all the more galling to
Satan now by the fact that today the church sits in power with Christ in
that very sphere. The church challenges all of Satan's principalities and
powers. Satan has already experienced the curbing of his power.

There are further falls ahead, all foreseen by Jehovah. Indeed, Satan
may be "the prince of the power of the air" (Eph. 2:2), but his throne
there is most insecure. He is to be cast out of that realm and down to
the earth one of these days (Rev. 12:7–12). Michael the archangel will
be the one to execute this drastic curtailing of Satan's power. Still later,
he is to be cast into the Abyss (Rev. 20:1–3) and, from the Abyss, into
the lake of fire (Rev. 20:7–10). All this was foreseen by Jehovah, just as
Moriah, which loomed so large in Abraham's life, was foreseen by Jehovah. From beginning to end, the unfolding scenes anticipated Calvary.

2. The story of the great sacrifice

The key to this story is simple—everything was foreseen by Jehovah. He knew right from the start just what Abraham would do, just
what Isaac would do, and just what He, Himself, would do. Nothing
took Him by surprise.

Take for instance a clock. It is first conceived in the mind of an
inventor and laid out in a blueprint. The clock is designed so that the
movement of its hands can keep track of the passing of time. Its hands
move in harmony with the rotation of the earth on its axis. If it is a
sophisticated clock, it might even chime the hours and give the phases
of the moon.

It is possible, however, that the clock's hands might stop moving.

Or they might move too quickly or too slowly. The clock would then cease to perform the function for which it was designed. This possibility, however, was foreseen by the creator of the clock. Consequently, he made provision for it by including in the design a mechanism for rewinding it and for bringing its hands back into adjustment with the correct time.

It is just the same with us. We were created to have fellowship with God and to live in harmony with heaven. The fall of Adam and the resulting chaos was foreseen by Jehovah, as was the Cross, the instrument whereby God brings ruined people back into harmony with His will.

Dark indeed was the word that came to Abraham: "Give Me thy son!" But "behind that frowning providence God hides a smiling face." Thankfully God never allows us to be tested beyond our endurance. And He always has a way of escape ready for us—as Abraham discovered in the end.

We can well imagine that Abraham's soul was in turmoil. Surely God did not want him to slay his son! Not only would it be a crime but also it is contrary to the character of God. Besides, if he slew his son, what would happen to God's own word, "In Isaac shall thy seed be called" (Heb. 11:18)? The light dawned. Of course! He would raise him from the dead. But no one has seen someone raised from the dead. How could it be? All things are possible with God. He is God, Most High. He is the everlasting God, without beginning or ending of days. So, doubtless, the debate ebbed and flowed in Abraham's soul until, at last, he came to the settled conviction, based on a lifetime of experience, that he could trust God no matter what. The Isaac story could not come to a terrible end on some accursed hill. It could not be that he, broken and bereaved, would have to stumble homeward to break the news to Sarah that Isaac was dead. No! It simply had to be that not only was all foreseen by Jehovah but that somehow God would make provision for Abraham in His trusting pilgrim patriarch's most desperate hour of need.

It was thus, too, with our Lord—broken and sobbing, with blood-soaked tears in dark Gethsemane.

a. The place

The place! How it must have haunted Abraham! "Abraham," we read, "rose up early in the morning . . . and went unto *the place*" (Gen. 22:3). "Then on the third day Abraham lifted up his eyes, and saw *the place* afar off" (v. 4). "And they came to *the place* which God had told him of" (v. 9). Then, later, "Abraham called the name of *that place* Jehovah-jireh" (v. 14, all italics added), but by then the ordeal was over, and Abraham would never have to go to that dread place again.

Let us walk awhile with Abraham as he set out with Isaac, with an ass, and with a couple of men. Abraham himself chopped the wood for the fire. Mental pictures of the place would loom up in his mind. He would see, perhaps, a towering crag, its face blasted by lightning and gouged into fearful shapes by tempest, earthquake, and storm.

At other times, maybe, he saw a tortured, twisting path leading down into a gorge in the mountain and ending near some dark cave, a wild beast's lair, where bats and scorpions lurked. And over yonder, a mound suitable for an altar of sacrifice stood by.

Or was it that he saw a gruesome grove amid the peaks where the pagan Canaanites offered up their sons in sacrifice, where hideous Moloch scowled down on little children waiting, little did they know it, to be seared on Moloch's red-hot lap while vultures patrolled the sky, and jackals dug for blackened bones—a place where a million horrendous memories lurked and where the blood of these small children cried aloud from the ground for vengeance.

Now mark this. If the place, now known as Mount Moriah, haunted Abraham's dreams, how much more did that other place, the place called Calvary, intrude into the mind of God. Calvary was ever before Him. His omniscience made it so. The place that tormented Abraham was a mere shadow, cast upon a moment of time, compared with the place foreseen by Jehovah.

Calvary! It towers higher than the Himalayas. The snow-crowned Andes are mere molehills compared with Calvary. With the right skills, with the proper equipment, with courage and determination, men can master mountains such as these. But Calvary! Ah, there is a mountain so vast, so high, that only God can reach its peak.

God gazed out across the ages. Ah! There it was! A hundred billion galaxies might lie between, but they were a woven carpet beneath His feet, no obstacle at all. Ten thousand ages might likewise lie between, but so what? They are but a day or so to God. Calvary! From the moment in a past eternity when it was chosen and foreseen by Jehovah, it was never out of His sight.

In the old days, when the London underground railway issued tickets bearing the names of the various stations it served, there was one route that had a quite unintentional significance. The ticket bore the words "King's Cross to Mansion House." It entitled the passenger to board the train at the King's Cross station and to get off at the Mansion House station. It became a collector's item—a ticket from King's Cross to Mansion House. Of course, one could also buy a ticket to go the other way—Mansion House to King's Cross. For long, long ago, and far, far away, just such a journey was planned. Then the time came. The Lord Jesus came from the mansions of glory to a cross on Calvary's hill—the King's cross, we may well call it now. It is Luke who pinpoints the place and gives it a name—"the place, which is called Calvary" (Luke 23:33). Matthew calls the place "Golgotha" and says it was the "place of a skull" (Matt. 27:33).

But we must go back to Abraham. Again, we have the insistent beat of the *polysyndeton*: "*And* Abraham rose up early in the morning, *and* saddled his ass, *and* took two of his young men with him, *and* Isaac his son, *and* clave the wood for the burnt offering, *and* rose up, *and* went unto the place of which God had told him" (Gen. 22:3, italics added). The relentless "ands" sound like the drumbeats of doom. They herald the dawn's early light. They point to the patient beast awaiting bit and bridle. They call attention to the two witnesses needed to bear testimony to it all. The "ands" make us pause as we read, so that we might appreciate the acquiescence of the son in all of this. They herald, too, the commencement of the pilgrimage.

b. The plea

"They went both of them together," the Holy Spirit says. He says it
twice (Gen. 22:6, 8). There was a perfect understanding between the
father and the son. Isaac was not dragged, protesting, to the appointed
place. He was old enough to have mind and will of his own. The picture would not have been complete had Isaac rebelled. Up in heaven,
no doubt unseen by Abraham and Isaac, Father and Son, likewise,
went both of them together to "the place."

At last, the small caravan came to a stop. There was a point beyond
which the servants could not go. Thus it was in Gethsemane when
Jesus withdrew Himself a stone's cast (the distance of death—the Jews
put people to death by stoning) from His disciples and asked them to
watch and pray. With all the will in the world, Peter, James, and John
could not watch and pray for a short hour or so, still less could they
enter into Christ's agony, as He saw the Cross just up ahead.

Just so with us. There is a point beyond which we cannot go ourselves. There are depths in the sufferings of Christ we can never know.
As the old hymn says:

> But none of the ransomed will ever know,
> How deep were the waters crossed,
> Nor how dark was the night that the Lord passed through
> Ere He found His sheep that was lost.[2]
> —Sankey, "The Ninety and Nine"

When at last we stand on Canaan's shore, when we see the land
from whence He came, and when we see the glory that was His before
time began, we will only find the mystery deepened.

So Abraham called a halt. The wood for the fire was taken from his
servants and given to Isaac. Their load became his. Suddenly, he himself felt its weight, while they went free. The wood, of course, had
been there all the time. Isaac was aware of it. But now, suddenly, it
was to be his burden, his to carry the rest of the way.

Above and beyond, that is the case of our Lord. The Lord Jesus had always known all there was to know about sin. He knew about sin as an omniscient, omnipresent, and omnipotent God knows everything about everything. In Gethsemane, however, everything came into sharper focus. Christ had His first personal experience, His first fore-taste of the unspeakable horror of sin. His instinctive cry was, "Father, if it be possible, let this cup pass from me" (Matt. 26:39). On the cross, it was immeasurably worse. The sins of the whole were suddenly heaped upon Him. Psalm 69 gives us His reaction, anguish, and woe. So does Psalm 22. He who knew no sin was made sin for us. We can never enter into that.

But there was something else. Isaac saw in his father's hands the knife and the fire. The knife spoke of death. The fire spoke of that which, for the sinner, comes after death. To the weight of the wood was now added the menace of the knife and the fire. Isaac spoke. "Where is the lamb?" he cried, "Behold the fire and the wood: but where is the lamb?" (Gen. 22:7). Abraham was ready for the question he knew must come. "My son," he said, in words both simple and sublime, "God will provide himself [to be the] lamb" (v. 8).

Then, perchance, Isaac saw a look upon his father's face that silenced all further speech. It was with a full understanding now that they went on, "both of them together" in holy harmony.

Gethsemane lay behind. Golgotha lay ahead. Both for Abraham and Isaac, and for God—Father and Son.

c. The pledge

Out of eternity and on into time, Father and Son came, in step amid the galaxies, heading for a planet called Earth. Down from the high halls of heaven they came, to a little town called Bethlehem, known among scholars as the place where God would become man. Galilee! Gethsemane! Gabbatha! Golgotha! The Grave! What a woeful way it was—out of the Garden and into the hands of Judas and his gang. On to Annas, Caiaphas, Pilate, and Herod; Father and Son together. The Father saw the Son beaten, bullied, bruised, scourged, and scorned. Then there was the wood—that heavy rough-hewn cross dumped on His torn and bleeding shoulders. On they went through the milling multitudes, the shoving crowds, the air filled with curses and catcalls. Still "both of them together."

So it was with Abraham and Isaac. "*And* they came to the place . . . *and* Abraham built an altar there, *and* laid the wood in order, *and* bound Isaac his son, *and* laid him on the altar upon the wood" (Gen. 22:9). Abraham seized the knife and raised his arm. He steadied himself for the fatal plunge of the knife. Then, God reached out His arm and stayed the blow—thus assuring that He would, indeed, provide Himself to be the Lamb. One day Mount Moriah would have to give way to Mount Calvary. "Jehovah-jireh!" cried Abraham. "The Lord will provide."

3. The sequel to the great sacrifice

Again we read the words: "And it came to pass after these things . . ." (Gen. 22:20). The offering up of Isaac was not the end of the story, just as Calvary was by no means the end of the trail. Passover was followed by Pentecost—and that's another story, a story introduced here in type and shadow by the words "after these things." The grave gave way to glory. God's answer to the Cross was the Resurrection. The Old Testament type foreshadowed it. When Abraham said farewell to his two servants on the way to Mount Moriah, he said: "Abide ye here with the ass; and I and the lad will go yonder and worship, *and come again to you*" (v. 5, italics added). It would seem that, by then, he had settled his own conflict—God would raise Isaac from the dead. The New Testament confirms this (Heb. 11:17–19).

Moses adds a postscript to the story of Mount Moriah. Once again, the *polysyndeton* controls the pace of the narrative: "*And* it came to pass after these things, that it was told Abraham, saying, Behold, Milcah, she hath also born children unto thy brother Nahor . . ." (Gen. 22:20). And so it goes on, until we come to this: "*And* Bethuel begat Rebekah" (v. 23). And that introduces another chapter in the story. The Holy Spirit next records the death of Sarah (a type of passing away of the nation of Israel) and the work of the unnamed servant (a type of the Holy Spirit) in the bringing in of Rebekah to be a bride for Isaac (a glorious type, recorded in detail in Genesis 24, of the coming into its own of the church, the bride of Christ).

In Genesis 22, we have a type for the love of the Father for the Son (v. 2). In Genesis 24, we have one for the love of the Son for His bride (v. 67). These, the first and second mentions of the word *love* in the Bible, give us the key to the eternal purposes of God in regard to the Cross.

Alas! and did my Savior bleed?
And did my sovereign die?
Would He devote that sacred head
For such a worm as I?

Was it for crimes that I have done
He groaned upon the tree?
Amazing pity! Grace unknown!
And love beyond degree?

Well might the sun in darkness hide,
And shut his glories in,
When the incarnate Maker died
For man, His creature's sin.

Thus might I hide my blushing face,
While His dear cross appears;
Dissolve my heart in thankfulness,
And melt my eyes to tears.[1]

—Isaac Watts (1674–1748)

CHAPTER 3

The Sin Offerings

Leviticus 4–6

1. Dealing with the principle of sin (the sin offering)
   a. Guilt finds us out
      (1) The ordained priest
      (2) The organized people
      (3) The officiating prince
      (4) The ordinary person
   b. Grace finds a way
2. Dealing with the practice of sin (the trespass offering)

UNDER THE MOSAIC LAW, FIVE MAJOR offerings were available to the people of God. All five pointed to Calvary. Each one shows a different aspect of the work of Christ on the cross. These offerings were divided into two kinds—the sin offerings and the sweet-savor offerings.

The two sin offerings depict what Calvary means to us; the three sweet-savor offerings reveal what Calvary means to *God*. The sin offerings deal with sin from the standpoint of our *guilt;* the sweet-savor offerings deal with sin from the standpoint of God's *grace*. The sin offerings reveal how the *holiness* of God is satisfied by the work of the Cross; the sweet-savor offerings tell us how the *heart* of God is satisfied by the work of Christ. The sin offerings set before us the *reasons* for the Cross; the sweet-savor offerings portray for us the *results* of the Cross. In the sin offerings, God deals with our *wickedness;* in the sweet-savor offerings, He deals with our *worship.* In the sin offerings, God deals with us as *sinners;* in the sweet-savor offerings, He deals with us as *saints.* In the sin offerings, we learn how *vile* we are; in the sweet-savor offerings, we learn how *virtuous* we now are in Christ.

There were two kinds of sin offerings. Both were designed to bring before us the enormity of our guilt in the sight of God. We tend to take a complacent view of our own sin. God does nothing of the kind. Our sin kindles His wrath on the one side and His compassion on the other.

In the sight of God, our sin is so horrendous and the enormity of our guilt is so great that some remedy had to be found that was commensurate with the guilt of the whole world, on the one hand, and with outraged holiness of God, on the other. That is what the sin offerings were all about. There were two of them. One was actually called the sin offering; the other was called the trespass offering. The sin offering dealt with the *principle* of sin; the trespass offering dealt with the *practice* of sin.

1. Dealing with the principle of sin (the sin offering)

We do what we do because we are what we are. That is true of every creature in the universe. It is even true of God Himself. We, ourselves, are not sinners because we sin; we sin because we are sinners. An apple tree, for instance, is not an apple tree because it bears apples. It bears apples because it is an apple tree. This is the principle underlying the sin offering. It makes provision for what we are by nature—sinners of Adam's ruined race.

a. Guilt finds us out

The fourth chapter of Leviticus makes that perfectly clear. Again and again, God uses the word *guilty* to remind us of our culpability. There are no exceptions, for "all have sinned, and come short of the glory of God" (Rom. 3:23). Even after we are saved there is no state of holiness in this life that puts us beyond the reach of temptation and the possibility of sin.

God begins with *the ordained priest:* "If the priest that is anointed do sin according to the sin of the people . . ." (Lev. 4:3). God demands a higher standard of behavior from those who have been consecrated to the ministry than he does of others. This is evident in the kind of sacrifice a guilty priest was to bring to God. An ordinary sinner could bring a sheep, a goat, a dove, or even some flour. The priest had to bring a bullock. His sin loomed so much larger. His offering had to be commensurate with his greater calling and greater responsibility.

Next we view *the organized people,* the congregation of God's people, as a body of believers. "And if the whole congregation of Israel sin . . ." (v. 13). The corporate sin of the gathered people of God is regarded as seriously as the sin of a priest.

The elders of God's assembled people were to take the blame and were required to act representatively on behalf of the people. It was their duty to make sure that the gathered people realized their guilt and were made aware of the cost of their restoration.

Sin in the congregation is always a serious matter. It calls for a mature measure of appreciation for the death of Christ to effect reconciliation with God in such a case. The bullock, the largest of the sin offerings, reminds us of that. Failure on the part of the organized people of God to confess their corporate sin and seek cleansing leads eventually to apostasy. The Holy Spirit leaves them to their own self-will. An unsaved person can resist the Holy Spirit (Acts 7:51), a believer can grieve the Holy Spirit (Eph. 4:30), and a corporate body (Israel in the Old Testament, a church in the New Testament) can quench the Holy Spirit (1 Thess. 5:19).

Where the Holy Spirit has been quenched, the congregation might go on functioning as though nothing had happened, but there are no results except carnal and worldly ones. The congregation settles down and carries on its affairs but "ichabod" can be written over the whole thing. The glory is departed. The Laodicean church is an example of that (Rev. 3:14–22).

We look next at *the officiating prince.* What happens when sin is discovered in one of the rulers of the nation? The prince in Israel was ordained the secular ruler of God's people. His exalted position sometimes exposed him to powerful temptations. The case of David and that of Solomon come readily to mind. David tried for a while to sweep his sins under the rug. Solomon acted with high-handed recklessness that called for divine reproof.

Serious as sin was in the life of a prince, it was not put on a par with that of a priest or that of God's people viewed corporately. The sin offering for a secular ruler was to be a kid of the goats.

Finally, there was the sin offering for *the ordinary person,* a member of the rank and file of those who made up the nation. The sin offering of an individual was the same as that of a ruler. For all are leveled by the Fall—small and great, rich and poor, young and old, men and women, bond and free. All need the cleansing and forgiveness that can only be found at the Cross.

Throughout much of this Old Testament legislation, the Holy Spirit frequently emphasizes the fact that much of our sin is caused by our ignorance. It runs like a refrain through these verses: "If a soul commit a trespass, and sin through ignorance . . ." (Lev. 5:15). Ignorance is no excuse. Suppose an American tourist in Britain were to be stopped by the police for driving on the wrong side of the road. Would it help him in court to plead that in the United States everyone drives on the right-hand side? Of course not! The judge would remind him that he was not being judged by the laws of the United States but by the laws of Great Britain. "You should have acquainted yourself with the law by which you would be judged." Ignorance is no excuse.

God, likewise, holds people responsible for knowing His Word and His laws. Most people could not quote the Ten Commandments, let alone the entire Bible legal code of 613 commands. Nor is God impressed by the glib statement, "Just let your conscience be your guide." Conscience, indeed, is God's vice-regent in the heart of humankind, but a conscience can be silenced. It can also be seared. Consciences are often subjective and, therefore, need to be monitored by an outside, objective, absolute standard—in other words, it has to be kept in line with God's Word. There is no escape from the Word of God. It is the final arbiter in all matters of faith and morals. We are liable before God just as much for sins of ignorance as we are for sins we commit with malice and aforethought. God sees to it that our sins always find us out (Num. 32:23). Thank God, then, for the sin offering!

b. Grace finds a way

God is holy but He is also love. His holiness says, "Punish!" His love says, "Pardon." Calvary is the place where the holiness of God meets the love of God and where they kiss each other (Ps. 85:10). It was God's matchless, everlasting love that moved Him to provide us with a means, commensurate with both His holiness and our helplessness, to put away our sin and guilt.

The sin offering had to be without blemish. If the Lord Jesus had harbored in His heart for one fleeting moment just one single sin, He would have been disqualified as our substitute. Calvary would have been in vain. The Lord Jesus was sinless in thought and word and deed. He was "holy, harmless, undefiled, separate from sinners" (Heb. 7:26).

The sinner's guilt was brought home to him in the ritual of the sin offering. He had to place his hand upon the sacrifice, symbolically transferring his sin to the substitute. Then he, himself, had to kill the sacrifice. By so doing, he proclaimed that it was his sin that made such a drastic remedy necessary—just as it was our sin that took Jesus to the tree (1 Peter 2:24). Once the sinner had done the dreadful work of slaying the sacrifice, the priest took over. The entire process of cleansing was in the hands of the priest for there is no way we can cleanse ourselves from guilt.

The sacrifice of the sin offering now entered another stage. The body of the victim was taken to an isolated spot outside the camp where it was burned to ashes. Thus it was that Christ suffered outside "the camp" (Heb. 13:11–13) in loneliness and despair. He was cut off from God and humankind and plunged into abysmal darkness. His "orphan cry" echoes down the ages, "My God, my God, why hast thou forsaken me?" (Matt. 27:46).

In the order in which the five offerings are introduced, the burnt offering and the other sweet-savor offerings come first; the sin offerings come last. God begins with the highest of the offerings, the one that was all for Him. Then he moves steadily forward to the sin offerings.

In the actual order of experience, however, the opposite is true. We begin with the sin offering and progress toward the burnt offering. Consciences quickened by the Spirit of God cry out for a sin offering. It is not until people have grown in grace and begun to increase in the knowledge of God that they appreciate the worship aspect of things as represented in the burnt offering. Even at that, there will be various stages of growth. That is suggested by the various sizes of the animals used—a bullock, a sheep or a goat, a turtledove or a pigeon. The various values of these creatures suggest the different levels of apprehension and appreciation of the offerer. Some of God's people have a much greater comprehension of the work of the Cross than others.

Newly awakened sinners cannot see the fine points of all this. All they know is that they are under deep conviction of sin and desperately need a sacrifice, a substitute, a Savior. The Old Testament sinner learns God has provided a way of escape. It was probably rare for a sinner to see beyond his ritual sacrifice to the Savior.

2. Dealing with the practice of sin (the trespass offering)

We are sinners by nature. That is the message of the sin offering. The sin offering deals with our standing before God, which is perfect in Christ. The trespass offering deals with our state, which is often deplorable. The sin offering deals with the principle of sin and, hence, with our standing. The trespass offering deals with our practice of sin and, thus, with our state. The sin offering has to do with sin; the trespass offering has to do with sins; the sin offering deals with the root of sin; the trespass offering deals with the fruit of sin.

One of the distinctive features of the trespass offering is the way it called not only for redemption but also for restitution. A simple illustration will make that clear. A Hebrew citizen is nagged by his conscience, which drives him at last to the priest. He brings a lamb to offer as a sacrifice.

"What kind of an offering is this?" the priest asks. "Are you bringing a burnt offering, a peace offering, a sin offering, or a trespass offering?"

The man looks bewildered. He confesses himself ignorant of all these options.

"Have you brought your lamb because you wish to worship God—because you want to express to Him the love and devotion you have for Him?"

"Well," says the man, "I should like to do that, of course, but I'm not ready for that kind of thing. The truth is, I have sinned, and I need to get right with God."

"Ah!" responds the priest. "You will need to offer a sin offering or a trespass offering."

Again the man is at a loss.

"Do you want to confess to God that you are a sinner, or do you wish to get right with God over some specific sin?"

"That's it," the man replies. "About a year ago I stole a hundred sheep from a man, and I know God is displeased with me."

"Well, then, your lamb is to be a trespass offering. Tie it up to the post over there. You will need to make restitution with your victim. Leave your lamb here and restore to your neighbor the hundred sheep you stole. Get a receipt and bring it with you."

After a while, the man comes back. The priest looks at the receipt. "This is just for a hundred sheep," he says.

"That's all I stole."

"I understand that. The law of the trespass offering, however, requires that you add 20 percent to what you stole and that you give this extra to the man you wronged. That way he will become the gainer. God requires you to get right with your neighbor before you try to get right with Him. God wants you to learn that sin is a costly business."

The man comes back after a while with an additional receipt. His lamb is slain, and all is now well with the man, his neighbor, and his God.

Our own legal system could profit by incorporating into its penalties full restitution where possible and an extra bonus to repay some of the loss and inconvenience experienced by the one wronged by the crime. It would be a healthy deterrent to repeat offenses.

There are spiritual implications to all this. There is a sense in which God not only makes the wrath of man praise Him (Ps. 76:10) but the sins of men as well. Under the law of the trespass offering, the wronged party actually became a gainer. God Himself has become a gainer, so to speak, by what has happened. God can demonstrate His omniscience and omnipotence by His acts in creation. The fall of our race and God's awesome plan of redemption has given God a stage upon which to demonstrate, for time and for eternity, the unsearchable riches of His grace and everlasting love.

Moreover, we have become gainers. Adam might conceivably have lived in innocence in the Garden of Eden for a million years and then fallen into sin. Or he might have lived forever in a sinless state and brought a sinless progeny into the world. In time, one of them might have sinned. And even if they, too, were to live endlessly in sinless perfection, they would have remained children of Adam. God, however, as a result of the Fall, has devised something better than that. He has so thoroughly dealt with the sin question that His people are to be saved to sin no more. More than that, they are exalted above all creatures as sons and daughters of the living God.

Gainers indeed! The apostle Paul develops this trespass-offering truth in Romans 5. The phrase "much more!" is repeated five times— in connection with the government of God (v. 9), with the goodness of God (v. 10), with the gift of God (v. 15), with the glory of God (v. 17), and with the grace of God (v. 20).

Yes, gainers indeed! For all eternity we are to be "to the praise of his glory, who first trusted in Christ" (Eph. 1:12). For all eternity will be able to point us out as the supreme exhibits of His love.

Sweet the moments, rich in blessing,
Which before the cross we spend;
Life and health and peace possessing
From the sinner's dying friend.

Here we rest in wonder viewing
All our guilt on Jesus laid!
And a full redemption flowing
From the sacrifice He made.

Here we find the dawn of heaven,
While upon the Lamb we gaze,
See our trespasses forgiven,
And our songs of triumph raise.

Oh, that strong in faith abiding,
We may to the Savior cleave,
Naught with Him our hearts dividing,
All for Him content to leave!

May we still, God's mind discerning,
To the Lamb for wisdom go:
There new wonders daily learning,
All the depths of mercy know.[1]

—James Allen (1734–1804)

CHAPTER 4

THE SWEET-SAVOR OFFERINGS

Leviticus 1–3

1. The meal offering: A flawless man
2. The peace offering: A festive meal
3. The burnt offering: A fathomless mystery
   a. Apprehending Him
   b. Appreciating Him
   c. Appropriating Him

THREE OF THE OFFERINGS BROUGHT special delight to the heart of God. Because of this they are called "sweet-savor" offerings. They speak of what God derived from the work of the Cross, of the joy He derived from the sinless life of His Son, and from His Son's obedience unto death, even death on the cross.

The three sweet-savor offerings were the burnt offering, the meal offering, and the peace offering. The meal offering speaks to us of *the wonder of Christ's person.* It sets before us a flawless man. The peace offering speaks to us of *the wonder of Christ's provision.* It sets before us a festive meal. The burnt offering speaks to us of *the wonder of Christ's passion.* It sets before us a fathomless mystery, the enduring mystery of the Cross of Christ and the love of God.

1. The meal offering: A flawless man

Everything about the meal offering was designed to set before us the marvelous, sinless humanity of the Lord Jesus. The fine flour, the salt, the frankincense, the oil, along with the total absence of both honey and leaven. Each offering speaks to us about Him.

The flour, for instance, was to be fine flour, flour ground and ground until it was completely smooth and free from all unevenness. There was no roughness, no unevenness to be found in Jesus. No matter from which perspective we view Him, we find the same evenness of character. That is not so of sinful man. We are strong when it comes to this, weak when it comes to that. We are clever along these lines, clumsy along those. We like this one but cannot stand that one.

Not so the Lord Jesus. He loved everybody. He lived sinlessly. He was perfectly balanced, completely even tempered, always the same.

His body was perfect, a flawless instrument through which His impeccable holiness could be displayed, the embodiment of the Greek ideal of perfection. Never, since the fall of Adam, moreover, had the world seen such a man, "holy, harmless, undefiled, separate from sinners" (Heb. 7:26), the Jewish ideal of perfect humanity.

It says something about His physical strength that, even after a busy day and an exhausting ordeal in Gethsemane and then being marched here and there across the city—to the house of Caiaphas, to Pilate, to Herod, back to Pilate—Jesus was still able to stand up to foes. He had been scourged to the bone by a Roman scourge, a terrible instrument of torture designed to rip flesh off and tear at the organs within. Many a person died under the scourge. Yet the Lord not only endured the ordeal; He still had sufficient strength to pick up a heavy cross of rough-hewn wood and carry it halfway to Calvary.

But not only was His body in perfect balance, so was His soul—His intellect, His emotions, and His will. All were in perfect harmony. His emotions never ran away with Him. His thoughts were sublime, sinless, and wedded to God's revealed and published Word. He was never at a loss for words—the human and the divine existed in wondrous unity. His will was indomitable but never overbearing. He was always right but never objectionable. He was perfectly adjusted. He was never deceived, never wrong. There was never any trace of self-will. His whole innermost being was always in glad subjection to the will of His Father in heaven. He was all that was symbolized by the meal offering's fine and even flour.

Then, there was the oil. It was blended with the flour to produce a perfect mix, and then it was poured out in full measure on the batter. The oil symbolizes the Holy Spirit. The Lord Jesus was filled with the Spirit from His mother's womb. There never was a time when the indwelling Holy Spirit did not fill Him. He was man as God always intended man to be—man inhabited by God. He lived His life day by day, moment by moment, in harmony with the Holy Spirit, under the Spirit's control. At His baptism, when He was anointed by the Holy Spirit, the Spirit of God was poured out upon Him without measure.

The perfect blending of the human and the divine in the Lord Jesus was always in evidence for those who had the eyes to see. He was omniscient but never precocious. Though He was God, He grew up in a human home. He learned the alphabet, grew in knowledge, asked questions just like any ordinary boy. He was omnipotent but never aggressive. He was holy but never self-righteous. He was love incarnate, a friend of publicans and sinners, without ever compromising with sin in thought, word, or deed. The Lord Jesus was both man and God.

But that was not all. Frankincense was part of the meal offering. Frankincense was a fragrant gum. It was white in color and had a balsamic odor, especially when burnt. It reminds us of the fragrance of the life of the Lord. When Mary of Bethany poured out her alabaster flask of rare and costly perfume upon the Lord Jesus, the whole house was filled with the fragrance (John 12:3). The fragrance lingered on long after Jesus had gone. The frankincense as part of the meal offering tells us that the Lord Jesus carried with Him through life "a sweet savour unto the LORD" (Lev. 2:9). He brought with Him into every home, into every circumstance, into every contact, however casual, the fragrance of heaven.

To all this was added salt. Salt adds its own particular pungency to food. What otherwise would be insipid is often made palatable by the addition of salt. Salt is also used to arrest corruption. Salt itself is a miracle. Its chemical name is sodium chloride. It is composed of two chemicals (sodium and chlorine) both of which, taken separately, are deadly poisons. Turned into salt, however, they are a vital necessity to us. Indeed, salt makes up about 10 percent of our blood and our body cells.

How eloquently all this speaks of Christ! The Lord Jesus is a miraculous combination of two separate natures. From all eternity, He possessed a divine nature, eternal, uncreated, self-existing. He had all the attributes of deity. When He came into this world to be born of the Virgin Mary, He took upon Him a human nature just like ours except that it was sinless. He was both God and man, glorious in His deity, perfect in His humanity.

It was never a case of "Now I am acting like God," and "Now I am acting like man"—a case, that is, of two natures coexisting side by side. His two natures did not form a dichotomy but a single unity. They were perfectly combined so that always, in all places, under all circumstances, He was the God-man—God manifested in flesh.

Think again of sodium chloride. Each of its two components, separated, would kill us if it was imbibed. Even so, the deity of Christ would consume us or the humanity of Christ would condemn us, if encountered separately.

We could not endure for a moment an encounter with Christ in all the undiluted glory of His deity. He is a member of the thrice Holy Godhead (Isa. 6:1–3). He is "of purer eyes than to behold evil" (Hab. 1:13). Moreover "God is angry with the wicked every day" (Ps. 7:11). The omniscience of God, His blazing holiness, would consume us.

Similarly, the humanity of Christ would condemn us. Paul put it like this: "God sending his own Son in the likeness of sinful flesh, and for sin, condemned sin in the flesh" (Rom. 8:3). The life of the Lord Jesus has demonstrated once and for all that a sinless life can be lived on earth. What Jesus did was this: He took the law of God, holy, just, and good as it was (Rom. 7:12), raised it to impossible heights in the Sermon on the Mount, and then lived it! Lived it flawlessly, perfectly, to the very letter, in its sublime spirit, every moment of every day. He lived it flawlessly, perfectly, in all its 613 separate demands, through all the vicissitudes of life, from birth to death. We dare not test our own imagined goodness and self-righteousness alongside Him. What we have to offer is tinsel and tarnish, which is immediately exposed as such. "Wood, hay, stubble" is Paul's apt description of it in 1 Corinthians 3:12. The Lord's sinless humanity condemns us through and through. His life is our great indictment.

So, taken separately, the deity of Christ on the one hand and the humanity of Christ on the other hand would terrify us. But, at Bethlehem, God took deity and humanity and merged them into the glorious person of the Lord Jesus Christ, both God and man at the same time, one in essence, one in every sense of the word. Nor is He a threat to us. Paul puts it this way: "There is one God, and one mediator between God and men, the man Christ Jesus; who gave himself a ransom for all" (1 Tim. 2:5–6). The deity of Christ and the humanity of Christ merged into one, the God-man, is as essential to our spiritual life and eternal well-being as salt is to our physical life and temporal well-being. Thank God for the salt in the meal offering!

There was to be no honey in the meal offering. Honey speaks of natural sweetness. Solomon's comment about honey is thought provoking. He warns us against eating too much of it because overindulgence will make us sick (Prov. 25:16). Natural sweetness can pall. We tend to get sick of the person who oozes sweetness all the time.

The sweetness of the Lord Jesus was not natural but supernatural. The Bible says of Him that His words were "sweeter also than honey and the honeycomb" (Ps. 19:10). The supernatural sweetness of our Lord's personality is evident everywhere in the Gospels. He loved His enemies just as much as He loved His friends. He loved Pilate as much as He loved Peter. He loved poor lost Judas as much as He loved His dear friend John. His sweetness is such that we can never get too much of it. The Shulamite, in describing her beloved to the women of Solomon's court, saves the best wine to the last. She says, "His mouth is most sweet" (Song 5:16). James warns, "Out of the same mouth proceedeth blessing and cursing" (James 3:10). It was true of Simon

Peter (Matt. 16:16–17; 26:73–75), but it was not so with our Lord. "His mouth is so sweet," indeed. Even His enemies said, "Never man spake like this man" (John 7:46).

Honey then, a mere natural sweetener, was absent from the meal offering. So was leaven. In Scripture, leaven is uniformly employed as a symbol of sin and corruption. That is why it was banned from the meal offering. In the meal offering, all spoke of Christ, and in Him was no sin. Even Pilate declared, "I find in him no fault at all" (John 18:38). The Holy Spirit says of Christ that He "is holy, harmless, undefiled, separate from sinners, and made higher than the heavens" (Heb. 7:26).

There was one thing more—the meal offering had to pass through the fire. Some of it was baked in an oven; some was cooked in a pan. The meal that was cooked in the pan speaks of the more visible and evident sufferings of Christ; the part that was baked in the oven speaks of the hidden, unseen sufferings of Christ, those seen only by the eye of God. Part of the meal offering was offered up on the altar, and part became food for the priests. Thus both God and man can find something satisfying in the meal offering and the wonderful life of which it speaks.

2. The peace offering: A festive meal

In the meal offering, the matchless life of Christ is *shown* to us. In the peace offering, that life is *shared* with us. For the Lord Jesus not only gave His *life for* us on the cross; He now gives His life *to* us. Supremely, the peace offering was a fellowship offering. God, the priest, and the offerer all partook of the sacrifice. God and the cleansed sinner met together in peace. Paul declares that "being justified by faith, we have peace with God through our Lord Jesus Christ: by whom also we have access" (Rom. 5:1–2). By the peace offering the sinner was reconciled, and God was propitiated.

The peace offering made communion possible. For two or more people to have communion they must have something in common. What the sinner has in common with God is the Lord Jesus Christ.

The sinless life of Christ and His obedience unto death, even the death of the cross, is something upon which God can feast. God always intended to find an outlet for His love. He longed for one in whom He could find enjoyment down here on earth. The fall of Adam put an end to that. God's great yearning was for a person on earth to live a perfect life before Him, a person with whom He could commune and have fellowship. This divine yearning was satisfied at last when Jesus came, born of Adam's race, a man after God's own heart.

In the peace offering, ordained long centuries before but in anticipation of Calvary, God invites those who have some glimmering of the Cross to come and eat with Him.

The sinner could bring an offering from the herd or the flock—a bullock, a sheep, or a goat. The various degrees of value represented by the different animals depict the differing abilities of the offerers to grasp the awesome meaning of Calvary. Some people had a much greater capacity to understand the significance of Christ on the cross than others. Those who had but a meager understanding of Calvary brought a lesser sacrifice and, hence, had less upon which to feast. No matter! Both the strong believer and the weak believer, the babe in Christ and the mature saint of God, could come and be satisfied.

It is thus with us today. With Calvary already in view, the Lord Jesus in the Upper Room founded a new feast. He promised that, no matter how small the company, He would be there in the midst. We call it the Communion Service. The bread and the wine, emblems of His death, are placed upon the table. A feast of remembrance is spread before us. We take our places at the table, His honored guests, and the service begins. Some at the feast have very short attention spans. Their thoughts stray here and there and have to be dragged back to the worship. Some take a seat at the table but are in danger of eating and drinking judgment to themselves. They are not saved. They do not know Him. How can you remember someone you do not know? With others, their worship rarely rises higher than the chorus book. Some offer worship, but they have not spent time in private devotions or family worship all week so what they have to offer is skimpy and poor. Then there are those who come prepared, their cup overflowing and their souls aflame with thoughts of the person, the passion, and the position of the Lord Jesus. May we strive to be such.

3. The burnt offering: A fathomless mystery

The burnt offering was all for God. There was no sharing here. The burnt offering depicts the sufferings of Christ as they could be apprehended and appreciated by God alone. The fact that those of Adam's ruined race were invited to bring the offering shows that God does look for some responsiveness in the heart of the redeemed sinner to the deeper mysteries of the Cross. We may be limited in our ability to grasp it all, but we ought to be able to grasp something.

The burnt offering comes first. We would have started with the sin offering and ended with the burnt offering, since that is the way they impact us. The sin offering meets our need as sinners. God, however, starts with the burnt offering (Lev. 1). It was all for Him. God must always come first.

a. Apprehending Him

The people who brought burnt offerings to God had evidently grown in grace and increased in their knowledge of God. The burnt offering was purely and simply a worship offering. The offerers had progressed beyond a preoccupation with their sins. They wanted to express adoration and praise.

The burnt offering was all for God. It was also voluntary. There was no obligation for an individual to bring such an offering. The Holy Spirit says it was to be offered of the person's "own voluntary will" (Lev. 1:3). The sin offering and the trespass offering were required by law. The burnt offering was the response of love. It had to be without blemish. All its teaching had to do with Christ, the sinless Son of God. A person who desired to offer a burnt offering to God had to bring the best.

b. Appreciating Him

A person could bring a bullock, a sheep, a goat, or a pair of doves. As in the case of the peace offering, the varying types of animals mirrored the measure of devotion that prompted the sacrifice. A bullock, obviously, was a far more costly offering than a sheep, and a sheep or a goat cost much more to bring than a brace of doves. The principle involved here was expressed by David when Araunah the Jebusite offered his threshing floor to David, along with the gift of oxen and his threshing instruments, to enable David to offer a burnt sacrifice. It was a magnanimous gift. But it was not accepted. "The king said unto Araunah, Nay; but I will surely buy it of thee at a price: neither will I offer burnt offerings unto the LORD my God of that which doth cost me nothing" (2 Sam. 24:24).

Later on, the temple was built on this spot. We see the same spirit of costly giving demonstrated by Solomon at the dedication of the temple. Solomon "offered a sacrifice of twenty and two thousand oxen, and an hundred and twenty thousand sheep" (2 Chron. 7:5).

The Lord Jesus taught the same lesson to Simon the Pharisee. A sinful woman had burst into Simon's house, flung herself at Jesus' feet, washed them with her tears, and wiped them with her hair. Simon criticized her, but Jesus said to him, "Seest thou this woman?" (Luke 7:44). It was a fine piece of satire. The self-righteous, critical, and outraged man had seen nothing else for the past half hour!

Jesus compared the woman's treatment of Him with Simon's. Simon had studiously neglected to offer Christ the common courtesies due a guest. "I say unto thee," Jesus declared, "her sins, which are many, are forgiven; for she loved much: but to whom little is forgiven, the same loveth little" (Luke 7:47).

Coming back to the burnt offering—the bigger the sacrifice, the more the giver had a sense of appreciation for the sufferings of Christ. But even the smallest sacrifice was accepted. The poor man (mirrors the person with the poorest ability to grasp the portrayed truth of Christ's death) could bring two turtledoves or two pigeons. And more than that! In *this* case an exception was made to the general rule. The officiating priest slew the birds. The priest did not help anyone else, but he helped the poor.

c. Appropriating Him

If they were not poor, the offerer did all that needed to be done by himself. He placed his hand upon the sacrifice. He took the knife, no matter how inexpertly, and killed the sacrifice. After all—no one can worship for us. The priests were active at the altar, sprinkling the blood, building the fire, and arranging the sacrifice upon the wood, but the offerer did all the rest. He was personally engaged in all that had to be done during his act of worship.

Our worship must be the same. We should bring to God only that which we have personally seen in Christ. We do not bring to Him the result of someone else's labors but what we ourselves have learned about our beloved Lord. It may be clumsy. We may not be experts. But that is what He requires when it comes to worship—our own appropriation of Christ and the Cross. We see the same principle in a different context in the words of Joseph to his repentant and reconciled brothers: "Tell my father of all my glory . . . *that ye have seen*" (Gen. 45:13, italics added).

Just the same there were some things the priests had to do even for the mature believer. Matters having to do with the altar had to be handled by those called and trained for that work. The whole burnt offering was consumed upon the altar. All was for God. There was one remarkable exception—the *skin* of the sacrifice was given to the priest (Lev. 7:8). That speaks volumes! The priest represents the full-time servant of God, one called to handle holy things, one who spent his whole life engaged in spiritual affairs. Such was the Old Testament priest, but even he, for all his years of experience and study, could only comprehend and retain things that lie on the surface—as symbolized by the skin.

When it comes to the sufferings of Christ, no one, save God alone, can get beyond the surface. But God does. He and He alone can appreciate the deeper aspects of the work of the Cross. Perhaps He will reveal them to us in the endless ages of eternity.

Not all the blood of beasts,
On Jewish altars slain,
Could give the guilty conscience peace,
Or wash away its stain.

But Christ the heavenly Lamb,
Took all our sins away,
A sacrifice of nobler name
And richer blood than they.

We now look back to see,
The burden Thou didst bear,
When hanging on the accursed tree,
For all our guilt was there.

Believing we rejoice,
To see the curse remove;
We bless the Lamb with cheerful voice,
And sing redeeming love.[1]
                    —Isaac Watts (1674–1748)

CHAPTER 5

THE PASSOVER

Exodus 12

1. Stirring the will
   a. How the lamb was selected
   b. How the lamb was secured
   c. How the lamb was slain
2. Startling the mind
3. Striking the heart
4. Stabbing the conscience

PHARAOH'S GESTAPO KEPT ITSELF busy rounding up the Jews. They had already turned Goshen into a ghetto, a vast slave-labor camp. If the Jews wanted to survive, then they had to work. Why should they be allowed to live on the fat of the land? Why take the chance of having them side with the enemy should a war break out? And how many of them were there—a million? two million? What if they should suddenly decide to attack Egypt themselves?

Pharaoh's answer to "the Jewish question" was the same as Hitler's— genocide, mass murder, the systematic extermination of a race. So, the order was handed down from the throne: "All newborn Hebrew males must be thrown into the Nile." Within a generation there would be no Jews left.

Woe betide the nation that turns its hand against the Jews. Israel is the only nation with which God has signed a treaty. The treaty is called "The Abrahamic Covenant." Under the terms of this covenant, God has unconditionally guaranteed the survival and security of the Hebrew people. The treaty included a Promised Land stretching from the Nile to the Euphrates (Gen. 15:1–21). Any nation that turns against the Jews will have God to reckon with, as Pharaoh discovered in short order. This warning needs to be heeded because anti-Semitism is endemic in all Gentile societies. From time to time, it becomes epidemic and a holocaust ensues. One day it will become pandemic and will result in a global onslaught on the Jews.

God raised up Moses to confront Pharaoh and to redeem his people Israel. Rod and staff in hand, Moses stood before Pharaoh and demanded the emancipation of God's people from Egyptian bondage. Pharaoh refused to comply and Moses unleashed a series of mighty miracles to force Pharaoh's hand. These miracles only served to make Pharaoh more obdurate. Something more effective than miracles, signs, and wonders was needed to bring about redemption from "the house of bondage." The situation called for the shedding of blood—the blood of the Passover lamb.

Moses ordered that on the tenth day of the first month every Hebrew father was to take a lamb from the flock and set it apart. It was to be tethered where it could be watched and examined to make sure it was without blemish. On the fourteenth day, it was to be slain. The blood of the lamb was then to be applied to the lintel and doorposts of the house. The remainder was to be put in a basin and carefully placed upon the doorstep. The four points of the entrance to the house would thus be marked by the protecting blood of the lamb.[2] Note carefully, it was not splashed or sprinkled on the doorstep. There was to be no trampling on the blood—only apostates do that (Heb. 10:28–31). The family then could gather inside the blood-protected house, sheltered from the wrath to come by the blood of the Passover lamb. Safe and secure from all alarm, the family was to feast on the lamb itself.

The night of redemption came at last. The angel of the Lord, sword in hand, smote the Egyptians in a way the Hebrews would never forget but passed over the houses protected by the blood. God, moreover, wrote down a record of the "Passover" in His book. That way, the memory of it would never be erased, in time or in eternity. The Passover would be commemorated annually by the Jews in all the lands of their wandering, in all ages until the coming of Christ to reign. For what happened that first Passover night was a magnificent type, or picture, of the death of Christ as the true Passover Lamb. Judgment and salvation stalked side by side through the land. Judgment visited every home where the shed blood of the lamb had not been applied. Those who were sheltered behind the blood were saved.

This annual Passover feast was instituted by God as a picture of Calvary. God's plan of salvation has not changed. What was enacted in Egypt some thirty-five hundred years ago is as up-to-date now as it was then. In God's mind, it is but a short step in time and space from Goshen to Golgotha (1 Cor. 5:7).

1. Stirring the will

"Speak ye unto all the congregation of Israel, saying, In the tenth day of this month they shall take to them every man a lamb, according to the house of their fathers, a lamb for an house" (Exod. 12:3). We note that sometimes a house was too little for the lamb—in which case two neighboring households joined together—but the lamb was never too little for a house. Christ is always adequate. In all this, nothing was left to chance or choice. Everything was carefully spelled out by God.

We note *how the lamb was selected.* A man might have a flock of a thousand sheep, or he might have just a few sheep penned up near his house. He might have to beg or buy a sheep, but at all costs he had to select his lamb. "Your lamb shall be without blemish, a male of the first year: ye shall take it out from the sheep, or from the goats" (v. 5). A rich man was not to bring a full-grown bull, a poor man was not to bring a bird. God's Word made it clear that the sacrifice had to come from the flock.

All kinds of objections and arguments could have been raised. One person might say, "I'm related to Moses. That's good enough for me." Another might argue, "I'm a decent, moral, religious person, and a good husband and father, as well. I think that should be sufficient." Yet another might affirm, "I am the family priest. I have offered many a sacrifice in my lifetime. I stand on that ground for my salvation." Another might be skeptical of the whole thing. How could blood protect anyone? What kind of a god would demand the slaughter of millions of lambs? Why not continue with the miracles until Pharaoh gave in?

What it comes down to is this: We cannot select our articles of faith the same way that we collect our articles of furniture. When we choose our furniture, we select items that appeal to us. When we select our articles of faith, however, we had better make sure we are going by what God has said. And what God has to say about salvation is to the point: "When I see the *blood*, I will pass over you" (v. 13, italics added).

We note, also, *how the lamb was secured*: "And ye shall keep it up until the fourteenth day of the same month" (v. 6) ran the divine decree. Each morning, likely enough, the Hebrew father would go to where the lamb was tethered. He would examine it diligently to make sure it was free from any kind of blemish.

That lamb was a type for Christ, the true Passover Lamb. During His last week on earth, the Lord Jesus would go out as far as Bethany at night and return every morning to Jerusalem. In Jerusalem, He was under the constant surveillance of the authorities. He opened Himself up to their inspection so that they could see His sinless perfection for themselves. The Sanhedrin conspirators soon knew full well that they would have to depend on hired false witnesses in order to secure any kind of conviction against Him at all. Later, though they had a lineup of such perjurers take the stand against Him, they had to give up on that scheme and try something else. He was without blemish.

The Lord Jesus is the only sinless man to live on earth since the Fall. We have the testimony of His Father, His friends, and His foes that He was sinless. His Father declared Himself to be well pleased with Him (Matt. 3:17). Pilate said, "I find no fault in this man" (Luke 23:4). Peter declared that Christ "did no sin" (1 Peter 2:22). Jesus Himself challenged His enemies to prove He was guilty of sin (John 8:46).

We note, too, *how the lamb was slain:* "The whole assembly of the congregation of Israel shall kill *it* in the evening. And they shall take of the blood, and strike *it* on the two side posts and on the upper door post of the houses, wherein they shall eat *it*" (Exod. 12:6–7, italics added). All this was premeditated and deliberate. God would accept no excuses, no variations, no substitutions, and no argument. The decree was simple: Either the angel saw the blood, or he slayed the household's firstborn son. It had to be one or the other.

"The whole assembly of the congregation of Israel shall kill it," God said. That night thousands of lambs were slain. God did not see *them;* He saw *it.* He saw Christ the Passover Lamb (1 Cor. 5:7).

2. Startling the mind

It seems so unreasonable. Why did there have to be all this seemingly senseless killing? A skeptic once asked a Christian, "How can blood cleanse sin?" The Christian responded with a question of his own, "How does water quench thirst?" The skeptic said, "I don't know how water quenches thirst, but I know that it does." The Christian replied, "I, too, do not know how blood cleanses sin, but I know that it does."

God does not require that we understand His plan of salvation. He asks us to trust and obey. God's ways make little or no sense to the ungodly. The Holy Spirit says that "If our gospel be hid, it is hid to them that are lost . . . the god of this world hath blinded the minds of them which believe not, lest the light of the glorious gospel of Christ, who is the image of God, should shine unto them" (2 Cor. 4:3–4). Indeed, "the natural man receiveth not the things of the Spirit of God: for they are foolishness unto him: neither can he know them, because they are spiritually discerned" (1 Cor. 2:14).

Three kinds of blindness exist. One is *natural* blindness—the blindness to spiritual things that is humankind's legacy as a result of the Fall. It is this that stimulates false religions and cults, to which even intelligent people can fall prey.

Another is *willful* blindness—the blindness of those who choose of their own volition not to believe divine truth even when it is presented to them. People think up dozens of ways to pick holes in the gospel, and then they say that they can't believe. What they mean is that they won't believe.

Then, too, there is *judicial* blindness—the blindness that overtakes those who set themselves in defiant rebellion against God. An example of this is given by Moses in his description of the overthrow of Sodom (Gen. 19:9–11). There comes a time when God Himself blinds and hardens the human heart. Then the people who say they can't believe are confirmed in their unbelief and find themselves locked up in their lost condition, heading for certain judgment. Thus it was with Pharaoh (Rom. 9:17–18). And thus it was with King Saul, Israel's first king. Saul sinned against God once too often and was abandoned by God. Discovering that God would no longer speak to him, he sought out the services of a witch and, within a day, was dead (1 Sam. 28:5–25). The Holy Spirit clearly warns people not to trifle with spiritual things (Heb. 6:4–9).

The truth of salvation, full and free through the blood of Calvary's Lamb, is the greatest truth in the universe. The angels of heaven themselves desire to look into these things (1 Peter 1:12). It is astonishing. God, who is angry with the wicked every day (Ps. 7:11) and who requires from us a strict accounting of our past (Eccl. 3:15), is willing to blot out our sins (Isa. 44:22) and does so "freely by his grace" (Rom. 3:24). Moreover, He is willing to adopt us into His own family (Rom. 8:15–17) and seat us on high with Christ (Eph. 2:1–7), all because of the infinite price paid by the Lord Jesus on the cross of Calvary (1 Peter 1:18; 2:24). It is surely incredible to the angels that humanity, having been confronted by such truths, should respond by yawning in the face of God.

3. Striking the heart

God's demand was for a lamb. He did not want a full-grown mountain ram with large curling horns, brimming with fight and fire. Nor did He want a sheep, grown old and gray, tough of flesh, and set and stolid in its ways. He wanted a lamb, soft and gentle, lovable and trusting. The man's children could come out to where the little creature was tied. They would bring some fresh grass for it to eat. They would have a pet name for it. If it bleated, one of them would run to see if it was safe. They would inspect its bed to make sure it had enough straw. They would hug it before going in for the night. That was the lamb to be slain.

We can well imagine the horror in the house, the bitter tears when it was learned that the lovable lamb must die so that the oldest son might live. The whole family would look on in horror as the father unsheathed his great butcher's knife and headed for the pen. The father himself might have a desperate look in his eyes as he called to the lamb—and it came. Soon, the dreadful deed would be done, but the father would be left feeling like a butcher.

The process was all intensely personal and emotional. And so it was at Calvary. There, Christ's mother watched from the edge of the crowd, aghast. Faithful John's face ran with tears. Up in heaven, God the Father entered into it all—the anguish, the pain, the broken heart. God had called for a lamb, and there He was, the Lamb of God, God's Lamb, taking away the sin of the world (John 1:29, 36).

Once the family's pet lamb was slaughtered, and the dreadful deed was done, blood, fresh from the veins of the lamb, was carefully applied to the lintel and doorposts of the house. The basin was set before the door. The husband, wife, and children gathered inside while the lamb was roasted on the fire. The lamb was doubtless set upon a spit and placed over the open flame. Likely enough, the lamb was impaled on two pieces of wood. One piece ran through the lamb from front to back to hold it in place on the cooking irons. The other piece pierced the lamb through from side to side. This allowed the body of the lamb to be turned in the flame. Thus, the lamb was actually impaled upon a cross of wood.

But there was more! It had to be consumed. Garnished with bitter herbs, the lamb was eaten along with tasteless unleavened bread. The whole process, from start to finish, was designed to strike through every heart. It was intended to bring home to the Hebrews the cost of their salvation. In every house throughout all the land that night, there would either be a dead lamb or a dead son. The hushed people, keeping this first Passover, realized that sin and death were dreadful realities. The radical character of sin called for a radical cure. As they ate the lamb, another lesson was learned—one we can take right over to Calvary. As the Lord Jesus, the Passover Lamb, gave His life *for* us on the cross, so now He gives His life *to* us to sustain us on our pilgrimage to the Promised Land.

4. Stabbing the conscience

Why did that lamb have to die? Because of sin. Once the judgment angel was abroad, death had to occur. It was a matter of course. We can imagine that dark and dreadful messenger. He comes to a house. The agnostic lives there. He is an older son. This man has pinned a note to the door that reads, "I don't believe a word of it." In the angel goes, and in a terrifying moment of too-late awareness, the man is dead.

The angel of death inspects another door. It is the liberal's house. He had no use for Moses. He, too, has written a note. "I thank God I am not as other men are. I am a good man. I stand upon my merit." A flash of the angel's sword, and a choked cry comes from the cot in the corner. A young boy, the deceived man's firstborn son, is dead.

The next house has the blood displayed as required. The death angel passes over it. All is well. Sin has already been judged and canceled in that house. The people within are saved.

> God will not payment twice demand,
> First from my Savior's pierced hand
> And then again at mine.

So, the lamb spoke to the conscience and gave it peace. Suddenly, a great cry rose toward heaven. The Egyptians, with their bursting pantheon of foolish idol-gods, knew nothing of redemption by blood. There was death everywhere—in the bedroom, in the barn, in the mendicant's hovel, and in the Pharaoh's palace. Death reigned, indeed.

In Goshen, the Hebrews were packing their bags. As they came out of their houses, the blood was still there. It continued to speak to them, only now it spoke of sins forgiven, of peace with God, of judgment averted. And, to this day and hour in this distant land and around the world, that blood still speaks.

Rise my soul! behold 'tis Jesus,
Jesus fills thy wondering eyes;
See Him now in glory seated,
Where thy sins no more can rise.

There in righteousness transcendent,
Lo! He doth in heaven appear,
Shows the blood of His atonement
As thy title to be there.

All thy sins were laid upon Him,
Jesus bore them on the tree;
God, who knew them, laid them on Him,
And believing, thou art free.[1]
— J. Denham Smith (1817–1889)

CHAPTER 6

THE DAY OF ATONEMENT
Leviticus 16

1. Dealing with personal sin
2. Dealing with public sin
3. Dealing with persisting sin

ATONEMENT IS AN OLD TESTAMENT concept, not a New Testament one. It is a concept that has to do with the Hebrew people under the law of Moses.

Here is a young boy. His mother tells him to sweep the porch. He does so, boy fashion, but soon discovers he has a problem. What is to be done with the small pile of debris and dust he has collected? He dismisses the idea of finding a suitable bag, rounding up a shovel, and disposing of the remains in a garbage can. He spies the rug and, with a swift stoop and a deft swish of the broom, the problem is solved. The unwanted oddments are hidden under the rug!

This scenario is the basic idea behind the Old Testament notion of atonement. It provided a way to sweep the sins of the people under the rug. The sins were covered up, and covering up sins was precisely the idea that the word *atonement* was meant to convey. In fact, the word *atonement* means "to cover." The same Hebrew word is used in connection with Noah's ark. God told Noah to "pitch it within and without" (Gen. 6:14). The pitch was to completely "cover" the ark. Covering it in this way was what enabled it to survive the flood tide of God's wrath.

Everyone knows that sweeping things under the rug is no real solution to the problem of dirt. God allowed it in Old Testament times because, all along, He had the New Testament in mind. In the Old Testament, sin was covered. In the New Testament, it is canceled. The Day of Atonement in the Old Testament was a detailed enactment paralleling what was to take place on Mount Calvary.

Even the most casual reading of Leviticus 16 quickens our awareness of sin. There were some forty separate steps required by the ritual of the Day of Atonement, and all of them had to do with sin. The people of Israel assembled to watch and listen. They did nothing. There was nothing they could do, just as there is nothing we can do. Everything was done by the high priest in the Old Testament and, in our day, by Christ Himself.

1. Dealing with personal sin

The first part of the ritual had to do with the personal sin of the high priest. He was in no condition to act as the people's representative and as a type of Christ until God had first dealt with his own sin and guilt. What a revelation! Here was a man chosen and anointed by God, occupied daily with spiritual things, yet he was a poor sinner just like anyone else. In the sight of God he was no better than a murderer, a thief, or an extortioner. Being "full-time" in the Lord's work does not exempt even the choicest of God's saints from sin. Being an ordained minister of the sanctuary, however, makes any sin that much more serious and culpable. No less than fifteen steps had to be taken by the high priest before he could act on other people's behalf:

1. He took a young bullock to be used as a sin offering for his own sin.
2. He took a ram to be offered as a burnt offering for himself.

3. He washed himself.
4. He put on holy linen garments.
5. He took two goats and set them aside to be used as a sin offering for the people.
6. He took a ram to be used as a burnt offering for the people.
7. He brought his bullock before God and presented it.
8. He likewise presented the two goats to God.
9. He cast lots over the two goats. One was chosen to die—have its blood shed; the other, called the scapegoat, was to bear away the sins of the people.
10. The high priest sacrificed the bullock as a sin offering for himself and for his family.
11. The high priest took a censor and filled it with burning coals from the altar.
12. He filled his hands with incense.
13. He put the incense on the burning coals in the censor so that clouds of fragrant smoke might envelop him, hiding him from the Holy One enthroned within.
14. He then took the blood of the bullock in his hands and went into the Holy of Holies beyond the veil.
15. He sprinkled the blood on the east side of the mercy seat and seven times before the mercy seat.

What did all this elaborate and detailed ritual mean? The first thing that arrests us is that a goat, a very young goat, a kid, was sufficient to cover all the sin and iniquity of an entire nation (between two to three million people) but, for the high priest himself, a full-grown bullock was required—an animal in all its vigor and strength. Sin in one of the Lord's anointed servants calls for special and weighty measures. God sees the enormity of the sin when His consecrated servant is involved, and He cannot dismiss it lightly.

The bullock, then, was slain and the high priest took its blood into the Holy Place. To his left was the lampstand, to his right the table of showbread, straight ahead was the golden incense altar, just beyond that was the veil, and beyond the veil the Holy of Holies.

The high priest was protected from instant death by the blood once he stepped beyond the veil. He, thankfully, was blotted out by the billowing incense that filled the Holy of Holies and advertised his presence. He was arrayed in pure white linen, symbolic of righteousness and provided for him by God. Just the same he must have trembled in every limb as he stood in the immediate presence of a thrice-holy God.

Around him was great beauty. The drapes were of fine linen dyed scarlet, blue, and purple. The sacred ark of the covenant, the only piece of furniture in the Holy of Holies, was made of acacia wood, virtually incorruptible, overlaid with pure gold. The whole place was ablaze with the light of the Shechinah glory, the light of another world. Now that he was there, trembling and transfixed, he hastily sprinkled the blood beside and before the mercy seat—the golden lid of the ark, where God sat enthroned. The golden bells sewn into the hem of his garment jingled as he moved, advertising to those outside that he was still alive. Finally, he left. All this was to take care of his personal sin.

2. Dealing with public sin

Now that the high priest had symbolically taken care of his own sin, he could go on to do something about the sins of God's people. We can count fourteen steps that had to be taken in this regard.

1. The high priest took one of the goats, the one upon which the lot had fallen, and slew it as a sin offering for the people.
2. He went back into the Holy of Holies taking the blood of the goat with him.
3. He performed the same blood ritual he had enacted for himself. He was to do this alone, absolutely alone—stress is laid on that. He was to make atonement for both the Holy Place and the Holy of Holies. The Holy Spirit adds, "Because of the uncleanness of the children of Israel, and because of their transgressions in all their sins . . ."
4. He came out of the Holy of Holies and going to the great brazen

altar, he sprinkled it with the blood of both the bullock and the goat. Everything had to be cleansed this way—the Holy of Holies, the tabernacle itself, and the brazen altar.

5. He now took the remaining goat, the "scapegoat" as it was called, and put both of his hands upon its head.

6. Over the head of that goat he confessed all the sins, iniquities, and transgressions of the people for the past year, symbolically transferring the sins from the people to the substitute.

7. The high priest then delivered the goat into the hand of "a fit man" (the phrase occurs only here).

8. The fit man led the goat away from the outer court of the tabernacle, out through the gate, away from the camp, and on out into the wilderness. The people watched it go.

9. The high priest went back into the outer sanctuary ("the Holy Place") where he took off his linen robes and the garments he had donned for making atonement.

10. He washed himself.

11. He put on his garments of glory, the garments he had laid aside in order to make atonement. He reassumed them, taking back the glory that he had known before.

12. Next he offered the ram for his own personal burnt offering.

13. He offered another ram as a burnt offering for the people. This burnt offering was all for God. It pointed toward God's satisfaction in the finished work of Christ.

14. The high priest burned the fat of the sin offering on the brazen altar.

Having killed the sacrificial goat and taken its blood into the Holy of Holies where it would answer upon the mercy seat for the sins of the people, the high priest prepared for the most solemn and sobering ritual of all.

The people by the tens of thousands gathered around the tabernacle, craning to see, straining to hear. The second little goat was brought to the high priest who placed his hands upon its head. Then began the long recitation of Israel's sins. We can see the small creature as it cowered under the weight of the two hands, terrified by the sound of that solemn voice.

The catalog of sins went on and on—sins against God in His highest heaven, sins against all manner of people on earth. Sabbath breaking, profanity, child abuse, child rebellion, murder, adultery, theft, false witness, covetousness, sins of omission, sins committed in a flash of rage, and sins premeditated and cold-blooded—would the list never end? Some 613 specific commandments of the Mosaic Law were in force, and all of them were broken every day. No penitent crouching before some priest in a confessional ever had his soul searched and scorched like this—and there was no penance. That idea is foreign to God's Word. The penalty was to be borne by someone else, one of whom the goat was but a type. At last, the voice ceased, and the goat was handed over to another, one called "a fit man." (In the typology of the Old Testament, an unnamed man is often a type of the Holy Spirit.)

The unnamed man now took charge. He led the sin-bearing goat away into "a land not inhabited" (Lev. 16:22). On and on they went, past the brazen altar and the wide-open gate, past all the tents of Israel, past the tents of the farthest tribe, deeper and deeper into that waste howling wilderness. On and ever on until at last, looking back, the fit man could see not so much as a smudge on the horizon of the camp of Israel (Deut. 32:10).

He untethered the goat. The goat looked at him, and he looked back. Then the man turned his back and retraced his steps. The goat was now alone, alone with the sins of the people, alone in the desert—where there was not a single blade of grass, not a single drop of water, not a solitary patch of shade, where there was no eye to pity, no hand to save. The blazing sun beat down upon its head. Its strength was dried up like a potsherd, its tongue was cleaving to its jaws until at last it died alone, bearing the sins of others to a place where none would be able to find them.

But, when all is said and done, God still saw those sins. All the elaborate, intricate ritual of the Day of Atonement could not cancel those sins. The ritual was all a cover-up. The whole ritual pointed forward to Calvary.

In the meantime, the high priest had been busy. The sin question had been settled for another year. Before the solemn work of this Day of Atonement had begun, the high priest had divested himself of his garments for glory. The same was true with the Lord when He came to earth to deal fully with sin. He laid aside the glory that He had with His Father before ever time began. It had to be so. Had He come in blazing splendor, He would have blinded and dazzled the world. So He came divested not of His deity, never that, but of His glory. In the words of Robert Chapman (1803–1902):

> His life of pain and sorrow,
> Was like unto His birth,
> He would no glory borrow,
> No majesty from earth.[2]

He was known as "the carpenter's son." In humble guise, Jesus went about doing good. He became the sin bearer. He dealt with sin, not by a process of covering it up but by providing means whereby it could be canceled completely. The work is now finished once and for all. Once and for all time, once for all sin, once for all mankind. The Lord has now resumed His glory. That glory will indeed be displayed at His return and will fill people with fear (Matt. 24:30–31).

And that, in type and shadow, is how the Israelites saw their high priest when he reappeared.

3. Dealing with persisting sin

The problem with the sacrifices and offerings of the Old Testament was that they could not really deal permanently with sin. Another eleven steps had to be taken.

1. The fit man returned to the outskirts of the camp.
2. He took off his clothes, washed them, and bathed himself, demonstrating the defiling nature of sin.

3. He came into the camp thus signifying that the work of taking away the sin of the people was done.
4. The bodies of the bullock and the goat (the sin offering for the priest and people) were taken outside the camp.
5. The two carcasses were burned completely, including the skin.
6. When the burning was complete, the person who had taken care of it washed his clothes.
7. He then washed himself.
8. He came back into the camp.
9. The people were dismissed to their homes to mark the date on their calendars.
10. They spent the rest of the day afflicting their souls and observing the day as a Sabbath of rest.
11. They were then to note the day on next year's official calendar because it would all have to be done over again.

What a sobering reminder of the persistent nature of sin. We are now on this side of Calvary! There are no more sacrifices for sin. The Lord has finished that work. More! He has blazed a trail for us right into the Holiest where God sits enthroned. Thanks to Calvary we can come as sons and daughters where saints of old would not dare to tread. We can come whenever we like, stay as long as we like, talk about whatever we like. What more could we ask than that?

But what about those who profess themselves to be horrified by all this emphasis on sin and blood? They hurl insults in the face of God, accusing Him of cruelty and carnage. They forget two things—the awesome, blazing holiness of God, and the immeasurable sinfulness and culpability of sin.

PART 3

POETICAL

Crowned with thorns upon the tree,
Silent in Thine agony;
Dying crushed beneath the load
Of the wrath and curse of God.

On Thy pale and suffering brow
Mystery of love and woe;
On Thy grief and sore amaze,
Savior I would fix my gaze!

Sin atoning sacrifice
Thou art precious in mine eyes;
Thou alone my rest shall be,
Now and through eternity.[1]

     —H. Gratton Guinness
      (1835–1910)

CHAPTER 7

DARK CALVARY

Psalm 22

1. The loneliness (vv. 1–6)
   a. The distance (v. 1)
   b. The despair (vv. 2–6)
      (1) Utter abandonment (vv. 2–5)
      (2) Utter abasement (v. 6)
2. The laughter (vv. 7–18)
   a. What they said (vv. 7–8)
   b. What they saw (vv. 9–18)
3. The lion (vv. 19–21)
4. The Lord (vv. 22–31)
   a. As a priest (vv. 22–26)
   b. As a prince (vv. 27–31)

THE GOSPELS RECORD THE FACTS OF the crucifixion; the Psalms record the feelings of the Crucified. This is very evident in Psalm 22, one of the great prophetic and messianic psalms. The experiences David describes in this psalm were not his. They were Christ's.

1. The loneliness

Oh, the unutterable loneliness of Calvary! We have seen something of it in the story of the scapegoat. But that was only the shadow of Calvary. "Lover and friend hast thou put far from me," was the great sob that welled up from the soul of the Savior. There was no eye to pity, no hand to save. True, John, His beloved disciple, and Mary, His mother, came to the cross, but in His wisdom and love He sent them away. We can picture Him hanging on the cross, naked, wounds in His hands and feet, every bone out of joint, His whole body ablaze with pain, as He watched them wend their way through the mob. Again and again they would stop and look back. Then, obedient to His last will and testament, Mary would take John by the arm and continue on her way, a sword stabbing her own soul also.

With His mother gone, all He had left was His Father. His Father had been with Him each step of the way. Jesus had never a thought that had not been wholly centered on His Father. He had never spoken a word that had not come from His Father. There had never been an action of His that had not resulted from His communion with His Father. The life that He lived down here was His Father's life. "I and my Father are One," He could say.

He had been with His Father in the Upper Room. He had talked about Him continually, there, and on the way to Gethsemane. "In my Father's house are many mansions," He told the disciples, describing to them the home from whence He had come and to which now He was about to return. "I am the true Vine, and my Father is the Husband-man," He had told them, describing the new relationship that was soon to be theirs. They were to enjoy the same relationship to Him that He had enjoyed with His Father. His Father was with Him on the last walk along the Gethsemane road. "Father," He had prayed, "the hour is come; glorify the Son." His Father had been with Him in Gethsemane. The Father was with Him still when He was nailed to the tree: "Father," He said, "forgive them for they know not what they do."

So, He still had His Father. And, having His Father, He had all. He had been with His Father before the worlds began, in that dateless, timeless past, back beyond the beginning of time. There, in a past eternity, Father, Son, and Holy Spirit had enjoyed sweet fellowship together. No cloud had ever come into that sky, no shadow had ever fallen across the landscape of heaven. No discordant note had been introduced into their blissful harmony. So as long as He still had His Father, what mattered the hatred of hell and the malice and hatred of men?

But now came the loneliness. His father was no longer there. That is the first thing we note—*the distance*. The light had gone out. An eerie darkness fell on all the land. For the first time in His eternal existence, there was distance between Him and His Father in heaven. There was a great gulf fixed. He was engulfed in the horror of a great darkness. He was cut off, abandoned, alone.

We remember Fagin, the disreputable old man who made a living off the ill-gotten gains of young boys and girls he had seduced into a life of crime. In the end, he was caught and sentenced to death. Dickens pictures him vividly there in his cell awaiting the executioner's call. Dickens writes:

> He was searched that he might not have about him the means of anticipating the law; this ceremony performed, they led him to one of the condemned cells, and left him there—alone. He sat on a stone bench opposite the door, which served for a seat and bedstead; and casting his blood-shot eyes upon the ground, he tried to collect his thoughts. After awhile he began to remember a few disjointed fragments of what the judge had said though it had seemed to him at the time that he could not hear a word. These gradually fell into their proper places and by degrees suggested more, so that in a little time he had the whole, almost as it was delivered.
>
> He was to be hanged by the neck till he was dead—that was the end—to be hanged by the neck till he was dead. As it came on very dark he began to think of all the men he had known who had died upon the scaffold; some of them through his means. They rose up in such quick succession that he could hardly count them. He had seen some of them die—and he had

joked too because they died with prayers on their lips. With what a rattling noise the drop went down; and how suddenly they changed from strong and vigorous men to dangling heaps of clothes! Some of them might have inhabited that very cell—sat upon that very spot. It was very dark; why didn't they bring him a light. It was like sitting in a vault strewn with dead bodies— the cap, the noose, the pinioned arms, the faces that he knew, even beneath that hideous veil—light! light![2]

Thus Dickens described the last hours of this evil old man. At one time he raved and blasphemed; at another he howled and tore his hair. Then came the night of the last awful day. A withering sense of his helpless and desperate state came in its full intensity upon his blighted soul. Oliver Twist came to visit him. The demented old man thought he could use the boy as a means of escape. He laid his hands upon him in desperation. The guards came and rescued Oliver. "He struggled with the power of desperation for an instant," says Dickens, "and then sent up cry upon cry that penetrated even those massive walls and rang in their ears until they reached the open yard."

So, that old sinner faced death and damnation alone and in the dark, haunted by his sins. But the torments of that wicked man were nothing compared with the anguish of Jesus on the tree. In unspeakable horror of being abandoned, He gave voice: "My God, my God, why hast thou forsaken me?" (Matt. 27:46).

Then there was *the despair*. "Oh my God, I cry in the daytime . . . and am not silent" (Ps. 22:2). The only answer was silence. "Our fathers trusted in thee: they trusted, and thou didst deliver them. They cried unto thee, and were delivered" (Ps. 22:4–5). Again, the only response He received was silence.

There were two reasons why the heavens became as brass to Him in His terrible hour of need. They are highlighted by the word *but*— "But thou art holy . . . but I am a worm" (Ps. 22:3, 6).

"But thou art holy!" Surely Jesus was holy Himself. The Bible says so. He was "holy, harmless, undefiled, separate from sinners" (Heb. 7:26). It was flameproof holiness. Satan hurled every conceivable temp-

tation at Christ and found Him not merely innocent (as Adam and
Eve before the Fall) but holy! Holy as God is holy.

So why did the Lord say, "But thou art holy"? Because on the Cross
He not only died for us; He died as us—as every poor lost Fagin of
this fallen race. He did not become sinful—never that! Had He become sinful He could not have saved anyone. He was made sin for us,
He who knew no sin (2 Cor. 5:21). In that dread hour the altogether
lovely one knew *utter abandonment.*

And *utter abasement*—imagine it! The One whom angels worship
declared, "I am a worm, and no man." The word used here for worm
is an unusual one. Strong says it points to the grub that, when crushed,
yields a scarlet hue. "Though your sins be as scarlet," Isaiah had declared, "they shall be as white as snow" (Isa. 1:18). He whose personal
character was white as snow is now seen as scarlet so that we whose
sins are as scarlet might become as white as snow. These opening verses
of Psalm 22 give us what is probably the most terrible view of the
Cross to be found anywhere in Scripture.

2. The laughter

We notice first *what they said:* "All they that see me laugh me to
scorn: they shoot out the lip, they shake the head, saying, he trusted
on the LORD that he would deliver him: let him deliver him, seeing he
delighted in him" (Ps. 22:7–8).

The Lord's absolute and implicit trust in God was common knowledge. They threw it in His face as He hung upon the tree. It certainly
seemed that God had forsaken Him. The Lord's trust stood firm. He
was not trusting God to protect Him from the tree—that issue had
been settled in Gethsemane. He was trusting God to bring Him up
from the tomb.

If God had indeed delivered Him by bringing Him down from the
cross, then there would have been no salvation for them. Caught in
the very act of killing Him, the Father's well-beloved, their doom would
have been swift and sure. The Lord simply ignored these ignorant
and iniquitous men. He had known all along what they would say. He

had read it hundreds of times in David's psalm. At Calvary they said the very things David had said they would say.

We notice also *what they saw.* They saw what David had seen—the mob. "Many bulls have compassed me: strong bulls of Bashan have beset me round. They gaped upon me with their mouths, as a ravening and a roaring lion" (Ps. 22:12–13). Bashan was a stretch of farming country on the east side of the Jordan, famous for its cattle. Poetically "the bulls of Bashan" symbolized the bestial, raving mob, led by the priests and scribes, who stood around the cross, bellowing and taunting.

Centuries before the time of Christ, David saw the Man (Christ); he heard Him cry, "I am poured out like water, and all my bones are out of joint: my heart is like wax . . . my strength is dried up like a potsherd; and my tongue cleaveth to my jaws; and thou hast brought me into the dust of death" (Ps. 22:14–15). The physical agonies of the Lord were thus foreseen by David a thousand years before they happened. His bones were all out of joint—they had become a screaming mass of pain. His mighty strength, His glorious physique was broken and, to crown it all, He suffered a raging thirst beneath the blazing sun.

David saw the murderers. "For dogs have compassed me: the assembly of the wicked have enclosed me: they pierced my hands and my feet" (Ps. 22:16).

It is unlikely that David had ever witnessed a crucifixion. In giving him this psalm, however, the Holy Spirit allowed him to see clearly what one was like. David saw the pack of dogs (the Gentiles, specifically the Romans) who actually did the dreadful deed. He saw "the assembly of the wicked," a prophetic glimpse of the Jewish Sanhedrin, the ruling assembly of Israel, who closed in around the cross to snarl and sneer. He saw the hands and feet of the Holy One pierced by nails. We could go on and on. According to one count, no less than thirty-three distinct utterances in this psalm were fulfilled at Calvary.

So there He hung—on the cross. All about Him were wicked men who mocked and jeered. Their terrible laughter rang out until God turned their jeers to fears by putting out the sun.

3. The lion

The lion, the ox, the dog—all three were there at the place called Calvary. The lion and the wild ox are sworn enemies. They joined forces in their attack upon Jesus. We see them side by side harassing the dying Son of God.

The dogs were there. The Jews referred to Gentiles as dogs. Dogs hunt in disciplined packs. The reference to dogs may be a reference then to the military detachment of Roman soldiers that actually carried out the crucifixion.

The "strong bulls of Bashan" and the "unicorn," or, better, "the wild ox," which stood six feet at the shoulder and which, although formidable, was a ceremonially clean animal—these creatures may well symbolize the nation of Israel led by Caiaphas and his crowd.

Then there was the lion with its gaping mouth. The Bible readily identifies this foe. The lion refers to Satan (1 Peter 5:8). Paul tells us how the Lord Jesus on the cross triumphed gloriously over all of Satan's principalities and powers (Col. 2:15). For Satan was behind the whole terrible business as the prince of this world (John 12:31; 14:30; 16:11).

4. The Lord

The remainder of the psalm focuses on the glorious triumph of the Lord Jesus. In Scripture, "the sufferings of Christ" are never divorced from "the glory that should follow" (1 Peter 1:11). So it is with Psalm 22. The prophet-poet, focusing on the Lord's resurrection and on His return, saw ahead to the time when Christ would have all the ministry of *a priest* and all the majesty of *a prince*. People will remind each other during the golden years of the Lord's millennial reign of how much they owe to Him. "He hath done this" (Ps. 22:31), they will cry. The same word is used in 2 Chronicles 4:11: "And Huram *finished* the work" (of building the temple, italics added). "Finished!" said David. "Finished!" said Ezra the scribe. "Finished!" said Christ on the cross. Thus, this awesome psalm begins with one of the words of Christ on the cross: "My God, my God, why hast thou forsaken me?" It ends with another of the Lord's words on the tree, "It is finished!"

When I survey the wondrous cross
On which the Prince of glory died,
My richest gain I count but loss,
And pour contempt on all my pride.

Forbid it, Lord, that I should boast,
Save in the cross of Christ, my God;
All the vain things that charm me most
I sacrifice them to His blood.

See, from His head, His hands, His feet,
Sorrow and love flow mingled down;
Did e'er such love and sorrow meet
Or thorns compose so rich a crown?

Were the whole realm of nature mine,
That were a present far too small;
Love so amazing, so divine,
Demands my heart, my life, my all![1]
                    —Isaac Watts (1674–1748)

CHAPTER 8

IS IT NOTHING TO YOU?

Lamentations 1:12

1. The callous multitude
2. The crying man
3. The crowning mystery

THE BOOK OF LAMENTATIONS IS A hybrid, as much at home among the poets as among the prophets of the Old Testament. It is an elegy—a poem, a lament, a mournful contemplation of disaster; in actual fact it is a collection of five such sad elegies, all spoken by the prophet Jeremiah as he wept over fallen Jerusalem. The prophet loved both the city and its people as he loved his own soul.

The Jews read this book on the ninth day of the fifth month (*Ab,* our August). On that day, they annually commemorate the five great disasters that befell the nation in its long history. These disasters were (1) the rebellion of the children of Israel in the wilderness and their consequent forty-year wanderings; (2) the destruction of the first temple by the Babylonians; (3) the destruction of the second temple by the Romans; (4) the taking of Bether by the Romans under Hadrian, when no less than 580,000 Jews were slain; and (5) the plowing of Zion like a field in fulfillment of Jeremiah 26:18 and Micah 3:12.

Jeremiah's fivefold lament is arranged in an arresting style. The first two chapters consist of twenty-two long verses, each one commencing with a successive letter of the Hebrew alphabet. The next chapter has sixty-six verses, each triad commencing with the same letter—the first three verses begin with *aleph,* the next three with *beth,* and so on through the alphabet. The fourth chapter has twenty-two long verses but the acrostic is abandoned, probably because of an emotional outburst by poor Jeremiah.

In the Hebrew text, the name of the book of Lamentations is taken from its very first word, "Alas!" In it the prophet's broken heart is bared for all to see. Indeed, we are hardly into the book by a mere dozen verses when we come across a statement that we instinctively want to lift right out of its context and apply directly to Christ.

The prophet cries: *"Is it nothing to you, all ye that pass by? behold, and see if there be any sorrow like unto my sorrow, which is done unto me, wherewith the Lord hath afflicted me in the day of his fierce anger"* (Lam. 1:12).

Whether we look at this verse from the standpoint of the sorrows of Jeremiah or from the viewpoint of the sufferings of Jesus, the outline is the same. There is a callous multitude, a crying man, and a crowning mystery.

We can picture Jeremiah in his utter wretchedness. He had been called to the prophetic ministry when still very young. He was to foretell doom and gloom to his fellow citizens. Judgment was coming. We remind ourselves that this was in the thirteenth year of King Josiah (a good king who did his best to call his apostate people back to God). Jeremiah, young as he was, could see that Josiah's noble efforts would be in vain. He continued to preach until the capture of Jerusalem in the fifth month of the eleventh year of Zedekiah. Forty years of heartache! Indeed, his sorrows were to be so great that the prophet was told by God he must not marry. No woman should be expected to share the life of pain and suffering that was to be his lot in life. No wonder Jeremiah tried to excuse himself from such a call.

The first people to oppose him were the men of Anathoth, his own hometown. They threatened to kill him as a traitor for proclaiming the certain victory of Babylon over Judah and for urging Judah to surrender without a fight.

In the fourth year of wicked King Jehoiakim, the prophet began dictating to Baruch the scribe all the prophecies he had been uttering for some twenty years. As soon as the book was finished, Jeremiah told Baruch to take it to the temple and read it to the people who were coming and going there. The scroll was confiscated and taken to the king who listened to a few pages being read, seized it, cut it to pieces with a penknife, and threw it in the fire.

Probably Jeremiah expected no less from such a man as Jehoiakim. His response was to write another, longer scroll. For that, he was put in the stocks by Pashur the priest but was almost immediately released.

As we can well imagine, he was violently and bitterly denounced as a traitor. When the siege of Jerusalem was raised by the Babylonians because of their preoccupation with Egypt, Jeremiah made preparations to leave Jerusalem. He was seized, accused of being a deserter, and thrown into prison. He languished there for many days and then was committed to the callous attentions of the court guard. He was finally seized by the authorities, flung into a dungeon, and left there to die. In that wretched prison, he sank down into a miry clay where he would doubtless have perished had he not found an unexpected friend, an Ethiopian eunuch. This man persuaded the king to have Jeremiah pulled up from the horrible pit and once again remanded to the custody of the court guard.

The Babylonians, naturally enough, regarded Jeremiah as a friend. When they took Jerusalem, they deported many people but allowed Jeremiah his freedom. Before long, the behavior of those Jews the Babylonians had left behind called Jeremiah back to his thankless task. He denounced the schemes of those who nursed hopes of throwing off the Babylonian yoke. In the end, he was carried forcibly down to Egypt by some of his rebellious countrymen. There he delivered his final prophecies.

So, we can picture this desolate prophet standing at some busy intersection in Jerusalem, trying to warn his countrymen of judgment soon to come. He was an object of hatred and scorn, and his voice fell

on deaf ears. A few would curse him and cast stones and filth at him.
Most people ignored him. The fellow must be mad! Let him be!

Our thoughts run down the centuries. A new "man of sorrows"
comes. It is the same old city. There are the same old sins. A different
crowd runs the country, but they hate Jesus as much as their ancestors hated Jeremiah. We compare the great, heart-searching woes of
Jeremiah to those of Jesus. In the light of His sufferings, those of
Jeremiah were small indeed.

1. The callous multitude

The site of the execution was a skull-shaped hill just outside the
Jerusalem wall, with a well-trodden road nearby. Passover time had
arrived. People from all parts of the empire were there, curious for a
look at the crucified One. They could see the placard nailed over His
head—"JESUS OF NAZARETH THE KING OF THE JEWS" (John
19:19). Many joined the chorus of hate and scorn that was being leveled at that One as the crowds drew in closer for a better look. The
title had scalded the Jewish authorities, but the Roman governor refused to change it. It was a sardonic jibe at the Jews and gave him a
sort of sour satisfaction. He was through with that Man now, having
signed His death warrant, but Pilate's conscience plagued him just
the same. He shrugged his shoulders. He shook off his doubts. He
was Caesar's friend. What else could a Roman governor do? Besides,
why should he care? The Jews were to blame. He, Pontius Pilate, had
washed his hands of the whole affair.

"King of the Jews!" That was not the half of it. The One who hung
there in agony and blood was the Son of God. He was the eternal,
uncreated, self-existing second person of the Godhead. He it was who
had stooped down to fashion Adam's clay. He it was who had flung
the stars into space. He it was who had existed from all eternity, One
with the Father and the Spirit from everlasting to everlasting. The
song of the seraphim, the anthems of the angels, the worship of the
cherubim of principalities, of powers, of thrones, and dominions all
centered in Him. All were strangely silent now as a race of beings on a

distant planet went about the dark and dreadful work of murdering the incarnate Christ of God. As for men, they callously hammered Him to a Roman tree. Then, those who passed by either hurried on their way, carelessly indifferent to His sufferings, or callously stopped for a while to hurl dust or stones at Him or to throw a curse or a ribald joke at Him. It was nothing to them.

To this day, they pass Him by—people by the countless million. They come to church services. They hear the wondrous story. They pass Him by. It is nothing to them.

2. The crying man

"Behold, and see if there be any sorrow like unto my sorrow" (Lam. 1:12). The words "behold, and see" suggest the need for careful scrutiny, for diligent examination. There is more to this than meets the eye. The words can be rendered, "Look attentively." A casual, careless attitude will never do.

The Bible contains numerous stories of suffering saints. There are the sufferings of Jacob, for instance. His sufferings were *parental*. Although he was the father of the twelve tribes, poor old Jacob had his share of disappointments and sadness. Indeed, we see a sharp decline in the patriarchal family right from the start. Abraham excelled as a parent. "I know him," God said, "that he will command his children and his household after him" (Gen. 18:19). Isaac abandoned the gold standard. He and Rebekah had favorites right from the start (Gen. 25:28), and a sad mess they made of things before they were through. As for Jacob, his family life was in a perpetual state of upheaval (Gen. 29–30). When Jacob gave his testimony before Pharaoh, he confessed, "Few and evil have the days of the years of my life been" (Gen. 47:9).

Look at his family! There was the constant rivalry and bickering of his wives. There was the terrible sin of Reuben, the seduction of his daughter Dinah, and the criminal conduct of Levi and Simeon. There was the death of two of Judah's sons at the hand of God and Judah's episode with the "harlot." There was the general jealousy often of the boys against Joseph. Then there was the tragic loss of his beloved

Joseph and Jacob's deep suspicion that his sons had gotten rid of him. Then came the arrest of Simeon by the mighty and mysterious Grand Vizier of Egypt and his demand that Benjamin be taken to Egypt as a token for the good faith of the others. There were sorrows enough in Jacob's life. But those sorrows were not to be compared with the sufferings of Jesus.

Then, there were the sufferings of Joseph. His sufferings were *positional.* God had a high destiny for Joseph, but first He had to train him in the school of adversity. Joseph's brothers hated him. He was Rachel's firstborn and, as such, he monopolized Jacob's affections. Reuben eyed him with suspicion and dislike. Joseph was his rival. For Reuben was Jacob's firstborn, Leah's eldest. The firstborn son in a patriarchy was something special. This position brought unique rewards and responsibilities. So Reuben felt threatened by Joseph, beloved Rachel's firstborn, and responded accordingly. Dan, Naphtali, Gad, and Asher disliked Joseph because his goodness exposed their wickedness, and also because they were all sons of the slave wives, whereas Joseph was the son of Rachel, Jacob's beloved.

But those were only the beginning of his sorrows. The day came when the older boys seized him and sold him into Egypt as a slave. Purchased to be business manager of the affairs of one of Pharaoh's officers, Joseph faced further trials. The man's wife tried to seduce him, and when he resisted, she testified that he had tried to rape her. Her outraged husband threw him into prison and there he languished for years, forsaken and forgotten by all. The one spark of hope he had was the promise of Pharaoh's chief butler to remember Joseph once he, the butler, got out of prison. It was a hope that came to nothing. We can well imagine, as year followed year, how Joseph despaired of ever seeing the outside world again. But Joseph's sorrows were mild compared with those of the Lord.

And what about the sufferings of Job? His sufferings were *providential.* They burst upon him, wave after wave, without explanation and without mitigation. He lost his vast fortune. He lost all his children in one disastrous night. He lost his health. He lost the sympathy of his wife. His "friends" came to sympathize and then stayed on to sermonize. Poor Job! He wrung his hands! He wept! He prayed! He argued! He challenged God! But there was no explanation. He scorned the suggestions and accusations of his friends. His sorrows seemingly leaped upon him from nowhere and threatened to go on until he died. Great as they undoubtedly were, however, Job's sufferings cannot be compared with the sufferings of Christ.

We think, too, of the sufferings of Jonah. His sufferings were *punitive*. He reaped the due reward of his deeds. We see him aboard the boat on the high seas in a screaming gale. We see him hanging onto the rigging for dear life, confessing to the terrified mariners that it was all his fault. We see the sailors, at last, take him by his hands and feet and heave him overboard. His sorrows had only just begun. Oh, the horror of it! To be swallowed alive by a monster from the deep! How can we begin to describe the anguish and despair of this runaway prophet? The darkness! The stench! The burning gastric juices eating at his living flesh! The certainty of a terrible death! He, himself, said he was in "the belly of hell" (Jonah 2:2). So great were his sufferings that he is the only prophet to whom the Lord Jesus directly likened Himself. Even so, Jonah's sufferings cannot be compared with His.

We come back to the sufferings of Jeremiah. His were *personal*. All about him stretched a city sheltering the people he loved. His one great task was to weep and warn. He hoped and prayed that his words would be heeded so that the terrible judgment he foresaw might be averted. It was not to be. The Babylonians came at last, and Jeremiah saw his direst predictions fulfilled. The city was subjected to siege. The enemy sought to breach the wall and scale its ramparts. The Jews fought back with ferocity and ingenuity—and with growing despair. People were famished. All was lost. Then, with a wild yell, the Babylonians burst in, and the wretched city was given over to the sack. There was an orgy of rape, murder, and looting. When the first fury of lust was over, there came the more deliberate atrocities. The young, the weak, and the old were sorted out. With cold-blooded cruelty, babes were dashed to pieces against the stones. The healthy and able-bodied were chained in readiness for the long march to the slave markets of Babylon. Children were torn from parents, wives from husbands. Slave drivers with whips slashed away at the slightest provocation.

Jeremiah stood by and wept. Again and again, in the opening verses of Lamentations, he wrote down the horror and despair of it all—no rest! No pasture! No comforter! For every tear the wailing captives shed, he shed a tear. For every cry they uttered, he uttered a cry. "No sorrow like unto my sorrow," he wrote. But he was wrong.

We climb again that hill of shame, the hill called Calvary. High and lifted up on a cross of wood, nailed in agony to that tree, we see the One who was, indeed, "a man of sorrows and acquainted with grief." It was the end of a long and ordained road. The rising tide of His sorrow began ere time began when, in the council chambers of eternity, He took upon Himself the role of Redeemer for a lost and ruined race.

It rose higher when He came to this planet in space to be born. He entered into the hardships and heartaches of life on earth. All about Him were the marks of sin and death.

Now, at Calvary on the cross, His sorrows overflowed. He hung upon Golgotha's tree, and His heart broke. "Strong crying and tears" is how the Spirit Himself described it (Heb. 5:7). "Behold, and see if there be any sorrows like unto my sorrow." No, Jeremiah, we have seen your sorrows and terrible they were, but you must yield. There never have been, in all the annals of time, sorrows like unto His.

3. The crowning mystery

"Behold, and see . . . my sorrow, which is done unto me, wherewith the LORD hath afflicted me in the day of his fierce anger" (Lam. 1:12). Jeremiah did, indeed, live through one such day, the day when Jerusalem fell and the victorious and vengeful Babylonians burst in. God's wrath had been dammed up for a very long time. Jeremiah saw the dawn break and the tidal wave of doom break over city, temple, and people. But it was nothing like Calvary.

"The day of his fierce anger" was the day when God forsook Jesus on the cross. It was the day when, in utter darkness, Jesus was "made sin" for us, when the whole weight and guilt of this world's sin was heaped upon Him. It was the day when, out of the supernatural darkness, came that awful cry, "My God, my God, why hast thou forsaken me?" (Matt. 27:46).

When Jacob broke his heart over his wayward boys, he still had God. When Joseph ate his heart out in Pharaoh's prison, he still had God. When Job wrung his hands over his lost fortune and his dead children and his incurable disease and his estranged wife and his quarrelsome friends, he still had God. When Jonah's torment reached its climax, he still had God. When Jeremiah wept his way through chapter after chapter of his lamentations, he still had God.

But when Jesus broke His heart in the dark on the cross by Himself, He had nobody, not even God. It was the day of God's fierce anger. The waters of judgment closed over Christ's head. He sank in deep mire where there was no standing, and all God's waves and billows passed over His head. He had nobody, not even God.

"Is it nothing to you, all ye that pass by? behold, and see if there be any sorrow like unto my sorrow, which is done unto me, wherewith the LORD hath afflicted me in the day of his fierce anger."

PART 4

PROPHETICAL

O Christ, what burdens bowed Thy head!
Our load was laid on Thee.
Thou stoodest in the sinner's stead
To bear all ill for me.
A victim led Thy blood was shed;
Now there's no load for me.

Death and the curse were in our cup—
O Christ, 'twas full for Thee!
But Thou hast drained the last dark drop,
'Tis empty now for me.
That bitter cup, love drank it up;
Left but the love for me.

Jehovah lifted up His rod—
O Christ, it fell on Thee!
Thou wast sore stricken of Thy God;
There's not one stroke for me.
Thy blood beneath that rod has flowed:
Thy bruising healeth me.

The tempest's awful voice was heard,
O Christ it broke on Thee;
Thy open bosom was my ward;
It bore the storm for me.
Thy form was scarred, Thy visage marred;
Now cloudless peace for me![1]

    —Ann Ross Cousin (1824–1906)

CHAPTER 9

The Perfect Servant

Isaiah 52:13–15

1. The uniqueness of His person (v. 13)
   a. How lowly He was
   b. How lofty He was
2. The uniqueness of His passion (v. 14)
3. The uniqueness of His position (v. 15)
   a. He will startle the nations
   b. He will silence the nations
   c. He will sober the nations

THE JEWS—SCATTERED ACROSS THE face of the earth; the objects of endemic anti-Semitism and occasionally of epidemic anti-Semitism in various lands; loved; tolerated and hated in turn; made the scapegoat for the world's ills and the living embodiment of Deuteronomy 27–30—they have no trouble identifying the servant mentioned in Isaiah 52:1–15 and 53:11. The servant, they say, is the nation of Israel. However, those whose eyes have been opened by the Holy Spirit to recognize the truth of Isaiah 52:1–53:12 see very much more than that. Clearly, here we have a prophetic portrait of the Lord Himself—and the Holy Spirit Himself affirms that Isaiah 53 points directly to Christ (v. 7; Acts 8:32).

1. The uniqueness of His person

The prophecy begins with *how lowly He was*. But let us put things in perspective by asking a question. If God were to enter into human life how would He come? Now answer the question from the standpoint of human reasoning rather than from divine revelation in all four Gospels. We know that the divine revelation is true, but how close would we come to the truth, approaching it merely through careful thought?[2]

Would God come *as God?* If so, what would be the most obvious thing about Him? For one thing He would surely demonstrate power and authority over the animal creation and over the forces of nature. He would have an astounding ability to do the supernatural, to feed a hungry multitude with a few loaves and fishes, to still a raging storm, to walk upon restless waves of the angry deep—that kind of thing. We would also expect Him to be a healer of the ailments that afflict our race. Moreover, His thoughts and His ways would be of a higher, nobler quality than ours.

As to His arrival on this planet, there would surely be portents of His coming—a sign in the sky, for example—perhaps a new, spectacular star, or the sudden appearance of a celestial choir.

Should He decide to leave this world the way we do, by death, we would expect further wonders. There would be signs in the sky and on the earth—a sudden darkening of the sun, an earthquake, graves bursting open—things like that. Along with all this we would expect infallible proof that He had conquered death.

Or suppose He chose to come *as a man!* First of all, He would have no difficulty establishing an official family tree to link Him solidly with this world. He would have a mother. He would be a member of a family. He might even have ordinary brothers and sisters. As for His mother, we would expect her to be godly, pure, spiritually minded, and of considerable courage.

He would have a valid history. He would be born at a certain time and place, would go through all the stages of growing up—from being a babe, to becoming a boy, a teen, and a workingman. And in it all, He would be free from sin.

As a genuine human being He would get hungry, thirsty, and tired. At times He would be happy and sad, wrathful and forgiving, loving and kind—all without sin. He would have to be absolutely good.

He would have an ever-widening circle of friends and acquaintances and He would attract a smaller circle of committed followers. People would compare Him with this world's great heroes, important figures who would soon be seen to be far inferior to Him. His wisdom, charm, and power, along with His goodness, compassion, and love, would set Him apart from all others.

He would reach out to the poor, the sick, the bereaved, and the fallen, but He would not compromise with their sin.

If He came as a man, He would surely come *as a king*. He would be born in a certain place and at a given time. Moreover He would be born in a given social class, surely that of an emperor or king with a long line of royal ancestors. As the time of His inauguration approached, it would be announced by a properly accredited herald. Eventually He would announce His agenda.

The existing establishment would feel threatened by this king. The common people would cheer Him on approvingly—any king who could put food on the table, heal their ailments, and take on the establishment would certainly be popular. Those in power, however, would soon see this new king as a threat to their religious, political, and economic power. They would plot against Him. Attempts would be made to discredit Him and to get rid of Him. His various foes would come together in agreement, joining forces to find a way to get rid of Him. Some segments of society might try to force His hand, to make Him act too soon. He would resist such moves.

In the end, the conspirators might win, possibly by subverting one of His men. A mob rising might provide the opportunity to give Him a phony trial and arrange for Him to be executed.

Well, He *did* come as God. John tells us that. He *did* come as Man. Luke tells us that. He *did* come as King. Matthew tells us that. But, we ask ourselves, if God were to visit us and enter into human life, would He come as a servant? The prophet Isaiah foretold that He would, and Mark says He did. Hardly likely, we would say, but just the same, that's how He came, as God's perfect Servant. God never had such a servant like Jesus! "Lo, I come," He said, as He stepped off the throne of the universe, "(in the volume of the book it is written of me,) to do thy will, O God" (Heb. 10:7). "I do always those things that please him," He said (John 8:29).

Mark says of Him, "The Son of man came not to be ministered unto, but to minister"—not to be served but to serve (Mark 10:45). Mark's whole gospel is dedicated to the task of presenting Christ as the One who was "obedient unto death, even the death of the cross" (Phil. 2:8). We hear His words in dark Gethsemane: "Take away this cup from me: nevertheless not what I will, but what thou wilt" (Mark 14:36). From the very start, He had to be about His Father's business (Luke 2:49). He was, indeed, the lowly One (Matt. 11:29).

It all came into focus during Jesus' temptation in the wilderness. Satan had offered Him a completely unacceptable shortcut to the throne, one that promised to annul the Cross. The Lord's answer was brief and to the point—the answer of a true servant: "It is written, Thou shalt worship the Lord thy God, and him only shalt thou serve" (Matt. 4:10). We can almost hear God up in heaven say to the angels, "There! What do you think of that?"

Isaiah moves on to tell us *how lofty He was:* "He shall be exalted and extolled, and be very high" (Isa. 52:13). The path of obedience led directly from the cradle to the cross, and the way of the cross led Him home. When His work on earth was done, He led His disciples out through the gates of Jerusalem, down across the Kedron, up past the Garden of Gethsemane, and on up to Olivet's brow. He raised His hands in parting benediction then stepped into the sky. And He was gone! Received and enveloped in the Shechinah glory cloud! Up, up He went, through rank after rank of the angels. In, in He went through the gate of the celestial city. On, on He went following the golden highway to the great white throne. But what is this? There upon the throne sits God in all His glory, in a light unapproachable, in an aura of blinding holiness, amid the cherubim and seraphim, unleashing a thunderous anthem of praise.

Right up to that throne He went, a Man in a battered human body, the triumphant Victor over sin and death and hell! Room is made for Him upon that throne, His Father's throne on high. He seats Himself at the right hand of the Majesty on high where no created being would dare to sit. Lofty? Yes indeed! Exalted and extolled and very high? Yes indeed! For He who once was so lowly is what He always was and never ceased to be, God, over all, "blessed for evermore" (2 Cor. 11:31).

2. The uniqueness of His passion

The transition from Isaiah 52:13 to the next verse is sudden, startling, unexpected, and awesome: "As many were astonished (amazed) at thee; his visage was so marred more than any man, and his form more than the sons of men." The New Testament writers are seemingly reluctant to say much about the actual crucifixion itself and are restrained as to what they say about the beatings and physical abuse the Lord endured even before He arrived at Calvary. They tell us the bare facts but do not dwell on the details. We know that He was blindfolded at one point in the proceedings and punched by His captors who then jibed at Him to prophesy who had smitten Him. We know He was scourged so that much of His body became one dreadful wound. We know, too, that at one point His beard was wrenched from His face. And we know that one of the Jewish officials at His trial before Annas gave Him a slap in the face—the beginning of it all. This phase of His sufferings ended with the Romans smiting Him over and over again on the head with a cane. As He came staggering out of the building where He had been thus abused, carrying as best He could the heavy cross, He must have been an appalling sight. It is no wonder Isaiah says that "His visage was so marred more than any man, and his form more than the sons of men." He was hardly recognizable as a man.

But there was worse to come. Typical of the Evangelists, Luke gives his record of the actual crucifixion itself in four words—"there they crucified him" (Luke 23:33). Our history books fill in the rest. Death by crucifixion was excruciating and prolonged. We can barely imagine its torments. There was the tortured flesh, the unnatural position, the cramped muscles, the raging thirst, the ceaseless pain, the burning heat, the open shame.

Isaiah tells us that He, the Lord, who now sits enthroned on high, endured torments so great that even those callous, hardened men who sat around the cross looked on in amazement. And this was only the beginning of sorrows.

3. The uniqueness of His position

"So shall he sprinkle (startle) many nations; the kings shall shut their mouths at him: for that which had not been told them shall they see; and that which they had not heard shall they consider" (Isa. 52:15). In this verse, the prophet moves on to the second coming of Christ, to the time when He who once passed this way in lowliest of guise comes back in pomp and power.

He will startle the nations. Some translate the word *startle* as "sprinkle." The Hebrew scholar A. B. Davidson declared it treason against the Hebrew language to render it that way. Some suggest "silence" the nations; others suggest "sober" the nations as a possible rendering. At the time of His coming to reign, the various nations will all be drawn to Megiddo, mobilized for war. The precipitous return of Christ will startle the nations. His coming will be like a fearful lightning flash blazing across the sky. Earth will be convulsed. The heavens above will be emblazoned with terrifying signs. Angel hosts will be seen, rank after rank of them, in battle array. It will all happen in a moment, in the twinkling of an eye. This advent of Jesus in power and great glory (Matt. 24:27–31) will take this wicked world completely by surprise.

He will silence the nations. The nations will be dumbfounded, speechless, overwhelmed. The Beast (the Antichrist) and the False Prophet will be silenced forever, flung headlong into the lake of fire. Many will be silenced in death. Those who are still alive will be summoned to the Valley of Jehoshaphat in Jerusalem to answer for their crimes. They will have little to say, caught red-handed in their sins— though they have had plenty to say about the Lord in the past (Jude

14–15). In the past they used His lovely name as a curse word. Now they will fall paralyzed and silent.

He will sober the nations. Their eyes will be suddenly opened. They will suddenly realize the greatness of their folly down through the centuries in turning their backs on Him and in embracing falsehoods they have been told.

So, this segment of Isaiah's prophecy tells of the sufferings of Christ and, true to form, of the glory that is to follow.

"Man of Sorrows," what a name
For the Son of God who came
Ruined sinners to reclaim!
Hallelujah! What a Savior!

Bearing shame and scoffing rude,
In my place condemned He stood;
Sealed my pardon with His blood;
Hallelujah! What a Savior!

Guilty, vile and helpless, we;
Spotless Lamb of God was He;
"Full atonement!" can it be?
Hallelujah! What a Savior!

Lifted up was He to die,
"It is finished," was His cry;
Now in heaven exalted high;
Hallelujah! What a Savior![1]
　　　　　—Philip P. Bliss (1838–1876)

CHAPTER 10

MAN OF SORROWS

Isaiah 53:1–3

1. The seer (v. 1)
2. The Son (v. 2)
   a. How holy He would be (v. 2a–b)
      (1) His nature (v. 2a)
      (2) His nurture (v. 2b)
   b. How human He would be (v. 2c)
3. The sorrow (v. 3)

NOBODY HAS EVER KNOWN THE Bible like Jesus. As a boy of twelve He astonished the learned rabbis of Jerusalem with His questions. We can think of some of them—"What think ye of Christ? Whose Son is He?" "Of whom speaketh the prophet this? Of himself or some other man?" "If David in the Spirit called Him Lord, how is He then his son?"

By the time He was thirty-three years of age, there was not a person on earth who could hold a candle to Him. Doubtless, the prophet Isaiah would have been able to foresee that. It might well have been a source of solace to him.

1. The seer

"Who hath believed our report? and to whom is the arm of the
LORD revealed?" (Isa. 53:1). Page after page of what Isaiah called his
"report" came from the prophet's pen. Who believed it? Nobody—or
practically nobody! Day after day, he raised his voice to report to the
erring nations of Israel and Judah that God's wrath would assuredly
fall. Who believed him? Practically nobody! Now, in response to their
unbelief, the prophet had this great prophecy about the Messiah, about
His coming, and His coming again. And who would believe it? The
great seer was used to having his prophecies ignored. So, he begins
with the question, "Who has believed me?"

Nor were his doubts groundless. His own Hebrew people, not seeing the portrait of the Lord Jesus in this utterance, believed it was
simply a portrait of the sufferings of Israel down through the ages. In
the church the various chapters of Isaiah have been hacked asunder
by so-called liberals. "Isaiah?" they say. "Which Isaiah? There wasn't
just one Isaiah—there were two." Nonsense, of course, but this dis-
plays the disbelief the prophet had come to expect.

"Who will believe me?" the prophet cried. Back comes the clear
and emphatic reply, "I believe you! I, Jesus, Son of the living God!"
"He that hath ears to hear, let him hear" (Matt. 11:15). Nobody has
ever been such a Bible believer as Jesus was.

2. The Son

Isaiah's eyes ran down the centuries and he caught a glimpse of the
Lord Jesus entering into human life. In verse two he was taken up
with the glorious humanity of Christ. First he points out *how holy He
would be:* "For he shall grow up *before him* as a tender plant, and as a
root out of a dry ground" (italics added). Isaiah was impressed with
the Lord's *nature.*

Some years ago I was preaching in a retirement community in
Florida. The grounds of this place were kept in a beautiful condition
by a retired gardener, a certain Mr. Milligan. On a stormy winter's

night he would pull his chair up to the fire, open his seed catalogs, and dream about what kind of flowers he would need for the spring, what kinds of shrubs and trees he would order for this project or for that. He once told us an interesting fact about plants. "You know," he said, "all plants are catalogued in one of three ways; they are hardy, half-hardy, or tender. There are some very real differences I can assure you.

"A *hardy* plant is one native to the area. It will take ready root because it feels at home there. It likes the soil, and it finds the climate congenial. A hardy plant needs very little attention because it belongs where it is. Everything about the local environment suits its nature, so it will sink down its roots into the soil and flourish. A *half-hardy* plant is not native to the area, but it comes from a place that is similar. It will readily grow where it is planted because it finds the climate, the type of soil, the temperature, and the weather similar to what it has been used to. It can be planted in its new bed and will soon flourish, just as though it was a native. A *tender* plant, however, well that's another story. It comes from quite a different place. It does not find the soil in its new location congenial, nor does it like the climate. It really belongs somewhere else. The gardener knows that if he plants a tender plant, it will need special attention. It will have to be protected from the weather, it will need special nutrients added to the soil, and it will have to be guarded from disease. It is an exotic plant from far, far away.

"Now then," continued the gardener, "our Lord Jesus was on earth as a tender plant. He came here from far away. He was not a native of these shores of ours. His nature was not like ours. We settle down in this sinful world and soon feel at home here. But not Jesus! This world's social and spiritual climate was foreign to Him. As man, He was completely innocent; as God, He is absolutely holy. The character He displayed was simply and absolutely good. He went about doing good. Everything He said was good. He had no sin nature. This world was not His home." It was foreign to His nature.

Which brings us to Christ's *nurture.* He was "a root out of a dry ground." There was nothing here on which He could nourish His soul.

Think of the world of His day. The great world religions had been founded and had been given hundreds of years to show what they could do. Jesus certainly did not derive anything from them. The great philosophers had come and gone and had proved themselves empty. Nor was Judaism much better. True, the Word of God was at the heart of Jewish religion but the barren commentaries of the rabbis had practically buried it beneath endless traditions. Some of His strongest and most scalding denunciations of the scribes and Pharisees were aimed at their traditions. The Lord turned away from it all and drove His roots down deep into the Word of God. There was His nourishment. Just as the children of Israel ate manna—bread from heaven—in the barren wilderness, so Jesus found His nurture in God's Word sent down from heaven.

The prophet Isaiah not only saw how holy Jesus would be; he saw *how human He would be.* Jesus was holy. The very thought makes people back off because, when we think of a holy person, we tend to think of some half-starved ascetic, perched on some mountain spur, living on tasteless food, reciting the same prayers endlessly, and gathering disciples who can only imitate his example. Jesus was not like that. He was gloriously human. He was God, but He was God manifest in warm, vibrant human flesh, perfectly adjusted and down-to-earth.

Isaiah points out this very human side of Jesus, which all His days was the most evident thing about Him. His humanity was so genuine that His own family thought they had the right to advise and restrain Him, so much so that on one occasion Jesus virtually had to disown them (Matt. 12:46–50). They were unable to recognize His deity until after His resurrection.

Jesus was seen simply as an ordinary man—one who wore homespun clothes and spoke the native Aramaic with a thick north-country accent. The sophisticated Jerusalem Jews dismissed Him as a peasant. They saw no beauty in Him at all. Their Messiah? Him? Not on your life! He was a Galilean and a native of ill-odored Nazareth! They wrote Him off. They had their own ideas as to how a true Messiah should look, speak, and behave. They despised Him.

3. The sorrow

Verse 3 reads, "He is despised and rejected of men; a man of sorrows, and acquainted with grief." The expression "man of sorrows" literally means "man of pains." "Man of God?" Yes, we could readily accept that. "Man of war?" Yes, that makes sense. But "man of sorrows" or "man of pains"—surely there must be a mistake! As the old hymn puts it:

> "Man of Sorrows," what a name
> For the Son of God who came . . .

Here we touch on one of the great mysteries of the universe—the problem of pain. If ever there was a man who should not have experienced pain and suffering, it was Jesus. But that was precisely why He came—to deal with the great sorrow and suffering caused by sin and death. Everywhere we look we see chaos, disorder, and ruin. These things puzzle believers and give ammunition to those who reject God. It is hard to make any sense of it at all.

Not far from where I grew up in Britain, there stood the stark but impressive ruins of a magnificent abbey. This building had a history running back some seven or eight hundred years. It had been built by an agrarian order of monks and, like many other abbeys in medieval times, it became rich and powerful. By the reign of Henry VIII, the power of the abbeys of England compared with that of the throne. Henry decided to end the rivalry in his kingdom. He seized the vast abbey estates throughout his realm and distributed them among his favorite nobles. Then he ordered that all the lead roofs of the abbeys be torn off, melted down, and sold to enrich his own coffers. Stripped of their wealth, the abbots lost much of their power. Stripped of their lead roofs, the abbey buildings fell into disrepair and then ruins.

And that is what the visitor sees—ruins. They are impressive still, but ruins they are. Towering walls and transepts, carved columns, "poetry in stone," indeed—but ruins. Even in their present state, the abbeys bear witness to glorious feats of medieval engineering and to an impressive marriage of science and art. The visitor stands and stares at these abbeys. The ruins stand naked to wind and weather, all forlorn and desolate. But one thing never occurs to those who come to stand and stare. They never conclude that the abbeys were designed to look the way they do, that the architect designed them, right from the start, to be splendid ruins! No one would blame those who designed and built them for their present state. They never intended that the abbeys should be treated the way they were. They were designed to last. And even in their ruined condition, the abbeys bear testimony to their former splendor. They present us with a strange mixture of chaos and order.[2]

It is the same with the world in which we live. It is a ruined world, a world of sin and sadness, suffering, sickness, and death. It was not designed that way. Once, it was a paradise. Traces of its former splendor can be seen everywhere. What we see now is a strange mixture of good and evil, beauty and ugliness, love and hate, sordidness and splendor. An evil power has arisen, one the Bible calls Satan. He has been at work in this world. We can see many evidences of his handiwork (Matt. 13:24–30, 36–43).

Jesus came to deal with this state of affairs. He came here to get involved. He, Himself, became "a man of sorrows, and acquainted with grief." Isaiah points us to the Cross. The four Evangelists bring its scenes before us. We see the man of sorrows nailed to a cross, in torment, ridiculed and scorned—the One, no less, who created the universe. We see the uncanny midday darkness descend. Out of the darkness comes a cry, "My God, my God, why hast thou forsaken me?" (Matt. 27:46). There is no reply—just stony silence. It is as though God were dead. Yet Jesus was very much involved.

Some years ago, I read a book written by a man who went through the horrors of Auschwitz. As a young lad he was torn from his home and thrown into a boxcar. After seemingly endless miles of torture, he arrived, more dead than alive, at the concentration camp. Torment and fear became the substance of his life. His young eyes watched the black smoke from the incinerators unfurling in the sky. It was always there, the smudgy signature of the dead. His mother and little sister went that way. One of the black smudges he saw was theirs. Somehow he survived, always hungry, always terrified. Nevertheless, he survived.

One day, he witnessed the execution of a young boy. It took place in front of thousands of other prisoners. The camp commandant read the indictment but all eyes were on the boy. His face was livid, and he bit his lips. The gallows cast its shadow on him. His neck was placed in the noose; the chair on which he stood was kicked away. Because he was so light, the little half-starved boy took a long time to die. For more than half an hour, he hung by his neck, struggling between life and death, dying slowly in agony. That day, the youthful eyewitness of this atrocity felt God die in his soul. He heard someone in the ranks say, "Where is God now?" "Dead!" he said to himself. "God is dead." "That night," he wrote, "the soup tasted of corpses."

"Where is God now?" demands a skeptical world, faced with all kinds of horrors. "Where is God now?" demanded one of the witnesses. Yes, indeed—where was God the day that boy was hanged? He was just where He was when His Son was hanged, when His Son cried out "My God, my God, why hast thou forsaken me?"

For Jesus did not come to be a spectator. He came to get involved, to become "a man of sorrows, acquainted with grief." On the cross, He dealt the deathblow to the "mystery of iniquity." That is not always evident, especially to unbelief, but it will be one of these days. For He is coming back to get involved again in a different way, in pomp and power and glory. The cross will give way to the crown. The world will be His then, not only by right of Calvary but also by right of conquest. And the pristine order and splendor of things will be obvious to all.

There were ninety and nine that safely lay
In the shelter of the fold.
But one was out on the hills away,
Far off from the gates of gold.
Away on the mountains wild and bare.
Away from the tender Shepherd's care.

"Lord, Thou hast here Thy ninety and nine;
Are they not enough for Thee?"
But the Shepherd made answer: "This of Mine
Has wandered away from Me;
And although the road be rough and steep,
I go to the desert to find My sheep."

None of the ransomed ever knew
How deep were the waters crossed;
Nor how dark was the night that the Lord passed thro'
Ere He found His sheep that was lost.
Out in the desert He heard its cry—
Sick and helpless and ready to die.

"Lord, whence are those blood drops all the way
That mark out the mountain's track?"
"They were shed for one who had gone astray
Ere the Shepherd could bring him back."
"Lord, whence are Thy hands so rent and torn?"
"They're pierced tonight by many a thorn."[1]
                    —Elizabeth C. Clephane (1830–1869)

CHAPTER 11

WOUNDED FOR ME

Isaiah 53:4–6

1. The reality of Christ's sufferings (v. 4)
   a. He bore the burden of our sins
   b. He bore the blame of our sins
2. The reason for Christ's sufferings (v. 5)
   a. The character of sin
      (1) Defiance
      (2) Distortion
   b. The consequences of sin
      (1) Psychological
      (2) Physical
3. The result of Christ's sufferings (v. 6)
   a. How God sees our problem
   b. How God solves our problem

ISAIAH'S PROPHECY SUDDENLY BECOMES personal. *We* are brought into the picture. If it had not been for us, there never would have been a place called Calvary. Read the verses again (Isa. 53:4–6). Emphasize or underline in some way the use of the personal pronouns *we, us,* and *our.* It is all about *us.* As the old hymn puts it:

Was it for me, for me alone
The Savior left His glorious throne?
The dazzling splendor of the sky
Was it for me He came to die?

Years ago, I used to write advertisement copy for the Moody Bible
Institute Correspondence School. I discovered one basic principle
about writing advertisements—you don't try to sell the sausage; you
sell the sizzle! Also, you do not do much talking about the company;
you talk about the customers. You bring them into the picture; you
tell them how they will save, what benefits they will derive, and what
blessings they will get.

Here in these verses God very pointedly talks about *we, us,* and
our. Moreover, it is all about *Him.* He is in the forefront of the picture.
If it had not been for Him, there never would have been a place called
Calvary. Read these same verses again, and emphasize the personal
pronouns *He* and *Him.* It is all about Him.

1. The reality of Christ's sufferings

The Lord came into this world to bear *the burden* of our sins. "Surely
he hath borne our griefs, and carried our sorrows" (Isa. 53:4a). I remember the time when we had to have a water softener. The worst
part was that every so often I had to refill its hopper with salt. The salt
could be purchased at a store some miles away, and it came in hun-
dred-pound bags. It was easy enough to handle at the store because
the man dumped the bag into the car trunk for me. When I arrived
home, however, it was a different story. I had to haul that dead weight
out of the car. I had to hoist it onto my shoulders. I had to stagger
into the house and down the steps to the basement beneath that heavy
load. I learned one great lesson from that—a heavy burden takes the
spring out of one's step!

Sin is a burden, but blessed be God, Jesus has come! He says to us,
"Here, let me carry that for you!" "Surely," says the Old Testament
prophet, "Surely he hath borne our griefs, and carried our sorrows."

He has carried them to Calvary and, from thence, out into "a land not inhabited" (Lev. 16:22) where they have been buried out of the sight of both God and man. The hymn writer has put it thus:

> O Christ, what burdens bowed Thy head,
> Our load was laid on Thee,
> Thou stoodest in the sinner's stead
> Bore all my ill for Thee
> A victim led, Thy blood was shed,
> Now cloudless peace for me![2]

A missionary friend of mine was bumping along an African trail in a pickup truck when he saw a man up ahead carrying a heavy load on his back. He stopped and asked the man if he would like a ride. The fellow climbed into the back of the truck, and off they went. A few miles down the trail, my friend happened to glance into the rearview mirror and saw the man standing rigidly in the back of the truck, desperately trying to keep his balance by hanging onto his load with one hand and to the truck with the other. The missionary stopped the vehicle. "Why don't you put that heavy load down?" he said. "Oh!" said the man. "I didn't know the truck could carry me and my load!"

Well, blessed be God! Our Lord is able to do both.

Our Lord came to bear not only the burden of our sin but also *the blame* of our sin. "We did esteem him stricken, smitten of God, and afflicted" (Isa. 53:4b). The word for "afflicted" here means "humbled" or "degraded." One rendering reads, "We thought him suffering from a stroke at God's own hand."

Put all these ideas together: stricken! afflicted! smitten! humbled! degraded! suffering from a stroke at God's own hand! What a collection of words to describe the Son of God! It is the first word, however, that startles us most—"stricken!" and its companion phrase—"a stroke at God's own hand!" The Jews had a horror of what they called "the stroke of God." It denoted leprosy—like the time when King Uzziah was smitten with leprosy for intruding into the temple and when Gehazi was stricken with Naaman's leprosy. Nothing worse could happen.

But something worse has happened. The whole human race is under the stroke of God by reason of the leprosy of sin. At Calvary, God visited the stroke upon Jesus. Oh, how He suffered when He who knew no sin was made sin for us. Such suffering is beyond anything we could imagine or think.

2. The reason for Christ's sufferings

He was "wounded for our transgressions" (Isa. 53:5). The word for "transgressions" literally means "to revolt" and conveys the idea of sin against lawful authority. Fallen man is in a state of revolt against God. By contrast, Jesus always did those things that pleased the Father. The defiance of Adam has been completely offset by the obedience of Jesus. He took our place so that we might take His.

Moreover, He was "bruised for our iniquities" (Is 53:5). The word for "iniquities" means "perverseness," to be "bent" or "crooked," or "to be off course." All these words describe the state of fallen human beings. Crooked. How true! It reminds us of the nursery rhyme:

> There was a crooked man
> Who walked a crooked mile,
> He found a crooked sixpence
> Upon a crooked style.
> He bought a crooked cat,
> And it caught a crooked mouse,
> And they all lived together
> In a little crooked house.

The terrible bentness of the human race has been demonstrated supremely at Calvary. There the multitudes, having hounded heaven's Beloved to the cross, gathered around to joke and jeer.

The word for "bruised" can also be rendered "crushed." He was crushed beneath the weight of a whole world's sin. He was bruised, not only by humans but also by God. His bruising at the hands of humanity was terrible enough. A *Time* magazine article some years ago on Jesus stated that often the Romans, when hammering the victim's feet to the cross, drove the nail through the heels. If that was so, then the first prophecy in the Bible was literally fulfilled. "It (the seed of the woman; Christ) shall bruise thy head (the serpent's head), and thou (the serpent; Satan) shalt bruise his (Christ's) heel" (Gen. 3:15). The Lord Jesus was "bruised" by Satan, who worked through the hands of wicked men. He was crushed by the weight of the sin of the world. He was crushed when God Himself forsook Him in those tormenting hours as darkness enveloped not only Calvary but the whole country. The full horror of bruising and crushing cannot be grasped. We pray with the hymn writer:

> Oh, make me understand it,
> Help me to take it in;
> What it meant for Thee, the Holy One,
> To take away our sin.[3]

The prophet continues in the same verse: "the chastisement of our peace was upon him." It is not just "chastisement" the prophet foresees but *"the* chastisement," the appalling visitation of God's judgment upon the sin bearers—the fallen children of Adam's ruined race—which defies all description and eclipses all other chastisements.

The word for "peace" here is not just "peace" but *"our* peace." It refers to us as individuals. For God had long since determined to "make peace" through the blood of the Cross (Col. 1:20). The chastisement that makes peace was laid upon Jesus. Chastisement! Peace! Him! An *outrage* confronts us here, the outrage of our sin against a holy God that made the chastisement necessary. An *outcast* comes into view, crying in the darkness and desolation of His isolation on the tree, and He—the unique Son of the living God! An *outcome* follows—peace! Peace with God. Peace means that the war is over.

But there is more! "By his stripes we are healed." The healing of the body is part of the ultimate good that comes to us by way of the Cross. One day, we shall have a body "like unto his glorious body" (Phil. 3:21). The Lord Jesus healed people, multitudes of them. He never lost a case or charged a fee. It mattered not if a person was blind, or palsied, or lame, or demon-possessed, or dead. Jesus never failed. At the same time, He did not heal everybody. At the pool of Bethesda He picked out one man, a man whose case was hopeless, and healed him (John 5:1–9). There were multitudes of other needy people in the vicinity, but for some unstated reason He passed them all by. God gives no guarantee of physical healing in this age, not even to His own.

Isaiah's prophecy regarding the healing ministry of Christ (Isa. 53:4–5) was fulfilled by the Lord in His earthly sojourn (Matt. 4:23–24; 8:13–17; 1 Peter 2:24). The instructions given by James (James 5:14–16) refer to a person under church discipline whose illness is a consequence of his excommunication. The antics of modern so-called faith healers are completely foreign to the New Testament. Jesus healed lepers and lunatics with equal ease. It was as simple for Him to heal a poor woman suffering from a defiling and debilitating hemorrhage as it was for Him to heal a man with a withered hand or to restore the severed ear of Malchus.

3. The result of Christ's sufferings

"All we like sheep have gone astray; we have turned every one to his own way; and the LORD hath laid on him the iniquity of us all" (Isa. 53:6). That is the heart and soul of the Bible message. It tells us *how God sees our problem.* We have gone astray, turned one and all to our own way. Such waywardness God describes as "iniquity," referring to the essential bentness and crookedness of fallen humanity. The prophet calls us "sheep." A sheep is not strong, it is not swift, and it is not smart. It is its nature to go astray. In that regard it is a rather stupid animal. A lost sheep has no built-in mechanism to find its own way home. On the contrary, once lost it is at the mercy of its foes.

Years ago, D. L. Moody and Ira Sankey, Moody's song leader and soloist, were conducting a crusade and they were traveling together by train to their next destination. Moody was thinking about his next sermon. Sankey was reading a magazine. A poem by Elizabeth C.

Clephane attracted Sankey's attention. He clipped it out and put it in his pocket. That night, Moody preached on the Good Shepherd who gave his life for the sheep. At the conclusion of his message, he called on Mr. Sankey to sing. As he came forward Sankey suddenly remembered the poem in his pocket. The very thing! But it had no tune. So what? He'd make up a tune! And so he did. He propped the poem up on the portable organ he used and began to sing. The last verse drew attention to the result of Christ's sufferings:

> Up from the mountains thunder-riven
> And up from the rocky steep,
> There arose a cry to the gate of heaven,
> "Rejoice, I have found my sheep!"
> And the angels echoed around the throne,
> "Rejoice for the Lord brings back His own."[4]

Then, too, Isaiah tells us how the Lord *solves* the problem. "The LORD hath laid on him the iniquity of us all" (Isa. 53:6).

On another occasion, when the gospel crusade was over, Mr. Moody was leaning out of the window of the train saying farewell to his friends. A man came running down the platform just as the conductor was blowing his whistle and waving his flag. The train began to move. The man was alongside Mr. Moody now. "How can I be saved?" he cried. He had been to the crusade. He was under conviction. What can you possibly tell a man who is running ever harder to keep up to a train that is pulling away? Moody was up to the occasion. "Isaiah 53," he called. "Verse 6. Go in at the first 'all' and come out at the second 'all.'"

The man went home, found his Bible, and opened it to Isaiah 53:6. "*All* we like sheep have gone astray," he read. He accepted the truth of that. "The LORD hath laid on him the iniquity of us *all*." He responded to that and was saved.

That is *how God solves our problem* of sin so far as the fallen sinners of Adam's race are concerned. It is as simple and sublime as that.

Jesus is standing in Pilate's hall,
Friendless, forsaken, betrayed by all:
Hearken what meaneth the sudden call!
What will you do with Jesus?

Jesus is standing on trial still,
You can be false to Him if you will,
You can be faithful through good or ill:
What will you do with Jesus?

Will you evade Him, as Pilate tried?
Or will you choose Him, what e'er betide?
Vainly you struggle from Him to hide:
What will you do with Jesus?

What will you do with Jesus?
Neutral you cannot be;
Some day your heart will be asking,
"What will He do with me?"[1]
                —Albert B. Simpson (1843–1919)

CHAPTER 12

LEAD ME TO CALVARY

Isaiah 53:7–8

1. The silence of our Lord (v. 7)
   a. The trial before the Hebrews
      (1) Before Annas, the former high priest
      (2) Before Caiaphas, the functioning high priest
   b. The trial before the heathen
      (1) Before Herod
      (2) Before Pilate
2. The sufferings of our Lord (v. 8)
   a. How the death sentence was invoked
   b. How the death sentence was inflicted
      (1) It was a violent death
      (2) It was a vicarious death

NO MORE ASTONISHING WORDS, SURELY, have ever been written than these: "He is brought as a lamb to the slaughter." In the first place, it is astonishing that He should be brought anywhere. He was God, the incarnate Son of the Living God, the Creator of the universe. Ten thousand times ten thousand angels were at His command. All power, absolute power, was His. A word from Him and every sun and star in space would have vanished from the sky.

It is even more astonishing when we not only consider *who He was* but *where He went*. He was led as a lamb to the slaughter—as a lamb—to the slaughter! What amazing grace, grace beyond all thought!

Before the invention of sonar and other navigational aids, which have taken all the guesswork out of the business, sailors approaching an uncharted shore always set an experienced hand at a key place on the deck with a sounding line in his hand. His job was to report how shallow or how deep the waters were below the keel. It was music to the captain's ears when the leadsman called back to the quarterdeck, "No bottom with this line." Deep water was good news.

But when we come to Calvary, it is quite the opposite. We drop our sounding line into the dark mysterious depths of the verses before us. We report back the dreadful news, "No bottom here!" We tie on more sounding line, we tie on more and more, and always the result is the same, "No bottom here." Our lines are too short. We cannot measure these dark depths.

It is with this understanding of our inability to measure the deep sufferings of Christ as described in these verses that we try, at least, to feel our way.

1. The silence of our Lord

> He was oppressed, and he was afflicted, yet he opened not his mouth: he is brought as a lamb to the slaughter, and as a sheep before her shearers is dumb, so he openeth not his mouth. (Isaiah 53:7)

The Lord Jesus had a multiple trial. Isaiah's prophetic foreviews take in the whole terrible miscarriage of justice and the Lord's sovereign silence before His foes. First, there was *the trial before the Hebrews*. Isaiah's words, "He was oppressed, and he was afflicted," begin the record of miscarried justice. The word for "oppressed" means "hard-pressed." He had His back to the wall, so to speak, as His adversaries closed in on Him.

The Jewish leaders in Jerusalem had disliked Jesus from the very beginning of His public ministry. He brought down their ire upon Himself when He cleansed the temple of the merchants and money changers, those who had turned the outer court of the temple into a common market, and a dishonest one at that. Highly placed members of the Sanhedrin were hand in glove with this sacrilege, from which they profited themselves.

Down through the years that followed, the Sanhedrin continued to eye Him with suspicion and dislike and, as the end drew near, the authorities conspired against Him. All the same, they stood in awe of Him. There was no knowing what He might do if they resorted to violence. There was no denying that He had extraordinary powers. The whole country was amazed at His countless mighty miracles. Moreover, the mob had to be kept in mind. The Jewish leaders had a healthy respect for the mob. There had already been one popular attempt to make Jesus a king. If the Sanhedrin could mobilize the masses, well and good, but let Jesus incite them and there was no telling where it would end. The thing to do was to move against Him at night. What they needed was an accomplice. Surely one of His followers could be bought. It was then that Judas played into their hands. He led a motley crowd to Gethsemane and betrayed the Lord of glory into their hands. For one terrifying moment the Lord put forth His power and invoked His high name, Jehovah (I AM), so that those who sought to seize Him fell helpless to the ground (John 18:3–6). Then He surrendered Himself to their will.

They led Him along the rocky defile that skirted the steep eastern face of the temple wall, up the historic causeway at the southeastern angle of the city wall, and on to the headquarters of the Sanhedrin.

A great deal was illegal about this whole Hebrew plot and phony trial. It was illegal for the temple guard, acting as the official instrument of the high priest, to make the arrest. Jewish law called for a citizen's arrest—the witnesses themselves had to undertake the apprehension of the accused.

To try a capital charge by night was illegal, especially a charge involving a possible death sentence. To cross-examine the prisoner and then, after the testimony of the witnesses had broken down, to go on "a fishing expedition" to try to get something on Him was illegal. To accept the testimony of a false witness was illegal. On the contrary, if the testimony brought by the witnesses was proven false, then the law required that the false witness be put to death.

The Sanhedrin on that dark and dreadful night was not interested in seeing justice done. All that they wanted was a verdict of "Guilty!" and a sentence of death.

We come, then, to the arraignment before Annas. Annas was a former high priest and was father-in-law to Caiaphas, the incumbent high priest. Indeed, he and five of his sons in succession (not to mention his son-in-law, Caiaphas) had ruled the high priesthood for half a century. He was "an astute, tyrannous, worldly Sadducee, unvenerable for all his seventy years, full of serpentine malice and meanness which utterly denied the meaning of his name—'merciful.'"[2] Annas was the prime mover in the plot to crucify Christ. Farrar points to "his advanced age, his preponderant dignity, his worldly position and influence as one who stood on the best terms with the Herods and the Procurators, which gave an exceptional weight to his prerogative decision."[3]

As for the Sanhedrin itself, Farrar says, "If we may believe not a few of the indications of the Talmud, the Sanhedrin was little better than a close, irreligious, unpatriotic confederacy of monopolizing and time-serving priests . . . mostly of non-Palestinian origin who were supported by the government but detested by the people and of whom this conspirator was the very life and soul."[4] Avarice was the besetting sin of Annas. And he was the man who took the initiative in interrogating Christ.

This semiofficial hearing was a kind of lower-court hearing. Jesus simply ignored the questions put to Him, His only response being to remind Annas that His teachings were a matter of public record. For saying that, someone slapped Him in the face.

Then came the main trial before Caiaphas. Like Annas, his father-in-law, Caiaphas was a Sadducee. The proceedings, which took place in his house, were wholly irregular. At least twenty-three members of the Sanhedrin were required to make a quorum. The Sanhedrin itself consisted of seventy members. There were the chief priests (heads of the twenty-four priestly orders), the scribes (the legal authorities), and the elders (the tribal heads of the people). The high priest presided over the meetings. Membership seems to have been for life, and only those of impeccable pedigree were admitted. New members were appointed by the existing membership or by political pressure.

First, a number of false witnesses were heard. Jesus ignored them. His silence infuriated Caiaphas. "Answerest thou nothing?" he demanded. "What is it which these witness against thee?" (Matt. 26:62). By law, Jesus did not have to answer His accusers since no proven evidence had been introduced as yet into the trail. Caiaphas saw his whole case collapsing especially as he was running out of perjurers. Indeed, there was no case. Then Caiaphas had a diabolical idea. Why not create all the witnesses he needed by putting the prisoner under oath.

The high priest stood up and went to his place in the center of the court. Then he put to Christ the most solemn form of oath known and allowed by the constitution—the oath of the testimony. "I adjure thee by the living God, that thou tell us whether thou be the Christ, the Son of God" (Matt. 26:63).

It was a clever maneuver. This crafty ruse fulfilled the prophecy of Isaiah. Jesus was now "hard-pressed," as the prophet put it. He could not say that He was *not* the Son of God because that was exactly what He was. But if He said He *was* the Son of God, they would accuse Him of the capital offense of blasphemy. If He remained silent, He would open Himself to misinterpretation. Speak He must. "Thou hast said," He replied. Then for good measure, "Hereafter shall ye see the Son of man sitting on the right hand of power, and coming in the clouds of heaven" (Matt 26:64). With a violent gesture, Caiaphas rent his robe. "Blasphemy!" he cried. "What further need have we of witnesses?" (Matt. 26:65). All that remained was to wait until daylight when a session of the entire Sanhedrin could be convened and sentence be passed.

Now comes *the trial before the heathen.* The prophet Isaiah said: "He was taken from prison and from judgment: and who shall declare

his generation? for he was cut off out of the land of the living: for the
transgression of my people was he stricken" (Isa. 53:8).

When the Lord was first brought before Pilate, it did not take the
procurator long to discover that Jesus was a Galilean—and Galilee
was Herod's jurisdiction. Pilate had little or no regard for Herod, but
the fact that Herod was in town proved too much for Pilate. He would
send Jesus to Herod to be judged, a very convenient way for Pilate to
rid himself of an unpleasant predicament. When Jesus appeared finally before Herod, He again retired into silence. Herod had murdered John the Baptist. Jesus had nothing to say to him.

The Hasmonean Palace lay due east of the Herodian Palace. This
sudden and unexpected change of venue did not suit the Jewish leaders at all. Besides, Herod had no official business in Jerusalem. It was
no part of his realm.

Very likely, Herod was entertaining guests when news arrived that
Pilate had referred this notable prisoner to him. Herod doubtless
rubbed his hands. At last, he would get to see this wonder-working
preacher face-to-face. He might even get to see the man conjure up a
miracle. Rage and resentment boiled up in Herod's soul when Jesus
not only failed to produce a miracle but ignored him altogether.

The infuriated Herod turned his prisoner over to the guard to be
the butt of their buffoonery. "As a sheep before her shearers is dumb,
so he openeth not his mouth" (Isa. 53:7). The soldiers dressed Jesus
up in one of Herod's cast-off robes and pretended to pay Him hom-
age. Herod Antipas was indeed a despicable person—a dissolute
Idumaean Sadducee, a dangerous, devious fox of a man. He wanted
no more to do with Jesus. He bundled Him back to the procurator,
much to the disgust of the Jewish scribes and chief priests who had
begun to think Herod might be provoked into behaving rashly. After
all, he had already murdered John. Perhaps he could be goaded into
murdering Jesus. Herod was far too crafty to be caught like that.

Pilate thought that by sending Jesus to Herod he could wash his
hands of the case. But now the prisoner was back, looking much the
worse for wear.

A Roman trial was in three parts. There was the public accusation, followed by the interrogation—the cross-examination by the judge—and, finally, the defense made by the prisoner.

In Jesus' trial there were two basic charges. First, there was the charge of blasphemy, which seems to have greatly troubled Pilate. Pilate arranged a private session to question Christ and found himself faced with silence. Jesus said only enough to make Pilate aware of what he was up against—that he was sitting in judgment on the Son of God.

Then there was the charge of treason, a charge that really terrified Pilate. "If thou let this man go, thou art not Caesar's friend" (John 19:12), the chief priests and officers cried. On his finger, Pilate wore a prized ring of gold given to him by Tiberius Caesar. Engraved on the ring were the Latin words *Amicus Caesaris*—"Caesar's Friend." The ring marked him out as a man exceptionally honored by the emperor in Rome. In the end, Pilate made his choice. He chose to be Caesar's friend, even if that meant sending this mysterious, uncommunicative, and innocent man to a terrible and undeserved death. Throughout these various trials, the Lord responded for the most part with silence.

2. The sufferings of our Lord

The silence of the Lord Jesus opened the way for the appalling sufferings that followed. One word from Him and twelve angelic legions would have emptied heaven to wreak vengeance on the human race, then and there. It was either a silent Redeemer or a slaughtered race.

Isaiah's prophetic foreview of Calvary continues. We learn *how the death sentence was invoked.* "He was taken from prison and from judgment" (Isa. 53:8). This sentence can also be rendered, "By constraint and sentence he was taken away," or "By tyranny and law he was taken away," or "They did away with him unjustly."

Isaiah says that Christ was taken "by constraint." We see Pilate's side of things when we look at him with his awesome prisoner. Who, in fact, was the real prisoner? Surely it was Pilate. We see him being increasingly forced down a road by the sheer compulsion of circumstances. The more he shrank from making the final decision, the more the Jewish officials twisted his arm. They knew he was afraid of them. He was also afraid of the rabble. They were in a riotous mood, egged on by the agents of the priests. The last thing Pilate wanted was a revolt. He was afraid of the Jewish rulers. They had him in a tight corner, and he knew it. No Roman governor could afford to discount the power of the Jews. The Diaspora was everywhere. Jews lived abroad in all the Roman provinces, wealthy, and often in places of power. Some were close to Caesar himself and were a force to be reckoned with. Pilate dared not ignore the Jews' power to make trouble, especially as he had already had his lingers burned once or twice before in his dealings with this troublesome people.

It did not take Pilate long to make up his mind. By "constraint and sentence" Jesus was taken away. Pilate caved in to the pressure of Caiaphas and his crowd. Pilate detested them, and they detested him. They were already stirring up the rabble. Pilate certainly did not want influential Jews in Rome running to Claudius to say there was new rioting in Jerusalem because Pilate had been lenient to a man claiming to be the true King of the Jews. He scourged his prisoner and gave Him over to death.

Then Isaiah tells *how the death sentence was inflicted. It was a violent death.* "Who shall declare his generation?" demands the prophet, "for he was cut off out of the land of the living" (Isa. 53:8). That could be rephrased, "As for his generation, who among them considered that he was cut off out of the land of the living?"

The word for "cut off" is graphic enough. It means to be "wrenched." The sentence could be translated, "He was torn from the land of the living." In either case, the picture is that of a violent death indeed.

It would be hard to imagine a more cruel death than crucifixion. There was the fearful pain as the iron nails were driven through hands and feet. There was the sickening thud as the cross was dropped into its socket, the agonizing continuous pain as the weight of the body was thrown onto the nail wounds, and the torture of the unnatural position and of disjointed bones. In many cases, as with that of Christ, the whole terrible business came after the victim had been scourged to the bone. Every movement sent fresh stabs of pain through the nervous system. The sufferer had to cope with the lacerated veins, crushed tendons, inflammation, terrible cramps from tortured muscles and swelling arteries, especially those of the stomach. Added to all this were the swarming flies, the burning heat, the raging thirst.

As though all that were not enough, when the soldiers were called upon to speed up the execution, which when allowed to run its normal course often lasted several days, they chose a fearfully cruel way to hasten the end. They broke the legs of the malefactors. That threw the full weight of the body on the heart. The Lord was protected from this by a prophetic decree from on high that forbade the breaking of any of His bones (Ps. 34:20). The Lord Himself thwarted this savage final act of wickedness by sovereignly dismissing His spirit. The soldiers saw at once that He was already dead and contented themselves with thrusting a spear into His heart. Truly, He was wrenched out of the land of the living.

"Cut off out of the land of the living!" The prophet adds, "As for his generation, who among them considered that he was cut off?" "His generation"—what a guilty generation it was! It is referred to twenty-five times in the Gospels, often accompanied by an adjective such as "evil," "adulterous," "wicked," "faithless." Solomon foresaw this when he paused in his teaching to prophesy (Prov. 30:4–14). He was able to see that generation clearly enough and, by extension, our generation also. He describes it as bitter, blinded, boastful, and brutal. Of all generations the generation that murdered Jesus by cutting Him off was wholly without excuse.

Well over a century after Isaiah put down his pen, another Hebrew prophet actually foretold the exact date when Christ would be "cut off" (Dan. 9:24–27). The time envisioned by the prophet was a marked-out period of 490 years (70 x 7). The starting point for the period was clearly given. It would begin when a Persian king signed a decree authorizing the rebuilding of the wall of Jerusalem. We now know that date. It was the twentieth year of the reign of Artaxerxes (445 B.C.). From that specific date the Jews were to count off a total of 483 years (69 x 7). At the expiration of that period the Messiah would be "cut off." Precise calculation brings the terminus to the day Christ rode into Jerusalem as the

Messiah. Within a week He was dead. Truly the Jews of that generation were a culpable crowd. There was no excuse for them. Both Isaiah and Daniel had warned them. They paid no heed.

But that death was not only a violent death; *it was a vicarious death.* "For the transgression of my people was he stricken" (Isa. 53:8). It was what we call a substitutionary death. Mark Twain has given us a good illustration of what that means.

Tom Sawyer and his girlfriend Becky Thatcher had become estranged, and Becky set about snubbing Tom in every way she could. Their tyrannical schoolmaster, Mr. Dobbins, had a book in his desk that he kept under the tightest lock and key. Becky Thatcher had the misfortune to tear that book. She put it back in the schoolmaster's desk in mortal terror. Tom was witness to all this. The dreaded moment came when Mr. Dobbins discovered the torn page in his book. Becky was frozen with terror and Tom saw the haunted look on her face. The schoolmaster faced the class and every eye sank under his gaze. Writes Mark Twain,

> There was that in it which smote even the innocent with fear. There was silence while one might count up to ten. The master was gathering his wrath. Then he spoke, "Who tore this book?" There was not a sound. One could have heard a pin drop. The stillness continued. The master searched face after face for signs of guilt. The inquisition began. "Benjamin Rogers did you tear this book? Joseph Harper? Amy Lawrence? Gracie Miller? Susan Harper?" The next girl was Becky Thatcher. "Rebeccah Thatcher did you tear this book?" She sat there like a stricken rabbit and Tom, watching it all, knew that in a moment she would betray herself. A thought shot like lightning through Tom's brain. He sprang to his feet and shouted "I done it!" The school stared in perplexity at this incredible folly. Tom stood for a moment and then he stepped forward to go to his punishment. The surprise, the gratitude, the adoration that shone upon him out of poor Becky's eyes seemed pay enough for a hundred floggings.

Now come back to Calvary. There He is—our substitute. "For the transgression of my people was he stricken." He, the sinless Son of God, died for us. He took our place at Calvary. Evil people glowered on Him, jeered at Him, cursed Him, and blasphemed Him.

All that is over now. In yonder glory, He is surrounded by adoring multitudes who gaze upon Him with gratitude and surprise. Down here, He is worshiped by millions. We do the best we can. We say with the hymn writer:

> Unseen we love Thee, dear Thy name,
> But when our eyes behold,
> With joyful wonder we'll exclaim,
> The half was never told.[5]

King of my life, I crown Thee now,
Thine shall the glory be;
Lest I forget Thy thorn-crowned brow,
Lead me to Calvary.

Show me the tomb where Thou wast laid,
Tenderly mourned and wept;
Angels in robes of light arrayed
Guarded Thee whilst Thou slept.

Let me like Mary, through the gloom,
Come with a gift to Thee;
Show to me now the empty tomb,
Lead me to Calvary.

Lest I forget Gethsemane;
Lest I forget Thine agony;
Lest I forget Thy love for me,
Lead me to Calvary.[1]
  —Jenny Evelyn Hussey (1874–1958)

ONLY A BORROWED TOMB

Isaiah 53:9

1. The grave that was planned by His foes
2. The grave that was prepared by His friends
   a. The divine provision
   b. The divine proclamation
      (1) His blameless walk
      (2) His blameless talk

THE PROPHET DANIEL UNVEILS FOR US some of the things that exist in the mysterious world of good and evil spirits just beyond the range of our senses. He tells us that there are "watchers" out there in that extraterrestrial spirit world. Down through the ages they have seen many an extraordinary thing on this planet of ours. But never, surely, have they ever seen anything that filled them with greater astonishment and amazement than the sight of their Sovereign Lord and Creator lying still and cold in the darkness of a rock-hewn tomb.

The shining ones, who stand in the presence of God and fill the everlasting hills with their endless chant—"Holy! Holy! Holy is the Lord!"—hushed their hymn. How could heaven sing when creatures of another race, on a distant planet in space, had taken their Beloved and nailed Him to an accursed tree. The evil spirits, those principalities and powers, those wicked ones in high places, rulers of this world's darkness, instigators of all kinds of evil, must have held their breath. The word was already abroad that they had not really won at all. Jesus was going to rise triumphant over sin and death and hell. The flimsy attempt by Caiaphas and his cohorts to seal the tomb was ludicrous. Not bolts nor bars nor seals nor soldiers of Rome, nor all the machinations of fallen Lucifer would be able to prevent Christ from rising should He so desire. Already it was a known fact to all the spirit powers, good and bad, that no touch or taint of natural decay had been allowed to come near His body in the tomb.

For three long days and three interminable nights, the planet spun on its axis and described its orbit. In high heaven, twelve angels' legions fingered their swords while humans on earth continued their small affairs as though nothing out of the ordinary had occurred. The Sanhedrin hoped against hope that the tomb would hold its prey. Pilate felt the shadow of doom fall upon his soul. Herod added disgrace, day after day, to his vilified name. The soldiers who had done the dreadful deed doubtless discussed and debated in their barrack rooms the details of the past few days. Nothing seemingly had changed. In the city it was business as usual, though the holidays—Passover, Unleavened Bread, First Fruits, and, before long, Pentecost—would give more time for religious and family affairs. The Jewish calendar allowed for plenty of duties to occupy minds blind to the awesome realities now being worked out.

So the world went on, a leprous spot in the universe, where God's only-begotten and well-beloved Son had been tortured and entombed.

Three days! Three nights! The universe held its breath for twenty-four hours a day, for three stretched-out days, seventy-two never-ending hours, minute after minute for some 4,320 minutes, second after second for 259,200 seconds. Still, that lifeless form lay cold and unmoving. Round and round the world spun on its ordained path.

The disciples, who had scattered far and wide, drifted back to the Upper Room, scuttling down back alleys, terrified they might be recognized, arrested, and crucified themselves. In far-off Rome a depraved

Caesar continued with his excesses, wild enough to shock even that pagan city. All the time the body of the Son of God lay lifeless in the tomb, awaiting the appointed hour.

Then suddenly, untouched by human hands, the door of the cave rolled back. The tomb itself was ablaze with light from another world. Then a shining angel appeared and deliberately sat upon the stone. With one wild shout of terror, the soldiers guarding the tomb took to their heels and fled. Silence settled on the scene.

In all likelihood the garden tomb was just where General Gordon located it. Near Jerusalem there is a skull-shaped hill, the summit of which is now a Moslem cemetery. Probably this grim site was an execution spot in Roman times. Bearing off to the west, across the way from the Damascus Gate, is a garden and an empty tomb. Those who enter this tomb feel, like Moses at the burning bush, that they should remove the very shoes from their feet since the place where they stand is holy ground.

The tomb itself consists of a chamber, seven feet six inches high, fourteen feet six inches long, and eleven feet two inches wide. A low partition divides it into two parts. The eastern division of the tomb contains three receptacles for human remains, but only one seems to have been completed. The other two have surfaces that have never been smoothed, one for an adult and the remaining one for a child. Evidently, this sepulcher was originally intended to be a family tomb.

The western division shows traces of a receptacle that was planned but never completed. The only finished receptacle there contains a small cavity where a body was to rest. At each end there are ledges that might serve as seats. It was here, doubtless, that Mary saw the two angels in white sitting, one at the head and the other at the foot of the area where the body of Jesus had lain.

The body of Jesus was laid to rest wrapped in grave clothes, the head covered with a napkin. It had remained in place, so Joseph of Arimathea and the devout women thought, awaiting the end of the Passover Sabbath. Then they intended to come back and complete the embalming. The resurrection was the furthest thing from their minds.

True, the body of Jesus lay in solitary state. That body, however, was not waiting for Joseph. It was waiting for the moment when the Lord would rise from the dead, burst open the tomb, and prepare for His ascension to Glory.

Said Isaiah, "He [literally, "they"] made his grave with the wicked, and with the rich in his death; because he had done no violence, neither was any deceit in his mouth" (Isa. 53:9). This is the background for what followed.

1. The grave that was planned by His foes

Wicked hands had seized Jesus in Gethsemane. Wicked hands had blindfolded Him so that He could be mocked. Wicked hands had scooped up the money that Judas had flung at the feet of the priests. Wicked hands had invested that money in a potter's field. Wicked hands had punched Jesus in the face. Wicked hands had wrenched the beard from His cheeks. Wicked hands had torn a bunch of Jerusalem thorns from a wayside hedge, twisted it into a crown, and rammed it on His brow. Wicked hands had flung a mocking purple robe across His shoulders. Wicked hands had taken a tough cane and hit Him with it on the head. Wicked hands had taken a fearful scourge and plowed His back to the bone. Wicked hands had signed His death decree, hands that no water on earth could ever wash clean again. Wicked hands had dumped a great rough-hewn wooden beam upon His tattered and torn shoulders. Wicked hands had nailed Him to the tree. Wicked hands had offered Him a "drink" of vinegar and gall when, in His agony, He said, "I thirst" (John 19:28). Wicked hands had rubbed together in glee, hands that had been consecrated to the priesthood, to the service of the living God. Wicked hands had taken a hammer to smash His legs, but at *that* God drew the line. Wicked hands were allowed one more act—wicked hands took a spear and thrust it deep into His side to bring forth the blood that saves.

Wicked hands. How they would have liked to have seized that dead body on the tree. They had plans to do still more with those wicked hands of theirs. But to do what they wanted, they would have had to turn Isaiah into a false prophet. Once it had been demonstrated that the Lord was dead, only loving hands were allowed to touch His form.

The wicked men who had plotted His death also plotted His burial. They "made his grave with the wicked," Isaiah said (Isa. 53:9). They had their plans all right.

Outside the wall of Jerusalem was a dark and dreadful gulf. It was deep and narrow, with steep rocky sides, and it ran to the south and to the west of Jerusalem, separating Mount Zion from the "Hill of Evil Counsel." On the southern brow, overlooking the valley at its eastern extremity, Solomon had once erected the high places of Moloch. There the horrid rites associated with the worship of that demon god had been practiced. Little children, babes in arms, had been placed living on Moloch's red-hot lap, only to roll screaming into a great hole in the idol's belly from whence belched smoke and flame. The same hideous atrocities were carried out by later Judean kings at the same dreadful place. It became known as Tophet, and the word became a synonym for hell.

Good King Josiah sought to put an end to these ghastly practices by deliberately defiling the place. He rendered it ceremonially un-clean by spreading human bones all over the valley, along with other corruptions. From then on, it was the city's cesspool. Sewage was con-veyed there, some of it to be carried away by the Kidron, the rest to be burned in the undying fires that smoldered in that terrible place. The smoke and the stench of the place made it proverbial. It was known as Gehinnom, or Gehenna—a place where the worm never died, and where the fire was never quenched. It was a picture of the lake of fire, the ultimate home of the damned.

It is not at all unlikely that the Lord's enemies, not content that He had died accursed on a Roman tree (Gal. 3:10–14), would have flung Him headlong into that twice-accursed place to be eaten by worms and consumed in flames had they had the chance. Their wickedness and malice would have made them capable of even that. It is at least possible that the prophet Isaiah hinted at this in telling us that, even in death, the wicked would be there. Wicked hands would reach out to seize Him. That, however, was not to be.

2. The grave that was prepared by His friends

Only loving hearts could plan for Him now. Only loving hands might touch Him now. His sufferings and sorrows were gone forever. As the old hymn puts it:

> Ne'er again will God, Jehovah
> Smite the Shepherd with the sword;
> Ne'er again shall wicked sinners
> Set at nought our glorious Lord.[2]

The Lord is now famous for His gentleness and guilelessness. "He had done no violence, neither was any deceit in his mouth," which brings us to *the divine provision:* "He [was] . . . with the rich in his death" (Isa. 53:9).

That day in Jerusalem there were two men whose hearts had been prepared by God against this hour of direst need. Two things were required if these men were to circumvent the wicked plots of the Caiaphas crowd. They would need to be men of rank, and they would need to be men of riches. Only wealthy, powerful men of courage and conviction would be able, by bold, prompt, and decisive action, to thwart the plans of the Sanhedrin.

First, there was Joseph of Arimathea. He lived in Ramah, an ancient city sacred to the memory of the prophet Samuel and located about two miles northwest of Jerusalem. That the Holy Spirit prepared a man named Joseph to minister to Jesus at His birth and a man named Joseph to minister to Jesus at His death is of passing interest. Joseph of Arimathea was a wealthy member of the Sanhedrin. We can be sure he had no part or lot in the wicked schemes and plots of his fellow members.

He appears suddenly on the pages of Scripture to do just one thing—to protect the sacred body of Jesus from desecration by giving it an honorable burial in his own tomb. That task accomplished, he vanishes again. He was raised up by God for that one brief but glorious ministry. Each of the four Gospels mentions him, each one adding one more detail. Altogether it does not amount to much. He was a secret disciple. Often he has been blamed for that, but there may well have been a very good reason for him to have kept his convictions to himself. Fear of the Jewish officials? No doubt! But perhaps that fear was not necessarily a fear of what they might do to him but of what they might do to Him—desecrate His body.

It is well within the realm of possibility that Joseph of Arimathea, like Mary of Bethany, believed what Christ said about His forthcoming death and burial. Joseph had no illusions about the wickedness, malice, and depravity of Annas and Caiaphas. They would doubtless seek to gain possession of the body of Jesus, not only to prevent the disciples from absconding with it but also to further discredit Jesus by disposing of His remains in some dishonorable way. Well he, Joseph, would forestall them. He would make sure that he got possession of the body. He would beat the Sanhedrin at their own game. As for the burial of Jesus, blessed be God, he had a tomb to donate to the cause. He would bury Jesus in the tomb he had carved for himself and his family in Jerusalem. But no one must know! No one must suspect that he had a secret agenda! So, he would be a secret disciple.

Luke describes Joseph of Arimathea as "a good man, and a just" (Luke 23:50). That says a lot about him—a good man! Scarcely for a righteous man will one die, says Paul, but for a good man some might even dare to die. Joseph was that kind of a man. So this good man, afraid that the wicked men who ran the Sanhedrin might suspect what he was up to, kept his own counsel. A secret disciple—indeed, for fear of the Jews—yes, because it was only thus that he could be sure that he would not be prevented from doing the daring deed for which he has been honored from that day to this.

Then there was Nicodemus. Joseph provided the sepulcher, showing up at Calvary with the governor's warrant just in time. Nicodemus provided the spices, an enormous quantity of spices—a hundred pounds of myrrh and aloes. It must have cost a small fortune. It is suggested by some that the Nicodemus of the Gospels is identical with Nakdimon Ben Gorion of the Talmud, a man of enormous wealth.[3] Timidity seems to have kept Nicodemus a secret disciple. His one recorded attempt to dissent from the majority position of the Sanhedrin's members (John 7:50–51) was quickly smothered. His fear of the Jews was quite different from Joseph's. Nicodemus was afraid of what the Sanhedrin might do to his position; Joseph was afraid of what they might do to his plans.

What was it that finally brought Nicodemus out of hiding? It was the Cross. It is a remarkable fact that the power of the Cross accomplished, in the life of this man, what nothing else could. The Lord's many and marvelous miracles could not do it. The Lord's magnificent milestone preaching could not do it. The Lord's wisdom, love, and power could not do it, nor His flawless goodness and immaculate holiness. Nicodemus was afraid. But the Cross snapped his bonds and set him free.

When Bunyan's pilgrim arrived at the cross, that did it! The heavy burden of conviction he carried fell off him and tumbled down a steep place into the mouth of the sepulcher, and he saw it no more. Now, however, he could sing and sing he did:

> Blest cross! blest sepulchre! blest rather be
> The Man that there was put to shame for me.

When Nicodemus learned that Christ had been condemned to death and learned also, perhaps, of the evil cremation they were whispering about, he felt a new, sudden resolve. He would do what he could to put a stop to their plans. He was rich, and rich men wield power. Possibly he had seen Joseph of Arimathea leave the council chamber. Perhaps Nicodemus could guess where he had gone. He left and made haste. Spices would be needed. The Lord's disciples were poor people. He, Nicodemus, would make up for lost time. The fear of Annas and Caiaphas and the rest fell from him once and for all.

All of this focuses our attention on the divine provision. Nearly three-quarters of a millennium before, God had declared prophetically that the slain Messiah would be "with the rich in his death." All the plots and machinations of the Sanhedrin could not reverse that prophetic word. It was settled in heaven.

When Joseph of Arimathea showed up in Pilate's residence, the procurator seemed relieved. Doubtless Pilate knew the man. He was known as "a good man" (Luke 23:50), as "an honourable counsellor, which also waited for the kingdom of God" (Mark 15:43). He was bold. He was also a just man and, as such, had dissented from the majority vote with regard to the death of Christ (Luke 23:50–51). He was from Arimathea where the prophet Samuel had lived. Doubtless Pilate's police had a dossier on Joseph. Pilate probably knew about the man. So when this wealthy member of the Jewish nobility was announced, Pilate was impressed. Indeed, Pilate seemed glad of the chance to do something, however small, to express his regret for the way the trial had gone. Once he had been assured that Jesus was dead, he wasted no time in signing the warrant releasing the body of Jesus to Joseph. It was a way, too, of getting back at the Jews, and one that cost him nothing.

Finally, there was *the divine proclamation.* It explained why God would not allow the body of His beloved Son to be defiled or contaminated by wicked men.

The first reason was because the Lord was blameless in *His walk.* "He had done no violence" (Isa. 53:9). The Lord abhorred violence. Only once did His disciples suggest violence, and only once did they employ it. Interestingly enough, the disciples involved all came from the innermost circle of Jesus' disciples comprised of Peter, James, and John.

When some Samaritans treated the Lord with utter disrespect, James and John wanted the Lord to call down fire from on high and consume them. He nicknamed them "Boanerges," that is "sons of thunder," to remind them not to think any such thing again.

When Judas came with the mob to arrest the Lord in Gethsemane, Peter drew a sword and slashed out with it, cutting off the ear of the servant of the high priest. "Put up again thy sword," Jesus said. "They that take the sword shall perish with the sword" (Matt. 26:52). Then He graciously restored the poor man's ear.

It was not that violence was not a possibility. The Lord had already told Peter He had legions of angels at His command. He simply chose not to use them. Because the Lord chose the path of nonresistance, refusing to inflict injury even on His foes, His body was protected from His enemies' schemes.

The second reason why the Lord's body was held inviolate was because the Lord was blameless in *His talk.* "Neither was any deceit in his mouth" (Isa. 53:9). No matter what the situation, the Lord Jesus told the truth, the whole truth, and nothing but the truth. He never sought refuge in life's conventional disguises, the disguises we so readily adopt. He told the truth boldly, even when He knew it would bring down the wrath of the Sanhedrin upon His head. God protected Him in death because of what He was in life. When my grandfather was on his deathbed, he said to my father, "There's nothing to dying, Leonard. It's the living that counts."

The Lord's foes could not touch Him once He was pronounced dead. Loving hands took Him down from the cross. Loving hands embalmed Him. Loving hands put Him in that brand-new tomb. Death itself could not attack with corruption and decay that lifeless form of His. The wages of sin is death, and since Jesus never sinned, death itself had no claim upon His mortal clay. Had He remained in that tomb for a thousand years, it would have been the same.

So God kept His word with His Beloved. Thank you, Nicodemus. It was a kind thought and your name will forever be associated with it through all the ages of eternity, but no spices were needed. God Himself held *that* body in fragrant beauty even in death's own realm.

We have no guarantee that our mortal frames will not see corruption. That is part of the Fall. But we do have the blessed assurance that we shall rise again, rise from the dead in newness of life, changed in a moment, in the twinkling of an eye, sown in corruption, raised in incorruption! To be like Jesus! To have a body like His glorious body! To bear His image throughout the endless ages, now and forever more. Blessed be God, our God!

Low in the grave He lay,
Jesus my Savior
Waiting the coming day,
Jesus my Lord!

Vainly they watch His bed,
Jesus my Savior
Vainly they seal the dead,
Jesus my Lord!

Death cannot keep his prey,
Jesus my Savior
He tore the bars away,
Jesus my Lord!

Up from the grave He arose,
With a mighty triumph o'er His foes;
He arose a victor from the dark domain,
And He lives forever with His saints to reign.
He arose! He arose!
Hallelujah! Christ arose![1]

—R. Lowry (1826–1899)

CHAPTER 14

THE VICTORY SIDE OF CALVARY

Isaiah 53:10

1. The tragedy of Calvary (v. 10a)
    a. The unfathomable mystery of the Cross
       (1) The mystery of God's plan
       (2) The mystery of God's pleasure
    b. The unforgettable ministry of the Cross
2. The triumph of Calvary (v. 10b)
    a. The Lord's endless days
       (1) Materially
       (2) Mystically
    b. The Lord's endless delight

WHEN I WAS A BOY THERE STOOD in my father's library a prized, old engraved copy of *Pilgrim's Progress.* It had old pictures on almost every page. Pictures of Christian, Faithful, and Worldly Wiseman, of the man with the muckrake in his hand; pictures, too, of Obstinate, Pliable, and of Mr. Valient-for-truth. They were all there in Puritan dress, ageless and all of them unchanged to this day. Little-faith was pictured being robbed by Faint Heart, Mistrust, and Guilt, not to mention

Superstition and Envy who bore biased witness before Judge Hate-good against the pilgrims in the court at Vanity Fair.

The picture of Atheist showed him deriding Christian and Hopeful. What a picture that was! I can still see the old fool with his big floppy hat, his kneesocks, and his big shoes with the rosette bows. I see him yet, his sword by his side, his stick in his hand, standing on the edge of a precipice. He is looking back at the pilgrims, laughing mockingly at them and making a gesture of contempt with his outstretched hand. What he fails to observe is that the stick upon which he is about to place his full weight is not resting on solid ground but on thin air. For Atheist is so busy deriding Christian and Hopeful that he does not realize that he, himself, is about to pitch headlong into eternity.

There was another character, one that scared me as a little boy. I can see him yet in my mind's eye. The picture of Giant Despair had a whole haunted page to itself.

He was seated on a great wooden bench, leaning on his massive left hand. His face was ugly and a black scowl darkened his countenance. He had a crooked nose and horrible, staring eyes that seemed to look right into mine. He was poorly dressed, and his hair and beard were long and tangled. I was afraid of him. I knew exactly what page of the book he was on.

I would return time and again to that big book on my father's shelf. I would turn the pages looking at the pictures, studying Mr. Great-heart, Mrs. Bat's-eyes, Mrs. Know-nothing, Mr. Feeble-mind, and Mr. Ready-to-halt. I knew, however, exactly on which page Giant Despair lived and most times I would skip over that page and land instead on Mr. Ignorance's page. He was a pleasant-faced fellow with a lot to say.

But I never picked up *Pilgrim's Progress* without being aware that on a certain page in that book, waiting to frighten me, waiting to beat me with his great cudgel, lurked Giant Despair. I hated him. Sometimes in my braver moments, when the sun was shining and when there were other people around, I would deliberately open the book at the page and boldly stare the fellow down.

Calvary is like that in Isaiah 53. Calvary is there. Calvary is always there. We look at it and hastily turn away. Mount Calvary is a hideous place and the old Hebrew prophet keeps bringing us back to it again and again. For although the sight is dreadful, it has a horrible fascination about it that will not be denied.

Thus, in verse 9 of this awesome prophecy, Isaiah takes us to the tomb. At the end of verse 10 we are taken again to the tomb, only now it is an empty tomb, for Christ has risen indeed! But in between the burial of Christ and the resurrection of Christ, in verses 9 and 10, Isaiah brings us back to Golgotha's hill for another look at Giant Despair, another look at the Cross. He has taken us to Calvary in verses 3, 4, 5, 6, and 8. At last, Calvary is behind us! We have passed the page! But what is this? The prophet is bringing us back to Calvary. Indeed, before he closes this chapter at verse 12, he will bring us back for yet one more last look.

1. The tragedy of Calvary

> Yet it pleased the LORD to bruise him; he hath put him to grief: when thou shalt make his soul an offering for sin. (Isaiah 53:10a)

In the Bible we come across a "Holy of Holies," a "Song of Songs," a "King of Kings," and a "Lord of Lords." Here we have a "mystery of mysteries." Here it is—"It pleased the LORD to bruise him." That is a statement before which our boldest expositors pause.

There is *the unfathomable mystery of the Cross.* How could it possibly have "pleased" the Lord to "bruise him"? Whether we read that statement with Rotherham[2] or stay resolutely with the King James text, the mystery remains.

Let us look at the rendering. "Jehovah *purposed* to bruise Him." That takes us back to the mystery of God's plan. For God was by no means taken by surprise by the fall of man. It was foreseen by the living God. Omniscient foreknowledge took the fall of man into account before determining the form of man. After all, God wanted people not puppets. He could have patterned human life and society after the model beehive or ant heap, but that was the last thing He wanted.

God knew that once the mystery of iniquity was allowed to raise its head, it would grow to such vast proportions that it would have to be taken in hand by God Himself. The sin question would be localized on a certain planet in space; it would be allowed to fully express itself at a place called Calvary; and it would be dealt with to God's full and eternal satisfaction. Such awesome and monumental truths are made clear to us, not by a process of human reasoning but by a process of divine revelation. The whole process would give God a stage upon which to demonstrate to the entire universe the monumental truth that God is love.

> God is love I surely know,
> By the Savior's depths of woe.[3]

Love for us took Him all the way to Calvary. Amazing grace! Inexhaustible love! Only such love can explain why it was Jehovah's purpose to bruise Him. The word *bruise* comes from a Hebrew word meaning "to crush." God, having passed the severest sentence upon sin that His infinite holiness could demand, turned around and in the person of His only-begotten and well-beloved Son, He paid it Himself, at the Cross.

Now, let us look at it again as embedded in the King James text. "It *pleased* the LORD to bruise him." How could God derive pleasure from the death of His Son at the place called Calvary? Not simply death but "even the death of the cross" (Phil. 2:8).

Remember, Isaiah was a Jew, "a Hebrew of the Hebrews." Doubtless he knew his Bible by heart. He was well acquainted with the various offerings required of the Hebrew people under the demands of the Mosaic laws. There were five of them in all. The two that dealt with sin (the sin offering and the burnt offering) had little to bring pleasure to God. All was dark and dreadful about them. The three sweet-savor offerings each had an aspect to them that did bring pleasure to God, even though Calvary was at the heart of each one.

Communion is the predominant thought in connection with the peace offering. God had once had communion with Adam's race. In the cool of the day, He would come down and commune with Adam (Gen. 3:8). The Fall put an end to all that. The centuries came and went but God could not find a single person with whom He could commune and open up His heart in full. Then Jesus came.

As Jesus, at His baptism, came up from the water so the Spirit of God came down from on high. At last, at long last, here was One in whom could be all His delight—One who would be obedient unto death, even "the death of the cross" (Phil. 2:8).[4] Amazing wonder! God found pleasure in that.

The meal offering was next. Character was the predominant thought in connection with the meal offering. The meal was made of the finest flour. It was even, flawless, milled to a perfect texture. Its flawless, even texture symbolized the sinless life and perfect character of Christ. From the cradle to the grave, He displayed absolute perfection in thought, word, and deed. He did always those things that pleased the Father (Matt. 3:17; John 8:29; Heb. 10:7–9). God had pleasure in Him.

Above all, there was the burnt offering. The predominant thought in the meal offering was consecration, the kind of consecration displayed in dark Gethsemane. Jesus gazed into the dark and dreadful depths of the cup being offered to Him and begged and pleaded that it might be taken away. The prayer was immediately followed by the words, "Nevertheless not my will, but thine, be done" (Luke 22:42). God found immeasurable pleasure in that.

Next comes *the unforgettable ministry of the Cross.* "He hath put him to grief: when thou shalt make his soul an offering for sin" (Isa. 53:10a). That was the other side of the Cross, the sin-offering side. His soul was to be made an offering for sin.

Rotherham helps us here. He translates the expression "put him to grief" as "made Him sick." Our sin nauseated Him to the depths of His being. It was sin that broke His heart in Gethsemane. It was not just the thought of being crucified. He was a brave enough man for that. In those evil days the Romans crucified people by the thousands. The Lord could have taken death on a cross in His stride. It was being made sin that overwhelmed Him. The thought of it brought a sweat to His brow. His soul, His sinless, spotless soul, was to be made an offering for sin. The sin of the world was to be transferred to Him. It made Him sick to think about it.

2. The triumph of Calvary

> He shall see his seed, he shall prolong his days, and the pleasure of the LORD shall prosper in his hand. (Isaiah 53:10b)

In a single bound, Isaiah takes us to the other side of the grave. We stand breathless, on resurrection ground, beholding a risen Lord.

We think of His *endless days,* days prolonged beyond all count. But how could that be? He prolonged them in two ways. First, He renewed them *materially*—by rising from the dead.

Suddenly we see some women stealing through the Sunday morning gloom. From time to time, they stop to look around and listen. They fear that Sanhedrin soldiers might be lurking in the shadows. They intend to do a daring deed—to tamper with the tomb, to boldly break the Roman seal. More, they were venturing into a private cemetery, determined to take in hand a stiff and silent corpse. These are the very things of which fear itself is made. Holding hands, they press on their way, for "perfect love casteth out fear" (1 John 4:18), the apostle says. So it does!

Now the grave itself lies just ahead. Suddenly one-half of their difficulties are resolved. The stone has been rolled away from the door. The soldiers are gone. The women come closer. They peer inside. New doubts assail them. The tomb was empty! First they think of a robbery, but in a short time they know the truth. That empty tomb advertised not a robbery but a resurrection! Thus, He would indeed prolong His days!

But as the Son of God, what need had He to prolong His days? None whatsoever! He had existed from all eternity. He stood astride the ages. To enter into human life He had stepped out of eternity into time. As the Son of God, His future was as endless as His past.

As the Son of Man, however, He was born in Bethlehem in the days when Herod was king. He entered human life by way of a womb. He left it by way of a tomb, a tomb that had no power over Him. He burst its bands asunder, came striding out of the dark realm of death, and shortly afterward ascended into heaven where, to this hour, He prolongs His days materially in the power of an endless life.

There was more to it than that, however. He now prolongs His days *mystically* by means of the church, His mystical body. Ten days after the Lord's bodily ascension into heaven, the third member of the Godhead came down here to take His place. As the Holy Spirit had created a material body for the Son in the Virgin's womb, so He created a mystical body for Him in the Upper Room. From that momentous Pentecost until this very day, the Lord prolongs His days through us. He Himself is the Head of the mystical body, the church. We, baptized by the Holy Spirit, are its members. The church strides through the ages. The living God buries His workers but continues its work. Moment by moment, new workers are added to this mystical body so that the Head never lacks those through whom He can carry on His work. The mystical body of Christ was supernaturally injected into history on the Day of Pentecost. It will be supernaturally ejected back out of history at the Rapture. The church will then share the high places of the universe as the bride of Christ. Concepts such as these relating to the church were beyond what had been revealed in Isaiah's day. The Holy Spirit knew of these things, however, and buried them in numerous types and shadows to which the Old Testament saints did not have the key (Eph. 3:5, 9–12).

The prophet speaks now of the Lord's *endless delight*. He refers to "the pleasure of the LORD (that) shall prosper in his hand" (Isa. 53:10b). Now, that is pleasure of another sort. It is that wondrous joy that was set before Him, "joy unspeakable and full of glory" (1 Peter 1:8; see also Heb. 12:2).

Imagine the joy that now fills the soul of the Savior as He sits upon His Father's throne in heaven. He watches with the keenest interest as the Holy Spirit pursues His perfect work calling out a people for His name. Christ enters into the lives of His people down here, representing them as their great High Priest in the Holies and as their Advocate in the heavenlies.

Everything is prospering in His hand. We only see bits and pieces of it down here. He sits on high. The very gates of hell cannot prevail against Him or His church (Matt. 16:16–18). Well might we sing, "Hallelujah, What a Savior!"

The holiest we enter
In perfect peace with God,
Through whom we found our center
In Jesus and His blood:
Though great may be our dullness
In thought and word and deed,
We glory in the fullness
Of Him that meets our need.

Much incense is ascending
Before the eternal throne;
God graciously is bending
To hear each feeble groan;
To all our prayers and praises
Christ adds His sweet perfume
And love the censor raises,
These odors to consume.

O God, we come with singing
Because the great High Priest
Our names to Thee is bringing
Nor e'er forgets the least:
For us He wears the mitre,
Where holiness shines bright,
For us His robes are whiter
Than heaven's unsullied light.[1]
    —Mary Bowles Peters (1813–1856)

CHAPTER 15

THE TRAVAIL OF HIS SOUL

Isaiah 53:11

1. A redeemed people (v. 11a)
2. A royal priest (v. 11b)
   a. Infinite comprehension
   b. Infinite compassion

WE DO NOT USUALLY CONSIDER Samson to be a type of Christ. His faults and failings are too glaring. Still, we do not restrict the types to people who are free from iniquity and sin. The only full-length, perfect type in the Old Testament is Joseph (and possibly Daniel), and he is not even listed as a type in the New Testament. If a type has to be perfect, then we must write off Noah, Moses, Isaac, David, and Solomon—just for starters.

So, we approach those aspects of Samson's life and ministry that remind us of Christ with considerable care. There was, for instance, his miraculous birth—a birth heralded by an angel. That reminds us of Christ. There is the significant fact that the Holy Spirit is mentioned more in connection with Samson than with anyone else in the entire book of Judges, if not the whole Old Testament. Then, too, there was the glorious death of Samson. These things, taken together, point to a type. Moreover the Holy Spirit says of Samson something He says of very few people, indeed. He says that "time would fail . . . to tell of . . . Samson" (Heb. 11:32).

Samson was a Hebrew Hercules. The Spirit of God came upon Samson early in his life, way up in the northern tribe of Dan. His first act after that was to seek out the Philistines. These were the traditional and warlike ancient enemies of Israel. They were in the land but did not belong in the land. Samson went looking for them and found them at a place called Timnath where the central Palestinian mountains swept down to the sea. Samson's first contact with the enemy was one of peace, not war. He met a pagan woman there, one who was a stranger to the commonwealth of Israel and an alien to the covenants of God. Samson's heart went out to this spiritual outcast, and he determined to win her as his bride. That surely reminds us of Christ.

Samson set about achieving his goal in all the power of his might when a lion roared against him on the way. The lion speaks to us of Satan, our greatest foe, that roaring lion who goes about seeking whom he might devour.

The lion, however, was no match for Samson. He strode toward it and rent it asunder as though it had been a mere kid. But who can thus embrace a mighty lion and come away unscarred! We can be sure that Samson bore the tokens of that mighty battle to his dying day.

The battle won, Samson went on to woo and win his Gentile bride. We can picture her to ourselves, gazing at the marks left on his body by the lion. We can hear her say, "Where did those wounds come from? How is it that your back has been thus ploughed like a farmer's field?" Samson would reply, "These marks are the tokens of my love for you. I wear them because a lion roared against me on my way and because it stood between me and my heart's desire." Thus, our Beloved Lord came:

> Out of the ivory palaces
> Into a world of woe,
> Only His great redeeming love
> Made our Savior go.[2]

He came because He loved us with an everlasting love. And when Satan roared against Him, He threw wide His mighty arms and triumphed gloriously. But the battle scars remain. In the Upper Room after His glorious resurrection, He showed them to His own. He will show them to us too one of these days. We shall know Him by the print of the nails in His hands.

But it is time we returned to Isaiah. "He shall see of the travail of his soul, and shall be satisfied" (Isa. 53:11a), the prophet says.

1. A redeemed people

> He shall see of the travail of his soul, and shall be satisfied. (Isaiah 53:11a)

Travail—it is a word from the maternity ward, a word that speaks of pain soon to be forgotten in joy. It pictures suffering and struggle bravely endured, so that a new birth can take place and a new name written down in glory.

Travail—the prophet calls us to be present at the birth pangs of the church to witness the travail of *the Lord's* soul—there has been no such travail in all the world.

The old-time preachers would contemplate the miseries of those they saw struggling in a mighty battle with the Holy Spirit prior to their actual salvation. They had a word for it—*conviction*—conviction of sin! In God's wisdom conviction comes before conversion, repentance before rebirth, travail before trust.

Martin Luther is a classic example of how great the travail can be. All through his convent days, he was so tortured by the thought of his sin that his life was one long torment. As he crept like a shadow along the galleries of the cloister, the walls echoed back his groans. His body was reduced to a skeleton. His strength ebbed away. His brother monks would find him prostrate on the floor and pick him up for dead. He thought that by fasting and by fear and by penance and by pain he could atone for his sins.

He longed to see Rome. Penniless and barefoot he crossed the Alps, begging for his bread along the way. But Rome only added to his despair. He saw monasteries clothed in marble, monks living sumptuously on the fat of the land. He saw proud cardinals riding on horseback or sitting in carriages that glittered with precious stones. This was not the Rome of his dreams.

His tormented soul led him at last to Pilate's staircase where he hoped to find rest for his soul. This notable staircase, he was told, had been miraculously transported to Rome. The church assured him that if he ascended on his knees the twenty-eight steps of the staircase, wonders would be worked in his soul. After all, had not the blessed Savior Himself ascended and descended those stairs during His trial before the procurator of Rome? So, if he ascended those sacred steps on his knees, saying the proper prayers, step-by-step he would earn a full papal indulgence, complete absolution for his sins.

Complete absolution for his sins was the goal for which so long he had sought. We picture him, driven up from step to step by his travail of soul, praying devoutly to the Virgin Mary on each step of the way:

> Holy Mother, pierce me through,
> In my heart each wound renew
> Of my Savior crucified.

Step after step! "Holy Mother! Holy Mother!" Such was the travail of Martin Luther's soul. But poor Martin Luther's soul trouble was *nothing* compared with the soul trouble that seized the Savior when God "made him to be sin for us, who knew no sin" (2 Cor. 5:21). It was that soul torment that He expressed audibly, terribly, at Calvary. "My God, my God, why hast thou forsaken me?" (Matt. 27:46). There on the cross Jesus not only died *for* each one of us; He died *as* each one of us. The human imagination cannot picture what that meant to Him.

Think for instance of the Prodigal Son. There he goes with a swing in his step, a song in his soul, and bundles of cold cash in his purse. He devoured his living with harlots and ended up devouring slops from a garbage pail, slops left for pigs to eat. There he sat in his sin.

All along the broad highway was a trail of debauched young men and defiled, desperate young women. He had ruined them with his wit and wealth and wicked ways. There were aging parents grieving over daughters who had lost their innocence and sons who had ruined their family's good name—fathers and mothers with cause enough to curse the day this young charmer had come into town. Jesus died for him; died as him.

Think of the elder brother, a self-righteous hypocrite with sins of his own: nasty, mean, cheap sins of pride and jealousy and bitterness. Think of his anger when the Prodigal returned! Think of the acid that dripped from his tongue! Think how he resented the Prodigal's profligate past and resisted the father's warm pleas. What a nasty, spiteful, unforgiving spirit he displayed. Jesus died for him; died as him. Think of the travail of His soul.

"He shall see of the travail of his soul, and shall be satisfied." Webster gives a number of definitions for the word *satisfied*. We use the word when:

1. The terms of a contract have been fully met.
   It has been satisfied.
2. A financial obligation has been fully discharged.
   It has been satisfied.
3. The specifications of a blueprint have all been faithfully followed.
   It has been satisfied.
4. We find something to be completely adequate.
   We have been satisfied.
5. We are pleased and made happy.
   We are satisfied.
6. We have been gratified to the full.
   We are satisfied.
7. Reparation is made in full.
   The wronged party is satisfied.
8. When a doubt is laid to rest.
   The questioner is satisfied.

Some of these definitions are of a legal nature. The Lord Jesus, risen, ascended, and seated on high, is satisfied. He has met every demanding jot and tittle of God's law. He has met those demands both in the letter and the spirit of the law in its specific details and in its underlying intent. Satisfied—the law is satisfied. God is satisfied. Jesus Himself is satisfied.

Some of these definitions are more personal and go far beyond technicalities. The Lord in glory sees all those He has redeemed by His blood, sees them ransomed, healed, restored, forgiven; sees them saved to sin no more, seated with Him on high—and He is satisfied! He sees them wearing His image and likeness. He is satisfied, gratified to the full, pleased and made happy—satisfied indeed!

When we were young our favorite books were the fairy story variety. These stories told of wicked old witches who turned lovely princesses into toads and looked them up in a garden of weeds. Then along would come a prince charming. He would tear up the brambles. He would find the ugly toad. He would kiss the foul-looking thing and, wonder of wonders, in a moment it was a toad no longer but a beautiful princess. Then the gallant hero would hunt down the wicked old witch and kill her and take the princess away to a city of stars. Of course, they were married with all pomp and circumstance, and they lived happily ever after. We liked that part of the story best of all.

Then we grew up. Sad to say, in the real world of grown-up people, it isn't like that at all. Prince Charming turns out to be not nearly as charming as we pictured him. He sits around in his greasy overalls, he growls at the noisy children, he spends most of his time glued to the sports channel on television. Moreover, the beautiful princess has an acid tongue. She goes around all day with all kinds of oddments wound into her hair, and she plasters her face with foul-tasting compounds intended to keep her young. So much for fairy stories.

The fairy stories of our childhood were mostly idle daydreams. Sad to say, we read our stories from the wrong book. The stories we were told were collected by the brothers Grimm or Hans Christian Anderson. So we filled our make-believe world with fairy godmothers, fire-

breathing dragons, and beanstalks ascending to the sky. It was harmless and entertaining enough in its way.

But there is another book. It tells of giants and witches as well and
of a baby in a boat of bulrushes, rescued by a real princess, who grew
up to perform all kinds of wonders. This other book tells stories just
as marvelous, just as full of "magic," though miracles would be a better word since these stories are true.

For there is a Prince Charming, born in a small eastern town, described as "altogether lovely." His story is full of mystery, might, and
miracles. The people thought He was just "the carpenter's son" (Matt.
13:55), whereas He was the eternal, uncreated, self-existing Son of
the Living God. Oh yes, He will slay the great red dragon. He will
come back one of these days from that faraway land to which He has
gone. He will take us to be with Him. In His land there are no tears or
fears; there is no pain or death, only "joy unspeakable and full of glory"
(1 Peter 1:8).

He *is* coming back. We will be with Him where He is. We shall be
like Him. He will see in us the travail of His soul and be satisfied.

2. A royal priest

> By his knowledge shall my righteous servant justify many; for
> he shall bear their iniquities. (Isaiah 53:11b)

That Jesus was to be a *prince* is written in large letters both by Isaiah
and a host of other Old Testament prophets as well. That He was to
be a *priest* was a concept so daring, so different, so drastic that only an
occasional patriarch of the rank of Abraham, or prince of the rank of
David, or prophet of the rank of Isaiah or Zechariah or Daniel had
any concept of it all. The notion seems to have escaped the Jews completely. This truth was revealed in the Old Testament, but it is the
Cross that has brought it out into the broad light of day. It is the New
Testament that flashes upon it all the colors of the rainbow and makes
the truth blaze with the light of heaven.

Isaiah caught this one glimpse of it and expressed it in these words:

"By his knowledge shall my righteous servant justify many; for he shall bear their iniquities." That has to do, not with the finished work of Christ but with the *unfinished* work of Christ, His work at God's right hand as our "advocate with the Father" (1 John 2:1).

Our great High Priest is possessed of *infinite comprehension.* Isaiah refers to "his knowledge," and what knowledge it is—infinite, omniscient knowledge! He uses that knowledge to "justify many," all those who put their faith and trust in Him, many indeed!

In order to do that, the ascended Lord had to have two things. First, He had to have an absolute awareness of the fundamentals of God's throne. He must know all that God knows, all that God demands, the completeness of His holiness, the completeness of His wisdom, love, and power.

Second, He had to have an absolute awareness of the frailties of His people. He must know our frame and remember we are dust (Ps. 103:14). He must be "touched with the feeling of our infirmities" and He must be "tempted like as we are, yet without sin" (Heb. 4:15). He must know every detail of all our lives—know the place, the time, the occasion, the background, the outcome, and the continuing consequences of every soul and every sin. Such are His credentials. Such is His knowledge. Only One who is God can have such *infinite comprehension.*

Our great High Priest is also possessed of *infinite compassion.* His role is not to be the "accuser of our brethren" (Rev. 12:10). That is Satan's role. He is at God's right hand to plead our cause, to show His nail-scarred hands, to declare us righteous, justified, free from all guilt because of His finished work.

The Roman Catholic is taught that he is too great a sinner to come to Christ. He needs a mediator in the person of Christ's mother. If a suppliant wants a thing done by her Son, Rome declares that His mother might influence Him on that person's behalf.[3]

Some years ago I was in Vichy, France, a famous spa town where people go to be physically healed. At Vichy there is a Roman Catholic church called Our Lady of Healing. The shrine's central focus of worship is a black image of the Virgin Mary. The image is paraded through

Vichy with pomp and ceremony by bishop, priest, and the devout at certain times of the year. Plaques are built into the wall of the church by many grateful Catholics who believe that Mary has heard their prayers and healed them.

High up in the dome of the church is a giant picture. Christ is standing in the shadows of that picture, and Mary dominates the foreground. Her robes light up when the sunbeams strike them through the stained-glass windows. She is obviously the more important figure of the two. She is portrayed as standing triumphant, trampling a writhing serpent beneath her feet. Below her is a quotation from John 3:16, "For God so loved the world, that he gave his only begotten Son." Then, in much bigger letters, is the true message of this church. The message is a quotation from St. Bernard: "It is God's will that we receive all things through Mary."

The message is simply not true. For Mary to be the great mediator between God and humanity, she would have to have all the attributes of deity. She would have to be God.

Isaiah concludes this aspect of his great theme by bringing us back to the Cross. "He shall bear their iniquities." Our sins have all been dealt with at Calvary. When accusations arise against a believer, God simply brings the accuser back to the Cross. Let the great apostle Paul have the last word here. He says,

> What shall we then say to these things? If God be for us, who can be against us? He that spared not his own Son, but delivered him up for us all, how shall he not with him also freely give us all things? Who shall lay any thing to the charge of God's elect? It is God that justifieth. Who is he that condemneth? It is Christ that died, yea rather, that is risen again, who is even at the right hand of God, who also maketh intercession for us. (Romans 8:31–34)

Calvary covers it all!

Look, ye saints! The sight is glorious:
See the Man of Sorrows now:
From the fight returned victorious,
Every knee to Him shall bow:
Crown Him! Crown Him!
Crowns become the Victor's brow.

Crown the Savior! Angels crown Him!
Rich the trophies Jesus brings:
In the seat of power enthrone Him,
While the vault of heaven rings:
Crown Him! Crown Him!
Crown the Savior King of Kings.

Sinners in derision crowned Him,
Mocking thus the Savior's claim;
Saints and angels crowd around Him,
Own His title, praise His name.
Crown Him! Crown Him!
Spread abroad the Victor's fame.

Hark! those bursts of acclamation!
Hark! those loud triumphant chords!
Jesus takes the highest station;
O what joy the sight affords!
Crown Him! Crown Him!
King of Kings, and Lord of Lords.[1]
—Thomas Kelly (1769–1854)

CHAPTER 16

THE KING WITH THE NAIL-PIERCED HANDS

Isaiah 53:12

1. The reality of Christ's authority (v. 12a)
   a. Dividing the world with His friends
   b. Destroying the works of His foes
2. The reasons for Christ's authority (v. 12b)
   a. The dreadful intensity of Christ's sufferings
   b. The divine intention of Christ's sufferings
      (1) The indignity He bore
      (2) The iniquity He bore
   c. The daily intercession of Christ's sufferings

DRIVING THROUGH THE ROCKY Mountains, a motorist is surrounded by peaks reaching toward the sky. Before long, the driver realizes there is more than one mountain range barring the way. There are as many peaks before the car as behind it. The traveler can only guess at the nature of the valleys between the peaks. Are they wide or narrow, lush with grass or barren, mere shallow folds or deep ravines? Only later in his journey will he know. But there is no mistaking the peaks.

That was how Isaiah and the other prophets saw the future. They saw the main peaks clearly enough. They saw a *suffering* Christ, one torn and bleeding, shamed, spat upon, and crucified. They saw, too, a *sovereign* Christ, one reigning in power, with the nations prostrate in the dust before Him and Israel triumphing over all.

They did not realize that many centuries stood between the one and the other. Some Old Testament believers postulated two Christs, one coming to redeem, the other coming to reign. We now can see quite clearly the vast valley between the peaks. There was not to be two Christs but two comings. The Messiah would come, and then He would go and then come again. He would come first to bear the cross; He would come again to wear the crown. From where we stand in time we can look back to the first coming of Christ, back to the first mountain range of prophetic truth. We can also look ahead to the second coming of Christ. Events are hurrying us along to the second mountain range of prophetic truth. Indeed, everywhere we look we can see the signs of His coming again. Isaiah's perspective was quite different from ours, as he lived centuries before the birth of Christ. He jumped from one mountain range to the other. This is very evident in the last verse of this prophecy. One moment, Isaiah has us see the Lord dividing the spoil with the strong. The next moment, we are back at the Cross seeing Him pouring out His soul unto death. Isaiah cannot tear himself away from the Cross. He makes no attempt to sort out prophecies relating to the Lord's first coming and prophecies relating to His coming again.

1. The reality of Christ's authority

> Therefore will I divide him a portion with the great, and he shall divide the spoil with the strong. (Isaiah 53:12a)

First, the Lord is going to *divide the world with His friends.* "I will give him the mighty for his portion" is the way the Septuagint explains it. The word translated "divide" comes from a word that means "to apportion" or "to assign." The prophet here anticipates the day when Jesus will reign over the millennial earth, a theme often referred to by Isaiah in his great book.

It is fitting that this very sphere where once our Lord was crucified should be the scene of His ultimate triumph. Such a kingly triumph is in keeping with the poetic justice of God so discernible in His dealings with this world. If the Lord's withdrawal into heaven from Olivet's brow were the end of it, we would have a sense of incompleteness. There has to be more to it than that, more to it even than the coming of the Holy Spirit and the church. In a sense, Satan would be perceived as having somehow won after all. But that is not so! Christ, the King of glory, is coming back to reign. "The earth is the LORD's" (Ps. 24:1), and the universe itself eagerly awaits the day when that will be very evidently so (Rom. 8:19–25).

Accounts would not be properly settled with anything less. In accounting, every debit has to have a credit. That is a fundamental fact of bookkeeping. I worked for a bank long enough to know that; before one could leave the building, all the books had to be balanced. The institution would not settle for anything less than that. One of these days God is going to see to it that all the books are balanced. The great debit of the Cross is to be balanced by the great credit of the coronation. When that day dawns the Lord will divide the world with the strong.

Two kinds of people are going to have a special share in His glorious reign. He will have an earthly people (the nation of Israel), and He will have a heavenly people (the church). His earthly people will comprise the surviving remnant of the Jews at the time of His coming to reign. They will be instantly converted when they see Him in all His splendor. The new nation of Israel will be born instantly (Isa. 66:7–14). The surviving righteous Gentiles will be likewise born again instantly and will become the nuclei of the redeemed Gentile nations (Joel 3:1; Matt. 25:31–46).

His heavenly people will be those saved by His blood and baptized by His Spirit in this present age. We are already identified with Him in "the heavenly places" (Eph. 2:4–7). We shall reign with Him on high, the new Jerusalem being our eternal heavenly home.

When Jesus comes to reign, He will deal with two sets of foes. On earth there will be the massed Gentile armies, gathered by divine decree to the Battle of Armageddon. In the heavens will be Satan and all his assembled principalities and powers. The Lord will sweep them all away (Isa. 24:21). The Jewish remnant will be installed as head over the Gentile nations. The "times of the Gentiles" (Luke 21:24) will be over. The church will take the place in the high heavens presently occupied by those satanic forces who oppose us in so many ways in this age (Eph. 6:11–13).

Then, too, the Lord will *destroy the works of His foes.* "Therefore will I divide him a portion with the great, and he shall divide the spoil with the strong" (Isa. 53:12a). *He is going to carve up the world as it pleases Him.* The world will be in a terrible state by this time, as we learn from the Apocalypse. Three series of judgment will have swept the earth.

The home call of the church will herald the breaking of the seals (Rev. 4–6) and the removal of all divine restraint. The Holy Spirit will no longer act as the restrainer (2 Thess. 2:6–8). The world will rapidly descend into chaos. People will give way to despair. They will imagine that the great day of wrath has come (Rev. 6:12–17). Dreadful wars, famines, pestilences, and persecutions will be but the beginning of the sorrows (Matt. 24:4–8).

Universal upheavals will give rise to an outcry for a man, someone of great influence and power, to take over the affairs of this globe. The blowing of the trumpets will herald the coming of the Beast (or the Antichrist as we usually call him). In a series of planned maneuvers, he will sweep away all opposition and take over the reigns of earthly power. Once he is universally enthroned, he will reveal his true colors. He will throw off any pretense of befriending the Jews. He will seize their rebuilt temple, enthrone himself as god in its inner sanctuary, install his image in the temple, and inaugurate the Great Tribulation, "the time of Jacob's trouble," as it is called (Jer. 30:7). He will make all people receive his mark. A total economic boycott will be enforced against all who refuse to worship this image or receive this mark. There will be a global campaign to rid the world of all those who harbor any Judeo-Christian beliefs. The planet will become a suburb of hell.

Then will come the vial (bowl) judgments. Now, at last, the time of God's wrath will have come. This wrath will be concentrated, at first, on the power structure of the Antichrist. He will lose his grip. The eastern part of his empire (the nations east of the River Euphrates) will break away and mobilize against him. The armies of the world, East and West, will be drawn to Megiddo to decide the fate of the world. But suddenly the Lord will invade, ablaze with glory, accompanied by signs and wonders, surrounded by heavenly hosts, with all power at His command—and it will be over (Matt. 24:30–31; Rev. 19:11–21).

The terrible Pandora's Box of weird and wicked things introduced by Satan and his beast will be swept away. Jesus will have come! Isaiah catches a glimpse of it. He hints at it in this verse. Jesus will reign. The reality of Christ's authority will be acknowledged by all (Phil. 2:9–11).

2. The reasons for Christ's authority

The prophet is about to bring this majestic passage to a close. To do so he brings us back to the Cross. He wants to make sure we understand why it is that God has placed all authority and power in the hands of Jesus. It is because of Calvary. He reminds us again of *the dreadful intensity of Christ's sufferings.* "He hath poured out his soul unto death" (Isa. 53:12b), Isaiah declares.

Let us go back to an incident in the life of David. David was holed up with his mighty men in a cave. Saul's spies were everywhere. The Philistines held considerable stretches of territory in the neighborhood. Even David's hometown of Bethlehem was under Philistine control. The days were hot, long, and tedious. Suddenly, David exclaimed, "Oh that one would give me drink of the water of the well . . . by the gate!" (2 Sam. 23:15).

In a flash, three of David's mighty men were on their feet—Eleazar, son of Dodo, a man skilled in fighting Philistines; Adino the Eznite, who once took on overwhelming odds; and Shammah, son of Agee, who single-handedly had fought the Philistines to a standstill in defense of a patch of lentils.

Off they went. Past the Valley of the Shadow, over rocky hills where here and there a sheep or so could be seen. Then, like ghosts in the night, they crept toward the well by the gate. Now eyes had to be keen for King Saul's bloodhounds as well as for Philistine troops. Then, a sprint to the well—and away at full speed with a water skin filled to the brim! Back they dashed to David with the longed-for drink from the well.

David was overwhelmed! How he must have hugged those men! With what anticipation he raised the water skin to his lips. Then he stopped. He looked at the eager faces of his men. He thought of the fearful risk they had run. He thanked them with a full heart—and poured the water out onto the ground to the very last drop. He turned it into a drink offering to God. The whole camp watched the water, flowing swiftly from the water skin, cascading down to the ground. A costly sacrifice indeed!

That was what Jesus did. Only it was not just water that He poured out; it was His soul, His very life. He "poured out his soul unto death" was how the prophet put it. He poured it out drop by drop in fearful agony, in anguish, suffering, and pain. Slowly, the full tide of His life, His everlasting, sinless life was poured out as a drink offering to God Most High. Just as David, though he was aflame with thirst, kept back nothing for himself, so Jesus poured out His soul unto death.

Which brings us to *the divine intention of Christ's sufferings.* "He was numbered with the transgressors; and he bare the sin of many" (Isa. 53:12b). Think what that means!

In the Holy of Holies in the temple in ancient times, there resided the sacred ark of the covenant. The ark was made of incorruptible wood overlaid with pure gold. Among other things it contained an unbroken copy of the Mosaic Law. Moses had gone to the mountain to receive God's commandments. They were handed to him on stone engraved there by the finger of God Himself. Moses, however, had been gone from the camp of Israel for a very long time, or so it seemed to the Hebrews. They began to murmur and complain among themselves. Finally, rebellion broke out, and the people relapsed into idolatry, dancing and carousing around a golden calf they had made. Moses, coming back bearing his precious burden, heard the raucous noise and saw what the people were doing. He deliberately smashed to pieces the stone tablet of the law. It was a premeditated act, not an act of passion. The people below had broken the law and were exposed to God's wrath. Moses knew that they could not gaze at that unbroken law and live. It condemned them through and through, so he smashed it, broke it to pieces before their eyes, and took his stand as intercessor between them and God.

At a later date God gave Moses a fresh tablet of stone, likewise engraved with God's holy law, and told him to deposit it in the sacred ark. Moses did as he was told. He hid that unbroken copy of the law in the ark of God. The ark itself was a type of Christ—the acacia wood spoke of Christ's sinless humanity, the gold of His essential deity with God's unbroken law hidden in His heart.

Jesus kept every jot and tittle of the law from the moment He first drew breath until He bowed His head and died. His testimony rang clear. "I do always those things that please him" (John 8:29).

But the Sanhedrin, Caiaphas and his crowd, numbered Him with the transgressors. The word Isaiah used for "transgressors" speaks of revolt, rebellion, and sin against lawful authority. His delight was in the law of God, and in that law He meditated day and night (Ps. 1:2). Yet, He was numbered with the transgressors. Two thieves were crucified at His side. Pilate had His title nailed to His cross in three languages. His crime—simply that He was the King of the Jews, transgression enough for a Roman procurator enforcing Roman law. The very cross on which He hung was made for a true transgressor, Barabbas by name, a robber, murderer, and insurrectionist who had transgressed lawful authority. Such was the indignity Jesus suffered.

Think, too, of the iniquity He bore. "And he bare the sin of many" (Isa. 53:12b). The word for "sin" here is *chata*, which means "to miss the mark." It reminds us how short we all come of God's requirements.

I remember, when I was a boy in Britain, that to be a policeman or to be a member of one of the guards' regiments an applicant had to be at least six feet tall—far taller than most people in those days. A certain man who wanted to join the guards failed the entrance test. He was of good health and strong. He was intelligent and eager and educated. He had zeal and a will to obey orders. The problem was that he was five feet eleven and a half inches tall. Because of this he was rejected. He was short of the stature required. All his pleas and promises did not help. All his good points were swallowed up in that one negative fact—he came up short.

In all the history of this planet, only one person has ever come up to the standard. His name was Jesus. "I find in him no fault at all" was Pilate's verdict (John 18:38). Yet, Pilate crucified Him just the same. Little did that proud Roman know it but he, himself, had sadly come short and missed the mark. It never occurred to him, but on the cross Jesus was bearing "the sin of many" (Isa. 52:12b). One of the "many" was Pilate himself.

Finally, we have *the daily intercession of Christ's sufferings*. "And made intercession for the transgressors" (v. 12b).

Let us pause for a moment at a hill overlooking a green and well-watered plain. Down there in that lush vale, five cities can be seen. Those cities are wicked beyond words. Indeed, one of them has lent its name to a reprehensible vice to this day. God has just revealed to Abraham that He intends to overthrow those cities once and for all.

Immediately, Abraham becomes an intercessor. It is not Sodom and its neighboring vice capitals he cares for. It is his nephew Lot, whose home is in Sodom. Lot is a believer despite his backslidden condition. It is for him that Abraham prays. The record of Abraham's intercession is given in Genesis 18:23–33. Abraham becomes a prayer warrior. He makes intercession for the transgressor, besieging the throne of God like a man in the market haggling for a better deal.

God hears his servant and, as Abraham moves from one vantage point to the next, God goes along with his pleas, gives way before him. Abraham wins. For though God carries out His righteous determination to make a summary example of those cities, He spares Lot and those members of Abraham's family who could be persuaded to flee. Lot is saved "so as by fire," to use Paul's apt expression (1 Cor. 3:15). Indeed, all of Sodom might have been saved had there been, in that city, a prophet like Jonah whose awesome voice brought about the repentance of Nineveh years later. So, then, Abraham prayed.

Now, let us pause upon a hill far away that looks out upon this world of ours from the vantage point of God's Great White Throne. God looks out from a place "high and lifted up" (Isa. 6:1) with a commanding view before Him of all time and space. He sees there, amid the galaxies, the world that slew His Son and that, far from being repentant, goes on and on in its sins. For such a world God has a holocaust in store.

But for the moment His hand is stayed. Before Him stands One who has nail prints in His hands, One aptly called His "fellow" (Zech. 13:7), His Friend, His Equal, His Son, both God and Man.

What is this? Amazing grace! This One raises His pierced hands and makes "intercession for the transgressors" (Isa. 53:12b). "Not yet! Not yet!" He cries. "Holy Father I have a church down there on Planet Earth. I have loved ones down there. You cannot destroy the righteous with the wicked! You must let Me go and get them first. So, spare the wicked yet awhile for the sake of the righteous."

And that is what He is doing right now. This is Isaiah's last glimpse of Him in this heart-moving prophecy. There He is, making intercession for the transgressors. He has interposed Himself between God and humanity. He is holding back the floodtide of God's wrath. The Holy Spirit is fervently at work issuing the midnight cry. Jesus, our Advocate with the Father, is still at it to this very hour as time rapidly runs out. He is holding back the brimstone and the fire. Those arms, once outstretched upon the tree, are still outstretched to save. What more can He do? What more can be said?

PART 5

PORTRAYAL

On Calvary's brow my Savior died,
'Twas there my Lord was crucified:
'Twas on the cross He bled for me,
And purchased there my pardon free.

'Mid rending rocks and darkening skies,
My Savior bows His head and dies;
The opening veil reveals the way
To heaven's joys and endless day.

O Jesus Lord how can it be
That thou should'st give Thy life for me,
To bear the cross and agony,
In that dread hour on Calvary!

O Calvary! dark Calvary!
Where Jesus shed His blood for me,
O Calvary! blest Calvary
'Twas there my Savior died for me.[1]
    —W. M'K. Darwood (c. 1835–1914)

CHAPTER 17

THE CALVARY MIRACLES

Matthew 27:45–54

1. The sun (v. 45)
2. The sanctuary (v. 51a)
3. The stones (v. 51b)
4. The sepulcher (vv. 52–53)
5. The soldiers (v. 54)

CALVARY—THE MEETING PLACE OF two eternities. From beyond the beginning of time, everything pointed forward to Calvary. On, on, beyond the end of time, all will point back to Calvary. Calvary is the place where human sin confronted the wrath of God—the place, too, where heaven's love and heaven's justice met.

The cross stood out against the skyline like a lightning rod. Beneath its foot was a skull-shaped hill. Above its head were dark clouds laced with lightning, ablaze with menace. The thunder roared. Then the flaming fire of God's righteous wrath stabbed down. The end of the world had come. But no! The cross, a God-made lightning rod, stood astride the path of certain doom. The thunderbolt of wrath was caught and contained by the upraised stake of the cross, by its widespread arms, and by the One who was nailed there as a sacrifice for all sin. That fearful bolt of wrath burst in all its fury in the soul of the Savior

The world was there—Jew, Roman, and Greek. The worlds of culture, conquest, and creed were all represented. Priests and people were there, friends and foes, mourners and mockers—all were there. They huddled around the cross, appalled by the darkness, shaking with fear. They escaped. Jesus took the judgment that was ours. The darkness receded. The storm clouds rolled away. The earthquake ceased to make the hill called Calvary shiver and shake. A new day had dawned for us all.

The cross was nothing more than a gallows and a frightful one at that. The One who was nailed to that gallows was the Son of God. The work that was accomplished was salvation for Adam's ruined race. These are amazing truths, and many find them incredible. "So," they complain, "if Jesus was the Son of God as He said He was, and if He did what Scripture says He did, then surely there would be signs to prove to us that all this was so!" And so there were. Matthew, in his gospel, draws our attention to five mighty miracles, enacted at Calvary, miracles that were marked demonstrations of the deity of Christ.

1. The sun

> Now [says Matthew, a credible eyewitness,] from the sixth hour there was darkness over all the land unto the ninth hour. (Matthew 27:45)

The Lord reached out from that gallows on Golgotha and put out the sun. The darkness covered the last three hours of the Lord's agony on the cross, from high noon, when the sun was at its zenith, until three o'clock in the afternoon.

The sun had leaped from its bed that morning as it had done so many, many times during the period of our Lord's sojourn on this planet. It would watch with greatest interest the footsteps of Jesus. It would tuck itself into its bed each night. It would pull the blanket of darkness over its head. It would say to itself, "What a wonderful day this has been. I saw Him heal a blind man today! I saw Him cleanse a leper today! I saw Him raise a dead man today! I wonder what He will do tomorrow?"

For some thirty-three and a half years, it had watched its mighty maker grow from babyhood, into boyhood, and on to manhood. Every day with Jesus was sweeter than the day before. Then came this day. The sun looked down to see men murdering heaven's Beloved. It turned aside to hide its blushing face in shame. We echo the words of Isaac Watts:

> Well might the sun in darkness hide,
> And shut his glories in,
> When incarnate, our Maker died
> For man, His creature's sin.[2]

It was not until three o'clock that afternoon that the sun could summon up enough resolve to take another look—just in time to see the Savior die.

"Give us a sign from heaven," the skeptics cried. Well, when He was born He put a new star in the sky, and when He died He put out the sun. Signs enough we might well say!

Putting out the sun was, indeed, a mighty miracle. The sun is a vast sphere, 864,000 miles in diameter, containing 335 quadrillion cubic miles of violently hot gases, weighing more than two octillion tons. At its core, oxygen is fused into helium at a temperature of some 25 million degrees Fahrenheit. Jesus simply reached up and snuffed it all out like a candle. Instantly, the whole land was plunged into darkness.

We have no idea how it was done. It was certainly not a natural eclipse. Occasionally the moon, orbiting the earth, blots out the sun's rays causing an eclipse in some parts of the world. Whatever it was that happened at Calvary and all across the country was certainly not an eclipse.

For three long hours people sat in terror at this dreadful midday midnight. They must have thought the end of the world had come. It was a foretaste of that "blackness of darkness for ever" of which the

Bible warns (Jude 13). It covered all the land, every city, town, and village and every river, mountain, and plain. Everywhere scores of places were blanketed with this terrifying darkness—Bethlehem and Jericho, Dan and Beersheba, Nazareth and Cana, no corner of the country escaped. It was like the darkness Abraham once experienced—the "horror of great darkness" (Gen. 15:12). It was like the darkness that fell on all of Egypt except for Goshen where God's people lived, "darkness which may be felt," a "thick darkness" (Exod. 10:21–22).

Then, just before He died, in grace and kindness, Jesus turned the light back on.

2. The sanctuary

> And, behold, the veil of the temple was rent in twain from the top to the bottom. (Matthew 27:51a)

The veil separated the two sanctuaries; it divided the Holy Place from the Most Holy Place. The rending of the veil was a sign of tremendous significance to the Jewish people. It rendered Judaism null and void—a religion based on God-breathed law and sanctified by some fifteen hundred years of continuous history. The veil was rent by no human hand. It was not rent from the bottom to the top but from the top to the bottom.

The way through the veil into the Holy of Holies was jealousy guarded. It separated the Holy Place, where ordinary priests were allowed to venture when their turn came to minister, from the Holy of Holies, where only the high priest could go once a year and only then when protected by a most intricate ritual. But now, the veil between the two sanctuaries was suddenly rent asunder! The veil was as thick as a man's hand. A yoke of oxen could hardly have rent that veil. It was some sixty feet high. It spanned the temple from wall to wall. It had stood there (in tabernacle and temple) for fifteen hundred years. Its sole purpose was to act as a barrier between man and God, for beyond the veil was the sacred ark of the covenant and the mercy seat

where God Himself dwelt. No natural light and no artificial light penetrated into that awesome dwelling place of God. However it was ablaze
with the light of another world. The light of the Shechinah glory cloud
shone there, bathing the gold and the richly colored linen with hues
of glory.

Only a handful of people had ever set foot in there. Neither Moses,
nor Elijah, nor David, nor Solomon himself had ever gone in there.
Not even Jesus had gone in there. Only the properly constituted and
consecrated high priest could enter, and then just once a year, and
even then only after the most rigorous rituals had paved the way. In
some fifteen hundred years of continuous history, probably only a
scant fifty people had ever ventured inside the veil. Its sole purpose
was to keep people out.

But now, suddenly, stunningly, the veil was rent, and the way into
the Holy of Holies gaped open wide. The veil hung there, a torn and
tattered rag. We can picture the officiating priest of the day entering
into the first sanctuary. He would trim the lamps, attend to the table,
and approach the golden altar of incense, that stood by the veil. He
would put the coals in the censer, add incense and blot himself out, so
to speak, in the resulting billowing fragrant clouds. He would look
up. His jaw would drop; his hair would rise; his eyes would stare in
amazement. Horror would seize him. He could see beyond the veil
into the Holy of Holies. He would rush outside, summon some of the
attending priests. They, too, would stare in horror. Perhaps someone
sent for Caiaphas. Would even this callous and worldly soul be stirred
by such a sight?

It is doubtful that even a handful of people understood what it
meant until the apostle explained it some years later in his letter to
the Jewish church (Heb. 10:19–23). What it meant was that God, who
for fifteen hundred years had been saying to people down here: "Don't
you dare come in here! You are sinful and I am holy. Don't you dare
come in here," was now saying, "Come on in! Come as often as you
like. Stay as long as you like. Talk about anything you like and do
hurry back." Thus, the Cross put an end to Judaism.

3. The stones

> And the earth did quake, and the rocks rent. (Matthew 27:51b)

Just a few days before, the Lord had entered Jerusalem in triumph amid the hallelujahs and hosannas of the people thus fulfilling an ancient prophecy (Zech. 9:9). Jerusalem was packed with people from all parts of the world. It was almost Passover. Devout Jews from a score of countries were cheering and shouting as loudly as the Jews who lived there. "Blessed be the King that cometh in the name of the Lord!" (Luke 19:38) they cried.

The nation's leaders, Caiaphas and his crowd, were enraged. They demanded that Jesus tell the cheering multitude to stop this demonstration. "I tell you," Jesus said, "if these should hold their peace, the stones would immediately cry out" (v. 40).

Well, for now they were holding their peace at Calvary. They were strangely silent, cowed by a fear of Hebrew arrest and a swift Roman crucifixion. The only voice raised against the crime of Calvary was the voice of a crucified thief.

Where were they all—the multitudes who had feasted on the bread He had provided, who had been healed from illness and demon possession? Where was Bartimaeus and Jairus and Zacchaeus? Where was Andrew and Nathanael and Thomas? Where was Simon Peter? Perhaps he was in Gethsemane or down some back alley, seeking to cover his shame.

One and all they held their peace. They had nothing to say. So, the stones cried out. The rocks rent with a roar. The solid rock beneath that skull-shaped hill shook for fear of the dreadful deed being enacted there on its brow. The whole hill trembled down to its deepest foundations. Jerusalem felt the tremor as the stones cried out. Caiaphas doubtless fled outside his palace as the earth beneath that "Hill of Evil Counsel" (as the place of his palace has long been named, for it was the supposed site of some of Solomon's idolatrous temples) quaked and shook. Did Caiaphas, that man of evil counsel, flee that place of evil counsel? Did he stop his ears as the stones cried out? He might well have done so.

4. The sepulcher

> And the graves were opened; and many bodies of the saints which slept arose, and came out of the graves after his resurrection, and went into the holy city, and appeared unto many. (Matthew 27:52–53)

These resurrected Old Testament believers were the firstfruits of Christ's resurrection, the "wave sheaf" mandated by the Mosaic Law (Lev. 23:9–14). We do not know for sure what happened to these resurrected saints. The inference is that they ascended on high with Christ (Ps. 68:18; Eph. 4:8–10).

Death does not lightly yield up its prey. Step by remorseless step, it seizes on the bodies of the dead and returns them to the dust. Only three people were raised from the dead in all the Old Testament. Three people were raised by Jesus in the days of His earthly sojourn. In the book of Acts, two more were raised, making eight in all. Two others (Enoch and Elijah) escaped death altogether by means of rapture. Apart from these, until Jesus came to tear death's bars away, death reigned.

Then it happened. Jesus took charge of death, and all across the country graves burst open, and the bodies of many dead saints were exposed for all to see. It happened all over the land, from Dan to Beersheba, in hamlets and villages, in towns and cities. It must have caused curiosity and consternation. It was the talk of the country. As reports came in from all over, it was evident that this was no small matter. We hear Paul say, "For this thing [and many other things like it] was not done in a corner" (Acts 26:26). Everybody knew about it.

People would flock to the graveyards. They would gaze in amazement at the corpses of those recently entombed, at the corruption of those who had been dead for some time, at the dry bones and even drier dust of those who had been dead for centuries. "Who has done this?" would be the question on everyone's lips. "Who could have done this, desecrating tombs here, there, and everywhere?"

For a few short days the open graves were a herald of Christ's triumph. He was about to burst out of another tomb, His own—or rather ours, as His tomb should have been our own. Sure enough, before dawn, with a menacing rumble, the stone rolled back from the door of Christ's grave—not to let Him out; He had no need of that; He could walk through walls of stone—but to herald the fact that He was gone, alive forevermore! And, as at a given signal, all across the land, lo, those exposed bodies and bones came back to full and glorious life. More! As by a word of command, from every graveyard in the land, they came out of their graves and made a beeline for Jerusalem. Matthew could have filled a book with stories of close encounters of a terrifying kind or perhaps of a more blessed kind.

The whole astounding incident was of such common knowledge that Matthew treats it as a mere footnote, not deserving any commentary because everybody knew about it.

5. The soldiers

> Now when the centurion, and they that were with him, watching Jesus, saw the earthquake, and those things that were done, they feared greatly, saying, Truly this was the Son of God. (Matthew 27:54)

Roman soldiers were afraid of nothing. They and their kind had marched into every capitol in that part of the world. These men would lock their great rectangular shields together to make a solid wall of steel and then march boldly toward an overwhelming foe, fearing nothing. Yet, these were the kind of men that Matthew says "feared greatly."

Picture the Roman centurion in charge of the public execution at Calvary that day. Perhaps he was born near Rome or in one of the colonies. When he was a little boy his father would tell him all the great epics of the empire.

Like all other boys he would eagerly look forward to Roman holidays, to the days when he would go to the circus along with everyone else. Perhaps he had his favorite gladiators. Perhaps he eagerly strained to catch his first glimpse of some new attraction, Caesar's pet panther, perhaps, or a new pack of wild dogs. For a Roman circus was not convened to parade tame tigers around the ring or to watch acrobats and clowns perform their tricks. Romans wanted to see people die. They wanted blood to flow.

He grew up and decided to become a soldier. The barrack room would be his home. Hard-bitten veterans of Rome's foreign wars would teach him to drink and gamble, and to swear and fight without fear. He became a centurion, one of those noncommissioned officers who were the backbone of the Roman army.

He was sent to Judea, the most unruly and troublesome of Rome's provinces, and then on to Jerusalem where hatred of Rome was in the very air he breathed. Then came the particular morning when his assignment was to crucify three men. "Two of them are criminals," his commanding officer might have told him. "The other is worse. He claims to be the King of the Jews. I've heard He even claims to be the Son of God. Well, we've scourged Him, and He sure doesn't look like any kind of a god to me. Just show Him, soldier, how we Romans treat kings and gods of the Jews. Take Him to Golgotha and crucify Him." That is just what the centurion would do. He nailed Jesus to a cross of wood and hung Him up to die.

The centurion watched Jesus there, Matthew records. And the more he watched, the more evident it became. "Truly this was the Son of God!" he said (Matt. 27:54). And his words were echoed by his men. He had never seen such a death! Rolling thunder, shaking earth, darkened sky, and from what he could gather from the stories that were afoot, the sacrosanct temple itself incredibly violated right at its most holy heart. He had never seen such a death. Forgiven by the crucified Himself! Never had he seen a man under such torture speak with such love and grace. "This was the Son of God!" Can we doubt that the centurion, having thus confessed Jesus as Lord, will be in heaven now?

So that day, on that cross, the Lord Jesus saved a Jew and some Gentiles, and gave notice to all the universe that Calvary was the site of a great victory—and the precursor of many more victories to come.

I will sing of my Redeemer
And His wondrous love to me;
On the cruel cross He suffered
From the curse to set me free.

I will tell the wondrous story,
How, my lost estate to save,
In His boundless love and mercy
He the ransom freely gave.

I will praise my dear Redeemer,
His triumphant power I'll tell,
How the victory He giveth
O'er sin and death and hell.

I will sing of my Redeemer,
And His heavenly love to me;
He from death to life hath brought me,
Son of God with Him to be.

Sing, O sing of my Redeemer,
With His blood He purchased me;
On the cross He sealed my pardon,
Paid the debt and set me free.[1]
—Philip B. Bliss (1838–1876)

CHAPTER 18

A Ransom for Many

Mark 10:45

1. Giving His life in service
   a. Whence He came
   b. Why He came
2. Giving His life in sacrifice
   a. A supernatural life
   b. A sinless life
   c. A sufficient life

THE GOSPEL OF MARK REVOLVES around a single verse, just as our world revolves around a single star. Here is that verse:

> For even the Son of man came not to be ministered unto, but to minister, and to give his life a ransom for many. (Mark 10:45)

Mark ignores peripheral material and takes us straight to the heart of the matter, straight to the Cross. He shows us the Master, first giving His life in service ("the Son of man came not to be ministered unto, but to minister"), and then giving His life in sacrifice ("and to give his life a ransom for many").

Mark's gospel is singularly uncluttered. Perhaps one reason for this is that he was writing particularly for the Romans. The Romans were essentially people of action. They liked to get things done. Mark has fewer Old Testament quotations than either Matthew or Luke. Moreover, Mark interprets Aramaic words that would mean nothing to the Romans, and he explains Jewish customs with which Roman readers might not be familiar. A convincing argument for the Jew would involve prophecy, for the Greek it would involve philosophy, and for the Roman it would involve power. Even at that, while the Jews would be interested in power as well, they would primarily be interested in spiritual power. Likewise, the Greek would be interested in intellectual power. The Romans, by contrast, would be interested in dynamic power, the kind of power that conquers obstacles, that gets things done—the kind of power that moves men and mountains. The Romans would be convinced by the logic of deeds rather than of intellectual discussions. The Romans built bridges and aqueducts and roads. And because the Romans were doers, Mark shows them Jesus as a doer. There is little discourse in Mark but much movement.

We can see at once, then, that Mark's key verse is in keeping with all the rest. The Romans had enslaved much of the world. It would interest them to read of One who wielded absolute power but who, at the same time, was willing to take "upon him the form of a servant" (Phil. 2:7), literally the form of a slave.

1. Giving His life in service

When we stop to think about it, from our limited human point of view, it is extraordinary that Christ should be introduced as a *servant*. Introduced as a king, as God, as man—we can see Him in all those roles easily enough. But a servant, a slave—surely not!

"The Son of man came" (Mark 10:45). The readers would want to know *whence He came.* They also would want to know just who this "Son of man" was! The Lord Jesus generally used the title "Son of man" to describe Himself. The expression occurs some eighty-eight times in the New Testament, all but four of them being in the Gospels. The first occurrence is in Matthew 8:20 where we are told that the Son of Man "hath not where to lay his head." The last time is in the Apocalypse where our attention is directed to the golden crown upon His head (Rev. 14:14). The title occurs fourteen times in Mark.

He is come! Out of the ivory palaces He came—into a world of woe. He came because it was the Father's will that He should come, and He came because He chose to come. It had all been settled in a past eternity, before the foundation of the world, that He would come.

"The Son of man has come!" Jesus said so Himself. All creation, groaning because of the curse, heaved a sigh of relief. "The Son of man has come!" So might the stable have said to the star. So might the thistle have said to the thorn. So said the frightened Devil to his demon hosts. "We must kill Him in His cradle. In spite of all our efforts to corrupt the messianic line and to kill the seed before it could take flesh and come, nevertheless, the Son of Man is come!" The news shook Satan to the depths of his being. Ever since he learned that the One he should fear was the seed of the woman, he set out to corrupt that line and to prevent that One being born—beginning with the seed of the woman, then the seed of Abraham, the seed of Isaac, Jacob, Judah. The more focused the march of events became, the more relentless became Satan's attempts to search out and destroy the seed bearer. His great goal? To corrupt beyond recall the dreaded seed, to terminate once and for all the promise of the coming One—through David, Solomon, Rehoboam, Manasseh—all in the promised line. Instruments Satan had in abundance; Athaliah massacred all the royal seed except for one little boy she overlooked. Manasseh, the son of one of Judah's godliest kings, plunged Judah into religious apostasy, moral depravity, and almost total debauchery and decadence. The kingdom never recovered from his excesses.

But hundreds of years still lay ahead. So, down through silent centuries of widespread persecution of the Jews, somewhere, hidden from Satan generation after generation, the promised seed was kept alive. At last, came the sudden realization. "The Son of man is come!" So ended four thousand years of ceaseless war against the seed. Jesus was born! Satan had failed.

"The Son of man is come!" The shining ones from the high halls of heaven crowded around the cradle to see the wonder for themselves. They heralded the news from the surrounding hills. "He is come! At last, He has come!"

The coming of the Son of Man changed the balance of power on earth and on high. For many long centuries, Satan had wielded the weapons of his power virtually unrestricted and unrestrained. The fall of Adam meant that the human spirit was no longer indwelt by the Holy Spirit. Everything went wrong and from bad to worse. All creation was blighted. Plants became wild, some even became poisonous. Many animals became ferociously wild and savage. Harmful bacteria invaded living things. In the unseen spirit world, Satan's fallen angels took this world into bondage and darkness. They ruled over human affairs. They were the principalities and powers, the rulers of this world, along with countless hordes of wicked spirits in high places who held the world in thrall.

But now that "the Son of man is come," Satan has met his match and more than his match. Things will never be the same again. Satan is allowed a little space, a little time, a little power. He is still as malevolent as ever he was, still able to do damage and cause harm, but he is put under restraint. "The Son of man is come." Satan well knows what that means. God is working to a plan. The focus is now on our planet and on God's invincible purposes all centered in Christ. For the Son of Man has not only come but He is coming again. His coming again is what haunts the counsels of the gates of hell.

We not only want to know whence He came but also *why He came*. He came "not to be ministered unto, but to minister" (Mark 10:45). He came to live an absolutely obedient life. Jesus came to set before us an example of *unselfish living*. He did not come to be served. One of the best evidences of that took place in the Upper Room the night He was betrayed. The custom was that the feet of all the guests were to be washed and dried. It was work for a slave. But there was no slave there that night. Who would wash the disciples' feet? Not Peter, that was for sure! He aspired to greater things than that. Certainly not Judas! No money was to be made out of that. Not James or John; "Sons of Thunder" do not stoop to wash feet. So, the feet went unwashed—until later.

Later, Jesus took a towel and showed them what it was all about. It was about the Master taking the place of a slave. It was about coming, "not to be ministered unto, but to minister."

It is significant that Mark wrote the gospel of the servant for that was just where Mark himself so signally failed. At Antioch, the church decided to send its two best men to the mission field. Barnabas and Paul had labored greatly to build up that church. Perhaps it came as no surprise to the elders when these fearless, faithful men announced to them that they had been called by God to take the gospel to the regions beyond. After due spiritual exercise, the Antioch church gave these two men their blessing and laid their hands upon them in token of their full fellowship in this enterprise. The missionaries packed their bags and prepared to leave.

As a footnote to all this, we read, "And they had also John (Mark) to their minister (their servant)" (Acts 13:5). Evidently, Mark had volunteered to go along as their errand boy. He would take care of the chores, buy supplies, make the meals, pitch the tents, run the errands. A splendid idea! It would free up Paul and Barnabas to get on with the spiritual side of things. Barnabas was particularly pleased. Mark appears to have been his nephew. However, there was none of the spiritual exercise about the sending of Mark as there had been for the other two. He just seems to have tagged along.

Years ago, when I had some thought of going to a certain mission field, a veteran missionary, long a resident in that particular country, gave me some advice. "There are two kinds of missionaries," he said, "the *sent* ones and the *went* ones. Don't come out here until you are sure you are one of the *sent* ones." It was sound advice. Soon afterward conditions changed, and it became virtually impossible to obtain a visa to do missionary work in that country. John Mark was one of the *"went"* ones.

All went well initially. They went to Cyprus first, and exciting things happened. Barnabas had roots on the island. But, by the time the team crossed over to the mainland, it became increasingly clear to Mark

that some drastic changes were underway. Paul was now in charge
and Uncle Barnabas was obviously playing second fiddle. Worse still,
Paul was proposing a dangerous venture—to head up through the
Cilician Gates and the Taurus mountains into Galatia. Mark was
alarmed. People simply did not go to that part of the world without
an armed escort. The whole area was infested with brigands. Mark
made up his mind. He was going home to his mom.

This sad incident resulted in a great rift between Paul and Barnabas
later on. Barnabas was all for giving Mark a second chance on the
next missionary venture. Paul was adamant. On no account would he
take such a quitter with him. As a result, Barnabas took Mark back to
Cyprus, and Paul recruited a replacement for Mark.

Many years later, however, when Paul was in prison in Rome, he
wrote to Timothy urging him to come and to come soon, before winter, before his approaching martyrdom—to come and bring Mark
with him. Something must have happened! Paul gave Timothy a reason for bringing Mark with him to Rome. "He is profitable to me for
the ministry," he said (2 Tim. 4:11). Mark had become a faithful stew-
ard of the faith after all!

What was it that so moved Paul to change his mind about Mark?
Perhaps someone had given Paul a copy of Mark's gospel, a gospel written with a special burden for the Romans. Some are convinced that
Mark was the first to write down the gospel story. If so, Paul would be
all the more impressed at the enormous service Mark had rendered to
the church and the world in writing his book. Moreover, Paul was smart
enough to recognize Peter's hand on Mark as he wrote and penetrating
enough to recognize the servant character of Mark's gospel. One can
easily picture Paul, having read Mark's manuscript, putting it down
with a sigh. "Well!" he might have said, "Well done, Barnabas! You were
right after all! I never suspected the boy had it in him!"

So, Mark had failed as a minister, but he had succeeded in the ministry beyond all of Paul's expectations. And he had the genius and the
insight to present the Master as the Minister, as the One who came
"not to be ministered unto, but to minister, and to give his life a ransom for many" (Mark 10:45).

Jesus came to serve—to serve His Father in heaven, to serve His people on earth, and to labor unceasingly for the lost people of this world. Had He wanted to live for Himself, He could have stayed where He was, in a land of unfading day, where time is not counted by years and where ten thousand times ten thousand ministering spirits hang upon His words and rush to do His bidding.

But the Lord Jesus came into this world not only to exhibit *unselfish living* but also to demonstrate *unstinted giving*. He came "to minister," to serve, to give Himself wholly, to give of Himself for others at all times, in all places, under all circumstances. It is the view of some that Peter's speech in the house of the Roman centurion Cornelius summed up his preaching. It has been called the *kerugma*—that which is proclaimed by a herald. Mark's gospel followed what we have in Acts 10:34–43. Both begin with John's baptism, tell of the Lord's ministry in Galilee, Judea, and Jerusalem, recount His crucifixion and resurrection, and conclude with a call to personal witness, with the promise of the coming again of the Lord in judgment, and with an offer of forgiveness for those who, here and now, put their faith in Him.

How does Peter sum up the life of Jesus? The same way Mark does. Jesus "went about doing good" (Acts 10:38). And so He did. Mark wastes no time. He tells us about it at once. The key words in his gospel are "immediately" and "straightway." The Greek equivalents are used by Mark twenty-six times. The Lord never allowed Himself to be hurried but, just the same, He wasted no time. Mark emphasizes the swift and effective activities of Christ and the way He gave Himself to people unstintingly.

2. Giving His life in sacrifice

"The Son of man came . . . to give his life a ransom for many" (Mark 10:45). A ransom!

One of the most colorful periods in English history centers on the magnificent person of that great Plantagenet king known as Richard the Lionhearted. He was every inch a king—magnificent in person, invincible in war. He led the Third Crusade and his feats of martial skill became legend everywhere. His exploits won him even the grudging admiration of the Saracens. But his confederates in Europe were jealous and afraid of him. On his way back to Europe, he was seized by Leopold, Duke of Austria, who turned his royal captive over to the emperor, Henry VI, of Germany. Great Richard was flung into prison and held for ransom.

The ransom set was enormous—150,000 marks. It might, indeed, be called a king's ransom. Raising the sum taxed England to the very core. A heavy levy was placed on knights and landowners, and huge demands were made on the church. Even the monasteries, usually exempt from taxation, were forced to contribute.

A king's ransom! A sum of money that would tax a prosperous kingdom into bankruptcy! That was what was paid for Richard.

But that was nothing compared to the ransom Jesus paid for us.

First, the life He gave was *a supernatural life*. Our thoughts go back to the day when the Lord of glory stooped down to fashion Adam's clay.

He worked from the beginning with very big numbers and with very small parts. He required millions upon millions of cells, each one small enough to crowd into the circumference of the letter *o* in a line of type and each cell an engineering miracle.

Some of the parts would go to make more than one hundred thousand miles of blood vessels to be stretched over the body in a fantastically complex network of arteries and veins. And so it went on—a heart able to pump one hundred thousand times a day, moving at high speed enough blood to fill a swimming pool; a liver able to salvage various component parts of 10 million red blood cells a second; glands for the stomach, more than 35 million of them. And on and on—eyes and ears, kidneys and intestines, arms and legs, and of course, a brain and nerves. When it was complete, it was a complex mix of blood and mud—a magnificent body. But more was needed, for that magnificent human body was, after all, simply a corpse, a lifeless corpse unable to see or smell or hear or feel or taste. It needed life. So, God breathed into that still form the breath of life, and behold, that corpse became a man, a man endowed with natural life!

But what about the One who made him? Life began with Him, with God (John 1:4; 11:25; 14:6). God's life is not just natural life or human life but divine life, supernatural life. That very One who bestowed life on Adam came into this world to give *His* life as a ransom for many. How vast the ransom was.

Moreover, the life that He gave was *a sinless life.* It had to be. God sought to teach this truth to His ancient people Israel throughout the whole of the Old Testament. Every clean animal brought to the altar had to be inspected to make sure it was without spot and without blemish. The Gospels join their united testimony in bearing witness to the sinless life of Christ. He was sinless as a babe, as a boy, as a teen, and as a man, in the home, on the playground, in the classroom, in the synagogue, at the workbench, on the highway, in the marketplace—sinless!

He could challenge His enemies to find sin in Him (John 8:46). Three times over, in the space of perhaps half an hour, Pilate declared Him to be sinless. "I find no fault in this man," he said (Luke 23:4). The dying malefactor, crucified with his companion in crime along with Jesus, immediately detected the difference between his fellow criminal and the sinless Christ.

So, then, the life that Jesus laid down at Calvary was a sinless life. He gave Himself, the just, for the unjust, to bring us to God (1 Peter 3:18). He was made sin for us, He who knew no sin (2 Cor. 5:21). He could say that Satan had nothing in Him (John 14:30). The life He gave was a sinless life. It had to be. That is why the Bible says that no one can "redeem his brother" (Ps. 49:7). We are sinners, and any attempt we might make to exchange our life for our brother's life would be worthless. It would just be exchanging one sinful life for another.

Finally it was *a sufficient life*—a life for a life (Deut. 19:21). This was the rule under the Mosaic Law. The life that Jesus gave for our sins was an infinite life. Suppose it were possible for us actually to count all the people who have ever lived. Once we arrived at the final total, we would have a very large number indeed, but it would still be a finite number, a number with quite definite boundaries. There would be the first person (one whose name we know, Adam), and there would be a final person, the very last person whose name we do not yet know. We would have a number, an enormous number, but one that we could express mathematically.

The life that Jesus gave for us was an infinite life, a life without beginning or end, a life that was from everlasting to everlasting. A finite life cannot be given as a ransom for many. An infinite life can—and has been. Mark reminds us, "The Son of man came not to be ministered unto, but to minister, and to give his life a ransom for many" (Mark 10:45). Blessed be His Name!

Thou Son of God, eternal Word
Who heaven and earth's foundations laid,
Upholding by Thy word and power
The universe Thy hands have made.

As Lamb of God, Thy path we view,
Thy Father's will, Thy whole delight;
To Calvary we trace Thy way,
Each step of Thine with glory bright;

For us Thine untold sufferings there,
For us the darkness and the woe,
In love transcending all compare,
Thou Lord for us to death didst go;

Exalted to the Father's throne,
With glory and with honor crowned,
All at Thy glorious name shall bow
As Lord of all by each be owned.

We worship Thee, all glorious Lord
Forever be Thy name adored!
We worship Thee all glorious Lord,
Forever be Thy name adored.[1]

     —Inglis Fleming (1859–1955)

CHAPTER 19

THERE THEY CRUCIFIED HIM

Luke 23:33

1. The place
2. The people
3. The price
4. The person

THAT IS THE WAY LUKE PORTRAYS IT. It takes him just four words. He, says it all in short, stabbing syllables with never a word to waste. He hurries us to the hill and then describes the deed. "There they crucified him" (Luke 23:33). The brevity, the extraordinary economy of words leaves out a thousand details but says it all. All the Evangelists do much the same. They do not dwell on all the dreadful particulars of death by crucifixion. Luke leaves that to other historians. The whole appalling business was only too familiar to people living under the rule of Rome. They are all well known to us from our history books.

We arrive at that shameful, skull-faced hill. We wipe the perspiration from our brow. There all around us is the city wall, but we, for now, are "outside the camp," outside that wall. We listen for the blow of hammers, but it is all over. The cruel deed has already been done. They have taken the mighty Maker of the galaxies and nailed Him to a cross of wood. Already His cross has sunk into its socket. Already the weight of His body is tearing against the wounds in His feet and hands. Already they have hung Him there between earth and heaven. Soon they will sit themselves down to watch Him die.

Now, with hands dyed red from that precious blood of His, they have seized one of the thieves. His fearful agony is heralded in screams that defy description. Already his body is twisting in torment, and his anguished bellows have brought the rabble on the run. But of the nailing of our Maker to that accursed cross, of the actual deed itself, of the details of that sin of sins, that crowning act of wickedness— well, over that, God draws the veil. As Shem and Japheth, cloak in hand with averted eyes, walked backward into the presence of Noah, lying in a drunken stupor there, and covered thus his shame, just so God draws the cloak of silence over the actual deed of guilt of Adam's race. Indeed, no speech, no language is eloquent enough or has words enough to describe that deed as seen by the eye of God. The *Unabridged Oxford Dictionary of the English Language* runs to twenty large volumes. Yet all those words, thousands upon thousands of words, are not adequate to describe the nailing of our Lord to the tree. As for Luke, a man who talked to everybody about it, who doubtless took the most copious notes and who had seen many a poor wretch crucified—Luke says all he needs to say in less than half a dozen words.

1. The place

> When they were come to the place, which is called Calvary, *there* they crucified him. (Luke 23:33, italics added)

This is the only place in the King James Version where the word *Calvary* occurs. The word is made familiar to us by a hundred hymns. It has assumed a music of its own. Our familiarity with it is such that we feel it must be one of the more common words of Scripture. Not so. Once only did the King James translators employ it.

We know where the word comes from. "Calvary" is simply the Latin form of the Hebrew word *Golgotha*. Stripped of the poetry of the hymnbook and divorced from so many familiar hymns and melodies, the word stands naked enough. Calvary—the place of a skull. There's no glamour in that.

The name "Golgotha" is derived from the Hebrew word *gulgoleth*. One tradition has it that when David returned from the battle with Goliath he carried the gory head of the giant to Jerusalem and buried it there, at the place of the skull. Another ancient tradition is that Adam's skull was buried at this same place. Others think the name was derived from the skull-shaped hill itself. Whatever the truth of all that, there they crucified Jesus.

We step back another thousand years from David to Abraham. The time of his great testing had come. God called on Abraham to give up his son, his only son Isaac in whom was all his delight. Abraham did as he was told. He cut the wood for the altar. He summoned his servants. He sharpened his knife, saddled his ass, and snatched a flaming firebrand from the fire. He called his son, and off they went to find the place.

The thought of that ominous place must have haunted him at night and dogged his footsteps by day. At last, he saw the dread place on the far horizon. Step by weary step he plodded on, accompanied by his beloved son. They arrived at the place together.

But we must go back farther to Creation's morn. Galaxies, countless in their multitude, have exploded into being. Time has begun. The voice of the Son of God rings out, and the ten commandments of Genesis 1 bring light, life, and loveliness into the darkness, death, and disorder of our planet in space. Vast continents arise and throw off, as a mantel, the sea. God piles up against the cold skies the vast ramparts of the Himalayas. He piles high the hills of Judah.

Now, He pauses in His work. "My Father," He says. "Here am I, My Son," the Father responds. "Behold, My Father, behold the place." There it was, the place where the sin question would be settled forever, the place where heaven's love and heaven's justice would meet at last. It wasn't much of a place, as places go, but it was ordained by God as the place where heaven's Beloved would die for lost sinners of Adam's ruined race.

We can be sure that place, thereafter, was never out of His mind. The time came when not so very far from that place He was born. The cradle and the cross were near neighbors after all.

When Jesus was a boy of twelve, He came to Jerusalem for the Feast of the Passover with His mother and Joseph. We can be sure that He went and had a look at the place. Its shadow had rested on His soul from the counsel chambers of eternity. We can be sure that there was no place other than the temple in the Holy City that Jesus frequented as much. As for the temple, it was enthroned on Mount Moriah, the hill that had so tormented Abraham many years ago.

Now, battered and bruised and scourged and crowned with thorns, Jesus had come at last to the place. Trudging behind Him, dragging His cross for Him, was a man named Simon—Simon the Cyrenian. Where was that other Simon? we might well ask. Simon, son of Jonas, who had so loudly proclaimed his willingness to die for Him? Well, the Lord had this other Simon to help Him on His way to the place. Alongside, forcing the pace, tramped a line of Roman legionnaires, one hefting a hammer in his hand, an important part of the terrible business of the day. All about Him were the crowds, some sobbing, some sneering, some silent and subdued. So, at last, Jesus arrived at *the place.*

It had been a long journey—from glory to Galilee, from Galilee to Gethsemane, from Gethsemane to Gabbatha, from Gabbatha to Golgotha. Had we keener ears, we might well have heard His voice raised to speak to His Father. "Lo, I come (in the volume of the book it is written of me,) to do thy will, O God."

2. The people

Who, indeed, were those men and women of Adam's fallen race who crowded around that cross? Who, we might well ask, were those godless individuals who so successfully plotted His death? Who was it who dared to crucify *Him*?

In the first place the Roman was there—"the centurion, and they that were with him" (Matt. 27:54). The Roman was there with his law and his legions and his long arm stretched out across the world of his day.

The Greek was there. The title on the cross was written in Greek, as well as in Latin and Hebrew. The Greek was there with his culture and his creativity, his learning and his language—with his genius for saying clever things and creating beautiful things and believing the most incredible things as truth.

The Jew was there, rabbi and rabble alike. The Jew was there with his proud boast of being Abraham's seed and the heir of Moses and the prophets. The Jew with his Bible and his budding Talmud, with his Passover lamb ready for the coming feast.

Indeed, the world was there—the Roman representing the world of government, the Greek representing the world of culture, and the Jew representing the world of religion. At this time of the year, Jerusalem would have been host to a million Jews from all parts of the civilized world. A month or so later, Peter was able to append a list of some of the countries of the world represented in Jerusalem at that time. There were Parthians, Medes, and Elamites, and dwellers from Mesopotamia, Judea, Cappadocia, Pontus, Asia, Phyrgia, Pamphylia, Egypt, parts of Libya about Cyrene—and strangers from Rome, Jews and proselytes, Cretes and Arabians (Acts 2:6–11). The world was there.

We were there. Our representatives were there in the persons of those who took our place and acted our part and cast our vote and spoke for us and endorsed on our behalf, as well as their own, the dark and dreadful deed.

A farmer once bought a parcel of land despite the warnings of his friends who told him the ground was worthless. They said it would only produce scrub and sagebrush. The farmer fenced off a few acres. He plowed the ground and planted it. He fertilized it and cultivated it. At harvesttime it yielded only scrub and sagebrush. What need was there for him to plow and plant the rest?

Out of all the ages of time, God fenced off a period of thirty-three years. During this period He sent forth His Son, born of a woman, born under the law (Gal. 4:4–5). For the best part of a generation, that glorious Son of His trod the highways and byways of the Promised

Land. He went about doing good. He loved everyone. He performed countless miracles of which a bare three dozen are recorded in the Gospels. Others said, "Never man spake like this man" (John 7:46).

What was the world's response? "They crucified him," says Luke. There is no need to repeat that experience. That chosen people in that chosen period and in that chosen place acted representatively for us all. The human race stands forever exposed and condemned by its guilty representatives.

3. The price

"There they *crucified him*" (Luke 23:33, italics added). It was this fact that made Saul of Tarsus stumble in his unconverted days and held him in unbelief for years. That Christ should die was not the stumbling block. But that He should die on a *cross*! That was impossible! Saul knew his Bible. He knew how explicit the Law of Moses was. Anyone who died on a tree was accursed of God (Deut. 21:23).

Crucifixion was also a cruel way to die. Death by hanging is frightening enough. The Romans were not content with that. Death had to be filled with greater terror and torment than that, surely. Not content with using actual trees, they manufactured them. All it took was a wooden upright post and a crosspiece with arms outstretched. Then they nailed the screaming victim to that accursed cross and hung him up to die. Every form of agony assailed the sufferer. Open wounds, exposure to the weather, cramp, thirst, starvation, fever, flies, tetanus. Each torment increased the agony. Then was added the presence of the mob, the insults, the mockery, the shame. "They crucified him," Luke says. As a medical man he would know better than most just what that word "crucified" meant.

The children's hymn says it well enough:

> For such a cruel death He died
> He was cast out and crucified;
> Those loving hands which did such good,
> They nailed them to a cross of wood.

4. The person

"There they crucified *him*" (Luke 23:33, italics added). The One who was the center of attraction in the high halls of heaven and whose praise was sounded across the everlasting hills was crucified! The altogether lovely One, chiefest among ten thousand (Song 5:16). To think that people on our planet actually condemned Him to death and then carried out the sentence by way of crucifixion! Nobody could have invented such a story. It happened—and that is that. Reliable eyewitnesses have recorded the event.

"All things," says John, "were made *by him*" (John 1:3, italics added). He it was who hurled the stars into space—stars of all shapes and sizes, energized by almost deathless fires, traveling at inconceivable velocities, on prodigious orbits, throughout intangible space, with such mathematical precision that we can date an eclipse or the visit of a comet to the day and hour. Vast galaxies rush to do His will. They crucified *Him*.

"To *him* give all the prophets witness," the Holy Spirit declares (Acts 10:43, italics added). Each one in turn, Moses and Malachi, David and Daniel, Job and Jeremiah, Ezra and Ezekiel, by type and by shadow, by vision, voice, and visitation, in mystic utterance and direct statement, in sermon and in song—one and all they bore witness to a sovereign Messiah and a suffering Messiah. He was to come to suffer, bleed, and die. He was to come again to rule and reign over all the nations. He came, heralded by the combined testimony of prophets, great and small. As for men, they crucified *Him*.

"Let all the angels of God worship *him*," said Moses in his memoirs (Heb. 1:6, italics added; Deut. 32:43, quoting God from the Septuagint). And so they do! Their voices ring out in wonder, love, and praise. They proclaim His awesome holiness. "Holy, Holy, Holy," so sing the sinless seraphim that stand before His throne. Thrice holy! Holy Father! Holy Spirit! Holy Son! (Isa. 6:2–3). In like manner the chanting cherubim worship Him, proclaiming His holiness there beside the tideless sea, before the Great White Throne, casting down their golden crowns in deep humility. Thus, too, the countless angel throngs, when He stepped off the throne on high to descend to our small world in space—they, too, came hurrying down. They would be the first to worship Him. They crowded around that cradle in that crude cave that served as a birth room for heaven's Beloved. They swarmed across the silent hills of Judah and then burst into song. "Glory to God in the highest, and on earth peace, good will toward men" (Luke 2:14). Yes, yes indeed, the angels of God worshiped Him, but as for humankind, when He was fully grown, they crucified Him whose praise filled the universe.

"In *him*," says Paul, "dwelleth all the fulness of the Godhead bodily" (Col. 2:9, italics added). When Solomon dedicated the temple in Jerusalem, he expressed a great truth that had dawned upon him. The lavish use of gold and cedar and costly linen made the temple an unsung wonder of the world. It was worth the ransom of countless kings. It had taken seven years to build. Solomon had raised a tribute of men from the various tribes of Israel and put them to work on the temple—thirty thousand of them! But even as he was praying and dedicating it, and as he was sacrificing thousands upon thousands of oxen and sheep, the thought gripped him. He incorporated it into his prayer. "Behold," he cried, "heaven and the heaven of heavens cannot contain thee; how much less this house which I have built!" (2 Chron. 6:18). The far-flung starry heavens and the even more vast heaven of heavens, where God Himself had His abode, were far too small to hold an infinite God! Yet in Him, in the incarnate Son of the living God, dwelt all the fullness of the Godhead bodily.

We look at that tiny bundle of humanity, wrapped in swaddling clothes and lying in a manger. There dwells all the fullness of the Godhead bodily. We see a little boy playing with the shavings in Joseph's workshop in Nazareth or standing by the washtub alongside Mary helping with the washing. There dwells all the fullness of the Godhead bodily. We look again and, lo, we see Him, bigger now, coming home from school, singing a psalm perhaps, or with an arm thrown around the shoulders of a smaller boy, or disarming one way or another the school bully. There dwells all the fullness of the Godhead bodily. We see Him, a man grown now, pouring with perspiration, working at the carpenter's bench, His muscles hardened by labor and toil. There dwells all the fullness of the Godhead bodily.

He grew up. He moved out among people. A word from Him and storms were stilled. At His touch leprosy fled. At His will fish flung themselves gladly into Simon Peter's net. Loaves and fishes multiplied in His hands. Water turned into wine when He willed it. Everywhere there is the proof—in *Him* dwells all the fullness of the Godhead bodily. Amazing mystery, wickedness beyond all wickedness—they crucified *Him*.

"I saw the Spirit," said John the Baptist (and he is the only one who says any such thing), "descending from heaven like a dove, and it abode upon *him*" (John 1:32, italics added). That mighty eternal Spirit of God who had brooded over the darkness that gripped the globe prior to Creation, that Spirit of the living God came and abode upon Him. Brooding, century after century, over the deep darkness that reigns in human hearts, never finding one wherein He could abide, the Spirit at last found Himself a home down here on Him. John saw it happen. He told his disciples about it. They have told the world. As for men, they crucified *Him*.

"This is my beloved Son . . . ," God said. "Hear ye *him*" (Matt. 17:5, italics added)—not Confucius, Buddha, or Muhammad, not Mary, the pope, or one of the giants of the church—not them but Him. Those who paid heed marveled at the gracious words that came out of His mouth. Indeed, He spoke with authority and not as the scribes. Even His enemies were forced to confess, "Never man spake like this man" (John 7:46). When He hushed the raging storm with one authoritative command—"Be still!"—His disciples declared, "Even the wind and the sea obey him" (Mark 4:41). As for men, they crucified *Him*.

"There they crucified him" (Luke 23:33). Just four short words. It would be incredible except for one thing—it happened. But the crucifixion is not the end of the story by any manner of means. There is an epilogue. Says Paul, "God . . . hath raised *him* from the dead" (Col. 2:12, italics added). The terrible tragedy was transformed into a tremendous triumph.

In the year 1815 all England waited for the result of the Battle of Waterloo. The semaphore in France flashed the tidings across the Straights of Dover. "Wellington defeated," the signal read, and the fog came down. England went into mourning. The battle was lost! Then the fog lifted, and the message came through again. "Wellington defeated Napoleon." What had appeared to be a crushing defeat was actually a resounding victory!

As they took Christ down from the tree, as they wrapped His battered remains, as they rolled the stone against the mouth of the tomb, as Pilate's official seal was affixed, as the guard was detailed and as Joseph of Arimathea and Nicodemus and the women crept away, as the shadows lengthened and died in the west, the words "Jesus defeated" could seemingly be written over everything. For three days and three nights, it seemed to be so. The world turned. People went about their affairs. The silent Clay lay stiff and cold in death.

Then it happened. The mists rolled away. The tomb was empty. Jesus was alive! "I am he that liveth, and was dead," He says, "and, behold, I am alive for evermore, Amen; and have the keys of hell and of death" (Rev. 1:18).

Jesus defeated death! Blessed be God, our God!

Behold! Behold the Lamb of God,
On the cross! On the cross!
For us He shed His precious blood
On the cross! On the cross!
Oh hear His all-important cry,
"Eli, lamma sabachthani?"
Draw near and see the Savior die,
On the cross! On the cross!

Behold! His arms extended wide,
On the cross! On the cross!
Behold His bleeding hands and side,
On the cross! On the cross!
The sun withholds its rays of light,
The heavens are clothed in shades of night,
While Jesus wins the glorious fight,
On the cross! On the cross!

And now the mighty deed is done,
On the cross! On the cross!
The battle fought, the victory won,
On the cross! On the cross!
To heaven He turns triumphant eyes
"Tis finished" now, the Conqueror cries
Then bows His sacred head and dies,
On the cross! On the cross!¹
                    —Joseph Hoskins (1745–1788)

CHAPTER 20

CRIES FROM THE CROSS

1. Words of tenderness
   a.   A prayer (Luke 23:34)
   b.   A promise (Luke 23:43)
   c.   A provision (John 19:27)
2. Words of travail
   a.   His mental anguish (Matt. 27:46; Mark 15:34)
   b.   His physical agony (John 19:28)
3. Words of triumph
   a.   The past (John 19:30)
   b.   The prospect (Luke 23:46)

LAST WORDS ARE SUPPOSED TO BE heavy with meaning. Preachers of long ago had a great wealth of deathbed stories. D. L. Moody once took on all the atheist clubs in London, challenging the members to come to a meeting exclusively for them. Hundreds came, determined to make a fool of this upstart American preacher. Once he was in the pulpit, Mr. Moody volleyed broadside after broadside at their vulnerable souls—stories from his own experiences at the bedsides of dying men and women, saved and lost, told with compassion and concern and devastating effect. We don't hear such stories of deathbed happiness and horror anymore. It is probably rare today because most people die heavily sedated.

Edward Gibbon, who never wasted an opportunity to attack believers, died crying, "All is lost! Irrevocably lost! All is dark!"

Thomas Paine, who also did all he could to undermine the faith, said as he died, "I would give worlds that *The Age of Reason* had never been published. There is no God! But what if there is? Stay with me for God's sake."

Voltaire, the witty and famous atheist, died in soul agony. "I am abandoned by God and man," he said. The nurse who attended him and witnessed his torment of soul declared that not for all the wealth of Europe would she see another infidel die.

Sir Walter Raleigh, one of Queen Elizabeth's favorites, was greatly disliked by her successor, James I. James ordered the bold explorer beheaded. When Raleigh arrived at the block, the executioner advised him how best to place his head. Said Raleigh, "It matters little how the head lies, my friend, so long as the heart is right."

Queen Elizabeth also had a desperate death. She was terribly afraid to die. She refused to go to bed. Propped up by pillows, fighting death to the end, she sat bolt upright and cried out, "All my possessions for a moment of time."

Augustus Toplady, best known as the author of the hymn "Rock of Ages," exclaimed as he was dying, "Oh, what a delight! Who can fathom the joy of the third heaven. The sky is clear. There is no cloud."

D. L. Moody had a similar victorious death. "This is wonderful," he said. "I can see the children! Earth is receding! Heaven is opening! God is calling me!"

John Huss, the Bohemian martyr, while being burned at the stake, declared, "What I taught with my lips I seal with my blood."

Famous last words! But surely the most famous and significant last words of all were those of Christ spoken at Calvary. Words of tenderness, words of travail, words of triumph—three of them spoken in the broad light of day, four spoken out of the eerie supernatural darkness sent by God to veil Christ's deepest sufferings from the eyes of men.

Jesus spoke with authority and power. It can be said of the words He spoke in death what was said of the words He spoke in life, "Never man spake like this man" (John 7:46). These cries of Christ from the cross were no random utterances of a man dying in agony. They were the sayings of the incarnate Christ of God dying a predetermined death in complete control of all that took place.

1. Words of tenderness

The Lord's first three sayings were all concerned with others. The focus, however, narrowed with each one. The first saying had to do with His foes; the second one had to do with a felon; the third one had to do with His family.

The Lord's first utterance was *a prayer.* "Father, forgive them; for they know not what they do" (Luke 23:34). His final utterance was also addressed to His Father. The word *Father* speaks of *relationship.* He proclaimed this relationship at Calvary in the ears of friends and foes alike. It was because He claimed that God was His Father that the Jewish authorities wanted to kill Him. He was claiming equality with God. Father! It was the first recorded word that fell from His lips when, as a boy of twelve, He said to His mother, "Wist ye not that I must be about my Father's business?" (Luke 2:49). His Father's business was not that of a village carpenter. Joseph was not His Father. No one knew that better than Mary. Instead, it was His Father's business that brought Him all the way to Calvary. There, He spoke out boldly in compassion for those who nailed Him to the tree. "Father," He said, "forgive them; for they know not what they do" (Luke 23:34).

Father! The word speaks of *fellowship.* What a joy it is to a human father when his children grow up and are able to view their father as a friend rather than an authoritarian figure. What joy it was to our heavenly Father to have a Son down here who could say, "I do always those things that please him" (John 8:29). No wonder God could say, "This is my beloved Son, in whom I am well pleased" (Matt. 3:17; 17:5). Between the Son on earth and the Father in heaven, there existed a moment by moment and situation by situation *fellowship* of unbroken communion and love.

Father! The word speaks of *partnership*. The very word *Father* suggests an adult relationship. Sometimes a father will bring his child into his business as a partner. We would expect to see a sign that read, "Willman and Son," perhaps, but we would not expect to see a sign that read, "Willman and Child!" At Calvary, Father and Son were working together in partnership in order to bring redemption to a world of ruined humanity.

Thus, when Jesus arrived at the place called Calvary, He looked at the Roman soldiers and saw a hammer, a carpenter's tool, in the hand of one. Then He looked up to heaven above and saw something hidden from all human eyes—twelve legions of angels drawn up on the battlements of heaven, awaiting a word that never came. Instead of a word of command, which would have launched armies of angels against this world to make a final end then and there of planet and people alike, the people heard Him say, "Father, forgive them; for they know not what they do" (Luke 23:34).

This was no imprecatory psalm. This was the kind of prayer He taught us all to pray: "forgive us our debts, as we forgive our debtors" (Matt. 6:12). The Lord Jesus always practiced what He preached. Such, then, was His first word on Calvary's brow.

The Lord's second utterance was *a promise*. "Today shalt thou be with me in paradise" (Luke 23:43). This word was spoken to a dying thief, one who, only a short while before, had been cursing the crucified Christ as venomously as anyone else.

Something, however, arrested this man. He heard what the rabbis were saying and what the rabble was repeating: "He saved others; himself he cannot save" and "If he be the King of Israel, let him now come down from the cross, and we will believe him" (Matt. 27:42). He heard the gospel from Christ's bitterest foes.

The dying thief lifted his eyes. He could see what the Roman governor had written and nailed over the center cross: "THIS IS JESUS THE KING OF THE JEWS" (Matt. 27:37). He heard Christ pray for His foes. Slowly, it all condensed in his mind. He remembered, perhaps, Bible portions he had memorized as a boy along with bits and pieces he had heard over the past three years about the marvelous life of this Man.

The insensate rage ebbed out of his soul. Conviction and faith took root and sprang up to full flower and fruit. Seedtime and harvest came simultaneously in his soul. This was the Son of God. This was the King of Israel.

He turned to his companion in crime, who was cursing away at Christ like a mad fool. "Dost not thou fear God, seeing thou art in the same condemnation?" he demanded. "And we indeed justly; for we receive the due reward of our deeds: but this man hath done nothing amiss" (Luke 23:40–41). What a confession! What conviction! What comprehension!

He turned his head away from his cursing comrade to the Christ of God. "Lord," he said, "remember me when thou comest into thy kingdom" (Luke 23:42). Thus, in one great confession of faith, against all outward appearances, he put Christ on the throne of his heart and on the throne of the world. The man's sublime faith rang the joy bells in the heart of the Savior! All about Him was noise—the taunts and the blasphemies of the nation's rulers, the horrible curses that flowed like red-hot lava out of the mouths of those whose souls were as foul as the city sewers, the impure jests, the angry shouts. Christ turned away from it all. He faced the dying thief. He said, "Verily I say unto thee, Today shalt thou be with me in paradise" (Luke 23:43).

Such was the promise. A few hours later the Lord dismissed His Spirit. Shortly afterward this onetime thief arrived at the gates of paradise to be greeted with "joy unspeakable and full of glory" (1 Peter 1:8), the first convert of Calvary, a trophy of sovereign grace o'er sin abounding.

The Lord's third utterance made *a provision.* "Woman, behold thy son! . . . [John] behold thy mother" (John 19:26–27). Jesus' mother came to Golgotha. How could she have stayed away? Her husband, Joseph, is thought to have been dead. Her other children, the natural children of Mary and Joseph, were still unbelievers. The Lord had no intention of leaving her in their care. But there stood John, His closest disciple. Tenderly, the Lord committed His mother to John's care and, at once, John took her away from the scene.

That was not only a provision for His mother; it was a protection for the church, soon to be born and later to be corrupted. One of Rome's dogmas is that Mary is co-redemptrix with Jesus. In Rome, in the courtyard of the Church of Mary Major, there is a tall crucifix that depicts Mary hanging on the cross back to back with Jesus, dying for our sins along with Him. Well did the Lord know, as He hung on Calvary's tree, that well-meaning people would try to make her co-redeemer with Him. So, He sent her away. Even the word He used in so doing put distance between her and Himself. He called her not "mother" but "woman," a term of respect but not one of relationship.

Thus, Jesus deliberately declared His relationship with His Father and dissolved His relationship with His mother.

2. Words of travail

The next two words from the cross had reference to Himself and His anguish on the tree.

There was a reference to *His mental anguish.* "Eli, Eli, lama sabachthani?" (Matt. 27:46; Mark 15:34), He cried—the only cry from the cross recorded by two of the Evangelists. So significant was this central saying that the Holy Spirit summoned two people to affirm it.

The first, central, and final sayings were all addressed to God. The first and last referred to God as Father; the other referred to Him as Elohim, Creator-God of the universe. What was it that happened to the Father-Son relationship when He who knew no sin was sin for us?

Distance was put between the Father and the Son. We may not know, we cannot tell, how great that distance was—as far as the east is from the west, perhaps (Ps. 103:12). As far as heaven is from hell, maybe. We recall that man's first sin separated him from *God* (Gen. 3:22–24); his second sin separated him from *man* (Gen. 4:1–8). When Jesus became the sin bearer, He experienced for Himself the fact that sin separates.

Out of the darkness that fell upon the scene, there came a dreadful cry—"My God, my God, why hast thou forsaken me?" (Matt. 27:46; Mark 15:34). During those three dreadful hours of darkness, it would seem that Jesus experienced the horror of the lost—to be left alone in the dark, far from God, and in torment.

Jesus had never been forsaken before. Throughout all the ages of a past eternity, Father and Son had been together, coeternal, coexistent, coequal with the eternal Spirit of God. Now, sin had come between them. For the thirty-three years or so Jesus lived down here, He enjoyed unbroken communion with His Father. "I and my Father are one," He could say (John 10:30). Even in Gethsemane it was the same. "Father," He said, "if it be possible, let this cup pass from me" (Matt. 26:39). But now it was no longer "Father!" but "God!" His anguished cry, Emmanuel's orphan cry, rang out. "My God, my God!" and then the unanswered "Why?" Not all the ages of eternities as yet unborn will ever reveal the answer to the mysterious, unfathomable, incomprehensible depths of woe in that one word, "Why?"

Then, there was a reference to *His physical agony.* "I thirst!" He said (John 19:28). Fever is one of the torments of those crucified. So now the Lord experienced a raging thirst, one of the most terrible of torments. The rich man in hell summed up all his sufferings with the words "I am tormented in this flame," accompanied by an agonizing plea for just one touch of water on his tongue (Luke 16:24).

The Lord had now been on the cross for six hours. As He had begun His public ministry by being hungry (Matt. 4:1–2), He now ended it by being thirsty. His strength was "dried up like a potsherd," and His tongue clove to His jaws (Ps. 22:15).

Where are you, young people from Cana? Have you no water for Him? Did He not give you wine for water at your wedding (John 2:7–10)? Can you not spare Him a cup of cold water as a disciple and win an eternal reward?

Where are you, woman of Samaria? Did He not once before ask you to give Him a drink of water from the well? And did He not in reward give you living water from heaven's crystal sea, the very water of life, springing up into everlasting life in your soul?

Where are you Peter? Matthew? Thomas? Have you forgotten the time long, long ago when David was in the cave and breathed a sigh for a drink of water from the well of his boyhood days in Bethlehem? Have you forgotten how three of David's mighty men broke through the Philistine garrison, drew the water, filled their water skins, and made it back to David (2 Sam. 23:13–17)?

What! You disciples of Jesus, where are you? Can you not muster just three of you to dare the reaction of the guard to bring the agonizing Christ a drop or two of water on a sponge? Great would have been your reward in heaven. Ah, well! You're too late. Here comes a soldier with a sponge attached to a reed. It holds not water but the common beverage of the barracks. The soldier reaches up, despite the angry murmurs of the mob, and administers to the Lord of glory a meager drink mingled with gall.

"I thirst!" What an astounding fact! He who said that has been pouring two hundred thousand cubic feet of water a second over Niagara Falls for tens of thousands of years. "I thirst!" *He* said.

And more! Ten thousand times ten thousand angels, had it been allowed, would have rushed that instant to the crystal stream and brought to Him water from the river of life. But no! This was humanity's affair, not theirs. So He said, "I thirst," and He was given a drink of vinegar.

He could have commanded the clouds and summoned sweet, refreshing rain to pour upon Him there. But no! He would no more turn the clouds to rain without His Father's word than He would change stones to bread without God's permissive will.

3. Words of triumph

The last two words from the cross are full of victory. One of them concerned *the past.* "It is finished" (John 19:30). The English language requires three words for this expression, the Greek requires but one—*tetelestai.* This word expresses satisfaction. It occurs twice in the Bible. At the end of His work in creation, the Holy Spirit says, "Thus the heavens and the earth were *finished,* and all the host of them" (Gen. 2:1). Finished! The galaxy, the globe, the garden—all finished. Adam and Eve, fresh from the hands of God, their human spirits indwelt by the Holy Spirit—finished! Six days and ten commandments—and the work was done.

It was the same at Calvary with the work of redemption. Jesus said, "Finished!" *Tetelestai!* It is a word a shepherd would use to describe a newborn lamb, beautiful, shapely, without spot, blemish, or wrinkle. It is the word of an artist contemplating a completed painting or statue. Perfect! Finished! *Tetelestai!* It was the word the Savior used while hanging on the tree. There was not a single detail unfulfilled of all the many prophecies and promises concerning redemption in the Word of God. He had just fulfilled the last of them by proclaiming His thirst (John 19:28; Ps. 69:21). Everything was finished! The Lord Jesus pillowed His head on that. *"Tetelestai!"* He said. Done was the work that saves, done and forever done! Finished! You cannot add to a finished work.

Finished—as when a craftsman has put the final touches to a masterpiece. All the various parts of the desk or cabinet have been made with care, sanded down, and perfectly fitted together. The various coats of varnish have been applied. The polishing has been done. It is finished. But what is this? Here comes some carpenter's apprentice with a hammer and some nails and a bucket of paint. He thinks he can add some touches of his own. No he can't! All he would do to it would be to spoil it. A finished work cannot be improved. It is finished.

The great evangelist D. L. Moody had something like this in his mind when someone asked him, "Mr. Moody, what must I do to be saved?" He said, "I'm sorry, sir, you are too late. As a matter of fact, you are hundreds of years too late. All the doing has been done!"

But we must come back to the cross. When we launch a vehicle into space, the scientists first work their way through what we call "the countdown." They have a detailed checklist. Every item on that list is carefully and thoroughly reviewed and tested. Not until they are satisfied that every detail has been checked do they proceed to the final ten-second countdown to lift off.

Thus it was on the cross. As Jesus hung there on the tree, He did not bemoan His condition; He did not plot vengeance against those who had crucified and cursed Him. Not a bit of it! He was too busy doing a monumental countdown of all the details that had to be checked off on the list. "*Tetelestai!*" He said. "Finished!" He had reviewed every prophetic truth, every pictorial type. Nothing remained to be said or done. It was finished!

The final word from the cross concerned *the prospect*. "Father, into thy hands I commend my spirit," He said (Luke 23:46). The future was secure. The pain and suffering was over. Ahead lay resurrection, rapture, and a glorious return.

Jesus dismissed His Spirit. His death was as supernatural as was His birth and His life on earth. He did not die of a broken heart. He did not die of physical exhaustion, or of fever, or tetanus, or loss of blood, or heart failure, or of a stab from a soldier's spear. No person was allowed to take His life from Him. He laid it down of Himself. That was the Father's command (John 10:17–18).

Thus it was, as the soldiers came to make a swift and sudden end of their three victims, He was before them. He sovereignly dismissed His Spirit into the care and keeping of His Father in heaven.

Three days later He was back! Forty days later He ascended boldly and bodily into heaven. And there He sits enthroned on high, engaged in a countdown to the day of His promised return.

What, we wonder, will be His first word then?

PART 6

PRACTICAL

Death and judgment are behind us,
Grace and glory are before;
All the billows rolled o'er Jesus
There they spent their utmost power.

First fruits of the Resurrection
He is risen from the tomb;
Now we stand a new creation
Free because beyond our doom.

Jesus died, and we died with Him,
Buried in His grave we lay,
One with Him in resurrection,
Now "in Him" in heaven's bright day.[1]
—Mrs. J. A. Trench (1843–1925)

CHAPTER 21

THE OLD MAN CRUCIFIED

1. An old man (Rom. 6:6–7)
2. An old monarch (Rom. 6:12, 14)
3. An old master (Rom. 6:16)
4. An old marriage (Rom. 7:1–2, 4)

THE CROSS HAS A THEOLOGICAL AND intensely practical side. It is the instrument God uses to bring the believer into a life of victory. God's answer to worldliness and carnality in the life of the believer is the Cross. He does not take us back to Pentecost; He takes us back to Calvary. All kinds of highly suspect extrabiblical experiences are offered in the name of the Holy Spirit. They focus on shortcuts. God does not offer shortcuts. Nor does He hand out four-color glossy brochures offering wealth and health to those who will sign on someone-or-other's dotted line or join a "name-it and claim-it" religious club. God does not offer such things. Those who promote them and buy into them fail to see the difference between the blessing of the Old Testament and that of the New Testament. The Old Testament blessing is found in Proverbs 10:22. It is "the blessing of the LORD, it maketh rich, and he addeth no sorrow with it." The New

225

Testament blessing is found in the Beatitudes (Matt. 5:1–12). In the New Testament, God does not offer an exotic experience but an execution; not a charismatic experience but a cross.

The book of Romans is "the gospel according to Paul." Paul tells us what the Holy Spirit has to say about sin and salvation. He then turns to what God has to say about sanctification. As far as Paul was concerned, there was no room for debate. The believer is called to live a holy life, a supernatural life, a Christlike life. Paul deals with the principle of holy living in chapter 6, with the problems of holy living in chapter 7, and with the practice of holy living in chapter 8. He begins with a double illustration. First he gives a *biographical* illustration:

> What shall we say then? Shall we continue in sin, that grace may abound? God forbid. How shall we, that are dead to sin, live any longer therein? Know ye not, that so many of us as were baptized into Jesus Christ were baptized into his death? Therefore we are buried with him by baptism into death: that like as Christ was raised up from the dead by the glory of the Father, even so we also should walk in newness of life. (Romans 6:1–4)

The background to all this is found in the last clause of chapter 5, where Paul states that the believer has "eternal life by Jesus Christ our Lord." Chapter 6 ends with the same affirmation.

This teaching supports the doctrine of the eternal security of the believer. Some think this to be a dangerous doctrine. They claim that if a person is taught that he has eternal life in Christ, then he will think he can sin with impunity. Paul's answer to such a notion is expressed in a resounding "God forbid!" Exactly the opposite is true. The person who has eternal life through Jesus Christ our Lord was once dead *in* sin. He is now dead *to* sin. He is not free *to* sin but he is free *from* sin. Christ who died *as* that person now gives His life *to* that same person. We who were put to death in the death of Christ are now raised in Him to live in the power of an endless life.

This is the great truth that lies at the heart of Paul's biographical illustration in Romans 6:3–4. The illustration is that of baptism by immersion. When believers are baptized by immersion, they take their stand in the water, a substance alien to them and one that spells death to all that they are by natural birth. Water is not our element. Just let us get out of our depth, and water will drown us. Standing in the place of death, believers are immersed, put beneath the water, buried out of sight. Finally, they are raised up out of the water by the power of another's arm to live anew on resurrection ground.

That was Paul's biographical illustration. Baptism is much more than a symbol; it is the outward expression of an inward experience. We are baptized, Paul says, into Christ's death.

The Lord spoke of His own death as being a baptism. He said, "I have a baptism to be baptized with; and how am I straitened till it be accomplished!" (Luke 12:50). That baptism took place at Calvary when He was immersed beneath the icy waters of death. Our identification with Christ in His death, burial, and resurrection sets us free to live a new life in Christ. Spiritually and eternally, we stand now on resurrection ground.

Paul's second illustration is a *biological* one. "For if we have been planted together in the likeness of his death, we shall be also in the likeness of his resurrection" (Rom. 6:5). First Paul takes us to a funeral. We are going to a burial. When people are buried, that is the end of them. Then Paul takes us to a farm. Now we are going to a planting, but that is by no means the end of it. A seed is planted and buried out of sight. But it will be coming back, clothed in garments of glory.

Paul now paints four vivid word pictures to help us understand just exactly what it means to have eternal life through Jesus Christ our Lord. He likens the old nature to an old *man,* an old *monarch,* an old *master,* and an old *marriage.*

1. An old man

"Knowing this, that our old man is crucified with him, that the body of sin might be destroyed, that henceforth we should not serve sin. For he that is dead is freed from sin" (Rom. 6:6–7). The "old man" can be defined as "the man of old," the natural man, the man I was before I was saved. Everything the old man does is tainted by sin. The "body of sin" to which Paul refers has to do with the lusts of the body, the old nature that is the slave of sin. No wonder Jesus told Nicodemus that he needed to be born again (John 3:3). A person who accepts Christ is born from above, born of the Spirit, born "not of corruptible seed, but of incorruptible, by the word of God, which liveth and abideth for ever" (1 Peter 1:23). Born-again believers have two natures. They have an old nature derived from Adam, a nature that can do nothing right (Rom. 7:18), and they have a new nature, a divine nature derived from Christ, one that can do nothing wrong.

Once a young woman excused her hot temper by saying, "I can't help it. I was born that way." Her pastor wisely replied, "That is no excuse. You have been born again since then." The fact of the matter is that, so far as God is concerned, the old nature in the believer was put to death on the cross of Calvary. It has been crucified with Christ so *the old man is now dead.* A dead person cannot respond to temptation. You can stand alongside a dead person and call it, command it, or caress it. There will be no response.

The problem is that the old nature does not feel dead. That has nothing to do with it, as we are quick to point out to new Christians. We tell them that when God says something, that's the end of it. Our response to revealed truth is simple—we believe it. Faith is wedded to fact. Sometimes this is accompanied by feelings, sometimes not. In any case, feelings can be deceptive.

When I lived in the Chicago area years ago, I had to be out of the house by six in the morning to catch an early train into the city. It was often a struggle to get up and get going especially if it was still dark when the alarm went off and winter winds were blowing. One morning the alarm went off at the usual time of 5:00 A.M. My wife and I had been up several times in the night with restless children. When the clamor of the clock was finally stopped, my wife opened a bleary eye. "Is that five o'clock?" she asked. I assured her it was. She groaned. "It doesn't *feel* like five o'clock," was her final verdict.

Of course, it made no difference whatsoever that it did not *feel* like five o'clock. "The stars in their courses fought against Sisera" (Judg.

5:20). The sun, the moon, the stars, the rotation of the earth upon its axis all said it was five o'clock. It didn't feel like it was time to get up—but feelings had nothing to do with it! The machinery of the universe proclaimed that the hour was five o'clock. That was the end of it.

So the old man does not seem to be dead? He doesn't feel dead? No matter! He's dead all right! God says so! The entire machinery of redemption says so. That's the end of it indeed—or it certainly should be.

The story is told of a couple of men who got into an argument over a turtle. "Come here, Paddy," said Mike. "Look at this turtle. Its head's been cut off, but it's still alive, still running all over the lawn." "It can't be alive if its head's cut off," said Paddy. "It's dead." "It's not dead," said Mike. "It's still running all over the place." The disagreement began to escalate. They decided to ask O'Brien who was walking by to come and have the final say. O'Brien inspected the severed head. "Well," he said judicially, "he's dead but he don't believe it!" This is where many people are. The old man still seems to be very much alive to them. God says that the old man is dead. They simply don't believe it.

Paul says that the man of old is crucified with Christ. People can kill themselves in any number of ways. They can hang themselves. They can jump off high bridges or throw themselves from tenth-story windows. They can stab themselves or poison themselves. But they cannot crucify themselves. God does not tell us to put the old man to death. We cannot do so. In any case, God has done it for us. Our responsibility is to believe it to be so and to act on it day by day.

2. An old monarch

"Let not sin therefore reign in your mortal body, that ye should obey it in the lusts thereof. . . . For sin shall not have dominion over you" (Rom. 6:12, 14). God created Adam to rule and reign over the earth. He crowned him with glory and honor and set him over the works of His hands (Heb. 2:7–8). Adam was not elected president. He was anointed king. God said, "Have dominion . . . upon the earth" (Gen. 1:28). And so Adam was installed into his high and holy calling in the Garden of Eden. There he resided and ruled, in a perfect environment, under ideal conditions, with a loving helpmate, and in perfect harmony with God.

Adam, however, surrendered his sovereignty to Satan. Thus, world power and dominion passed into the hands of the Evil One. He is now "the prince of this world" (John 12:31; 14:30; 16:11) and "the prince of the power of the air, the spirit that now worketh in the children of disobedience" (Eph. 2:2). When Satan tempted Jesus in the wilderness, he showed Him all the kingdoms of this world and offered them to Him. The Lord Jesus did not dispute the right of Satan to dispose of the kingdoms of this world to whomever he pleased. Satan evidently had that right and was able to exercise it. However, he did not control the destinies of the nations because God gave him this power. He derived this prerogative from Adam. It was Satan's by right of conquest.

Every child of Adam's ruined race has been born into the wrong kingdom, into a realm over which Satan rules. As a result, sin reigns. This is evident in every person's life. The sin nature of defiance and disobedience is manifested by every babe born into this world. Babies do not have to be taught to display temper and self-will. As they grow older the Adamic nature in them becomes more assertive. They do not have to be taught to tell lies, steal, indulge their lusts, exhibit pride and rebellion, and defy authority—even divine authority. All this is part of our Adamic nature. Sin reigns.

But, blessed be God, *this old monarch is now defeated.* This world of ours has been invaded from outer space. The Son of God Most High came down to Earth. He defeated Satan at Calvary and took away from him the keys of both death and hades (Rev. 1:18). When we give our hearts to the Lord Jesus, God takes us out of Satan's kingdom and puts us into God's kingdom (Col. 1:12–14). Satan's authority over us ceases at the cross. Christ has "spoiled principalities and powers, he made a show of them openly, triumphing over them" in His cross (2:15).

Believers are aliens down here, called to be ambassadors for Christ (2 Cor. 5:20). Satan's power over them is broken. The old monarch is now defeated. Sin no longer reigns supreme in our hearts. It is not to have dominion over us. Our citizenship is in heaven. We obey the laws of another kingdom. Where once sin reigned, now Christ reigns.

3. An old master

"Know ye not, that to whom ye yield yourselves servants to obey, his servants ye are" (Rom. 6:16). We have been set free from bondage to sin so that we might become servants of righteousness. Like the children of Israel we were born slaves in a house of bondage (Exod. 13:3). "Whosoever committeth sin is the servant of sin," Jesus said (John 8:34, the word used is *doulos,* meaning "bond servant" or "slave").

We were born in a true house of bondage. Sin was our master. We were held enthralled by evil habits, sinful lusts, wicked beliefs, and wanton behavior. Time and time again, we have resolved to do better. We may escape for a while but often not for long. Our sin nature says, "Do this," and we do it, or "Don't do that," and we pass up on an opportunity to do good.

Paul has some more good news for us—*the old master is now deposed.* "Ye were the servants of sin, but ye have obeyed from the heart that form of doctrine which was delivered you [whereunto ye were delivered]. Being then made free from sin, ye became the servants of righteousness" (Rom. 6:17–18). The Lord Jesus came down into the slave market of sin, paid the price of our redemption, and set us free.

We now belong to Jesus! What a glorious and beloved Master He is! We no longer have to do what our sin nature says. We now can do what Jesus says. The motivation is love, the means is the power of the indwelling Spirit. We are Christ's purchased possession (Eph. 1:14). He owns us. He is our Master. Henceforth, we do what we do because we are what we are—bond slaves of Jesus Christ.

4. An old marriage

> The *law* hath dominion over a man as long as he liveth? . . . For
> the woman which hath an husband is bound by the *law* to her

husband so long as he liveth; but if the husband be dead, she is
loosed from the law of her husband. . . . Wherefore, my brethren, ye also are become dead to the law by the body of Christ;
that ye should be married to another, even to him who is raised
from the dead, that we should bring forth fruit unto God. (Romans 7:1–2, 4)

This passage does not refer to the question of divorce. In any case,
what is said here has to be taken in conjunction with passages that do
have a direct bearing on the question of divorce (Matt. 19:2–12, for
instance), not in isolation (2 Peter 1:20).

Certainly Paul is discussing here the dissolution of marriage. But it
is dissolution by *death,* not divorce. When Adam fell he contracted all
members of his race to be married to sin. We have lived on the closest
terms of intimacy with sin. As if that were not enough, the law has
stepped in and set the unhappy relationship in concrete. So now, not
only are we born married to sin; we are also bound just as rigidly to
sin by the demands of the law. What then is the solution?

Death! Happily, death puts an end to the law's tyranny but unhap-
pily it also puts an end to life itself! So that solution is of no help.
What can be done? What is Paul telling us? *The old marriage is dissolved.* "Wherefore, my brethren, ye also are become dead to the law
by the body of Christ; that ye should be married to another, even to
him who is raised from the dead, that we should bring forth fruit
unto God" (Rom. 7:4).

What frees us from the bondage of sin and the law is not *our* death
but *Christ's* death. It is the *body* of Christ that cancels the hold of sin
and the law upon us. He bore our sins in His body on the tree (1 Peter
2:24).

This brings us back to our identification with Christ, the predomi-
nating truth of this section of the Romans epistle. We were in Christ
when He died. When He died, we died. When He was buried, we were
buried. When He rose, we arose. So, now we stand on resurrection
ground "married to another," indeed! Even to "him who is raised from
the dead" (Rom. 7:4).

Surely, *that* truth should transform our lives. "Married to another!" It is not just a theological proposition. It is a life-transforming, heart-quickening, soul-stirring fact. We are married to yon glorious Man seated on high with God, now able to bring forth fruit unto Him. Jesus said, "Ye shall know the truth, and the truth shall make you free" (John 8:32). But how? That is the question.

Now we need to go back to the sixth chapter of Romans and mark three simple verbs that present us with a formula for holy living: "know" (Rom. 6:6–9), "reckon" (Rom. 6:11), and "yield" (Rom. 6:16).

There is something we have to know. We have to know that the old man is now dead, that the old monarch is now defeated, that the old master is now deposed, and that the old marriage is now dissolved.

Knowing, however, is not enough. We must also reckon. Years ago, I worked as an accountant for a lumber company in western Canada. As in many business operations, there were times when the company simply did not have enough cash flow to meet its current debts. The owner would then go along to the bank and talk to the manager. "Mr. Bank Manager, I have to meet a payroll. I need money to pay for royalties owed to the Forest Service. I have a number of other accounts payable. I need cash. I need to borrow fifty thousand dollars."

The bank manager would respond, "How much do you have in accounts receivable? How many board feet do you have of unplanned lumber and of planned lumber? How many boxcars are on the way to market but not yet sold?" Once his questions were answered, the manager would say, "Well, you are good for at least seventy thousand dollars. Sign here, and I'll put fifty thousand dollars in your account."

The owner would come back to me. He would say, "You can make out the paychecks. I've made arrangements with the bank. We have fifty thousand dollars in our account."

Presently, in would come the first lumberjack, looking for his pay. Suppose I were to say to him, "I have your check, but I can't let you have it. There's not enough money in the bank. Here, see for yourself. Here's the total payroll. It comes to twenty-five thousand dollars. Your check is included, as you can see. Now, look in this book. It is the general ledger. It sums up just where we stand. This is the bank page.

You can see the total amount of money in the bank comes to three hundred fifty dollars. That's obviously not enough to meet the payroll. I can give you your check if you insist, but it won't do you any good. There's not enough money in the bank to cover your check, much less everyone else's."

That would be wrong in every sense of the word. Not only would I be misrepresenting the company, but the statement itself wouldn't be true. What would I be doing wrong? I would be failing to reckon on the fact that adequate provision had been made to take care of every liability.

The old man is now dead. The old monarch is now defeated. The old master is now deposed. The old marriage is now dissolved. Adequate provision has been made at Calvary to take care of all our needs—and not just ours but everybody's. We must reckon that to be true. When temptation comes, we can count on God.

There is one step more. We must yield. We are made in such a way that when we are tempted we have to give in. However, we do not have to give in to sin. We must give in to the indwelling Spirit of God. "Resist the devil, and he will flee from you." How often we have read that verse and claimed it! But, as quoted, it simply isn't true because that is not what the whole verse says. It says, "Submit yourselves therefore to God. Resist the devil, and he will flee from you" (James 4:7). Yield to God! Submit to Him! That leaves Satan face-to-face with God, and he is no match for Him.

Beneath the cross of Jesus
I fain would take my stand,
The shadow of mighty rock
Within a weary land;
A home within the wilderness,
A rest upon the way
From the burning of the noontide heat,
And the burden of the day.

O safe and happy shelter,
O refuge tried and sweet
O trysting place where heaven's love
And heaven's justice meet;
As to the pilgrim patriarch
That wondrous dream was given,
So seems my Savior's love to me,
A ladder up to heaven.

There lies beneath its shadow,
But on the farther side,
The darkness of an awful grave
That gapes both deep and wide
And there between us stands the cross
Two arms outstretched to save,
Like a watchman set to guard the way
From that eternal grave.[1]
    —Elizabeth C. Clephane (1830–1869)

CHAPTER 22

GLORYING IN THE CROSS

Galatians 6:14

1. A great denial
   a. Paul: A remarkable man
   b. Paul: A religious man
   c. Paul: A regenerated man
2. A great doxology
3. A great divide

THE AMERICAN EVANGELIST D. L. Moody was a man with a one-track mind. He had a passion for souls. His death occasioned an outpouring of grief on both sides of the Atlantic. Though Moody began as a poor unlettered shoe salesman, his preaching moved thousands in both Britain and the United States. His education was minimal, and his grammar was atrocious, but his zeal was boundless and his enthusiasm infectious. His conversion to Christ, like that of the great apostle Paul, was wholly without reservation. No rivals! No refusals! No retreat! That was the quality of his commitment to Christ.

In 1874, two sophisticated Englishmen went to hear this unschooled American preacher, said by his critics to be the only man who could so massacre the English language as to pronounce the word *Jerusalem* as though it had just one syllable! One of the men who went to hear Moody was William Gladstone, the prime minister of Britain in the heyday of its empire. The other man was Matthew Arnold, the greatest intellectual in Victorian England.

They went. They listened. They came away. Said Gladstone, "I thank God I have lived to see the day when He should bless His church on earth with the gift of a man able to preach the gospel of Christ as we have heard it preached today." Matthew Arnold responded, "And I would give everything I have if only I could believe it."

When the World's Fair came to Chicago, so did D. L. Moody. Before long, Moody had the crowds, and the fair had to close on Sundays! They had the program, but Moody had the people. He chatted to thousands as though he were chatting to a half dozen. People from every walk of life came to hear him preach and went away trusting in Christ.

What was the secret of his extraordinary life? Commitment! He once said, "The main thing is to keep the main thing the main thing." He said, "I should rather say 'this one thing I do' than say 'these forty things I dabble with.'" The main thing was the Cross! Paul said,

> God forbid that I should glory, save in the cross of our Lord Jesus Christ, by whom the world is crucified unto me, and I unto the world. (Galatians 6:14)

Paul's view of the Cross was colored by his background. He was a Jew and as such had a thorough knowledge of the Old Testament. The fire on the great brazen altar was never to go out. It fed upon the sacrifices, but it was never appeased. It reduced the sacrifices to ashes and then demanded more. It went on like that, burning and burning. "More!" it demanded. "Give me more!" At Calvary, the Lord Jesus slaked those flames and put them out. As the old hymn says:

> No blood, no altar now,
> The sacrifice is o'er,
> No flame, no smoke ascends on high
> The lamb is slain no more.[2]

The Cross changed things for Paul. Right after his conversion he vanished into the wilderness, seeking the solitude of Sinai so that he could think through all the great truths of the Old Testament in the light of Calvary. Doubtless he took his Bible, probably the Septuagint version of the Old Testament, with him. He came back with Romans, Ephesians, and Thessalonians in his soul. Central to all these glorious new truths was the Cross.

1. A great denial

"God forbid that I should glory . . ." (Gal. 6:14a), Paul says. He was a *remarkable* man. He had plenty to boast about. He seems to have come from an influential and affluent family. He had been given a first-class education. He was at home in several languages. He possessed a rare and invaluable treasure beyond the price of rubies—he was a freeborn Roman citizen.

Paul was cosmopolitan, comfortable in three worlds. He was a Jew, a rabbi, and a Pharisee. He was raised in a Greek city and was conversant with Hellenism, its appeal and its problems. He was a citizen of Rome—an asset that not only opened doors for him but also protected him from persecution. It gave him the right, if need be, to appeal his case to Caesar. It also guaranteed exemption from crucifixion. When Claudius Lysias ordered Paul to be scourged, he backed off in a hurry when Paul claimed his rights as a Roman citizen (Acts 22:27–28). Similarly, the authorities at Philippi were terrified when they discovered that Paul, a man they had thrashed and incarcerated, was a Roman citizen (Acts 16:19–24, 35–40).

Paul once said he was a native of "no mean city." Tarsus was a busy seaport. Its harbors were thronged with sailors from all over the Roman world. A continual tide of commerce flowed through its docks—timber from Taurus mountains, for instance, and goat-hair fabric for the making of tents. Its schools were famous. The city rivaled both Athens and Alexandria as centers of learning, its greatest son being Paul himself.

Paul was also a *religious* man. He was a pureblooded Jew of the

tribe of Benjamin and of the strict sect of the Pharisees. His zeal for
the law was remarkable. He would fast three times a week. He tithed
all his income down to the mint in his garden. He kept the Sabbath
and all the feasts and fasts required under the Mosaic Law. He was a
trained rabbi, having sat at the feet of Gamaliel, grandson of the renowned scholar Hillel, whose reputation was so great that he was one
of a small circle of seven Jewish doctors honored with the title Rabban.
At the feet of Gamaliel he studied the Scriptures but especially the
oral law, the "traditions of the elders." Moreover, he was a zealot. He
saw in a flash that Christianity and Judaism were mutually incompat-
ible. He became the most feared persecutor of the church in his day.
His zeal took him to foreign countries where he made havoc of the
church abroad just as he had at home.

Paul described his zeal in his letter to his friends at Philippi. He
was indeed "a Hebrew of the Hebrews" (Phil. 3:4–6). The Cross made
short work of all these things.

Then, too, he was a *regenerated* man. Paul had plenty to boast about—
even as a Christian. Had he wished to boast of his achievements, he
could have filled volumes. He probably traveled more miles, visited more
cities, pioneered more virgin territory, won more souls, planted more
churches, and trained more people for the ministry than all the rest of
the apostles together. At a time when the apostles were sitting around
in Jerusalem and Judea, he was out evangelizing, pastoring, and teaching in Europe and Galatia. He was the first to take the Great Commis-
sion seriously. In miracles, tongues, and healings, he excelled them all.
In gifts of the Spirit and anointings of the Spirit, he outshone them all.
In writing the New Testament, he excelled them all. In being beaten
and bruised and left for dead, in playing the gambler with his life, in
being stoned and shipwrecked, in bearing witness before kings and
governors, in being disinherited by his family and disowned by his countrymen and even his fellow believers, in seeing heavenly visions, in hearing high callings, in being caught up to heaven, in prayer and fasting, in
bearing thorns in the flesh, and in waging war on principalities and
powers—rulers of this world's darkness and wicked spirits in high
places—Paul outshone them all.

Paul had one word for such boasting. He called it being worldly. And he had one way of dealing with it. He took it to Calvary, took it to the Cross, and crucified it. He said, "God forbid that I should glory, save in the cross of our Lord Jesus Christ" (Gal. 6:14). He had thoroughly mastered the technique of the great denial. Every time self asserted itself, he took it to the Cross. "I have died to you, O self. I died to you at a place called Calvary. I died when Jesus died."

Many believers never see themselves as God sees them. The story is told of an old fellow from way back in the woods who decided he would go to the market. He had heard about it ever since he was a boy, but he had never been anywhere or seen anything. While taking in the wonders of the market, he saw a small pocket mirror for sale. He had never seen a mirror before. He picked it up, looked at it, and saw his face reflected in it. "Well," he exclaimed, "what do you know! If it isn't a picture of my old granddad right here in the market!" He bought it and took it home. All evening long he would pull out the mirror, look in it, and murmur to himself, "Fancy that! It's granddad!"

His wife took notice. "What've you got there?" she asked. "Never you mind," he said, hiding the mirror in his pocket. "None of your business."

She waited until he went off to bed and then rummaged through his pockets until she found the mirror. She looked into it and gave a snort of disgust. "Some old hag he met in the market," she said.

There's nothing like a look at the Cross to show us what we are like. The Cross knows no compromise. It exposes us for what we are. The Cross denies all our imagined goodness while it exposes all our ingrained badness. Paul said, "If I am going to glory in anything, I am going to glory in the Cross."

2. A great doxology

"God forbid that I should glory, *save in the cross of our Lord Jesus Christ.*" We need to read these words as they would have sounded in the ears of these Galatians to whom they were first addressed. After all, Galatia was part of the Roman world. In the Roman world nothing was more despised, dreaded, or shameful than a cross. To glory in a cross in that day would be like glorying in a gallows or an electric chair today. The cross was an instrument of torture and death. It indicated the death of a felon, a particularly horrible death—death by execution, death by exposure. For a Jew it had the additional terror of being death by excommunication, the death of one accursed. There could be no hope for such a one.

Paul, however, was not viewing the cross as a Roman citizen or as a Greek intellectual or as a Hebrew rabbi. He was viewing it as a believing Christian.

John Bunyan will help us when it comes to the cross. His pilgrim, he tells us, had been awakened to a deep conviction of sin. "I dreamed," says Bunyan, "and behold, I saw a man clothed in rags, standing in a certain place, a book in his hand, and a great burden on his back." The man in Bunyan's dream talked to his wife about his burden. "O my dear wife . . . I am certainly informed that this our city will be burned with fire from heaven. . . ." His wife and children and his neighbors and relations thought he was mad.

Then he met a man called Evangelist who urged him to flee from the wrath to come and told him where to go. On his way he met various people including Mr. Obstinate, Mr. Pliable, and Mr. Worldly Wiseman who dwelt in the town of Carnal Policy, a very great town near the City of Destruction where Pilgrim lived. Worldly Wiseman directed Christian to the house of Mr. Legality who lived in the town of Morality. As he went in that direction, however, it only made things worse. His burden became heavier. Finally, he made his way to the cross.

"So I saw in my dream," said Bunyan, "that just as Pilgrim came up to the cross his burden was loosed from his shoulders and fell from off his back and began to tumble and continued until it came to the mouth of a sepulcher where it fell in and was seen no more."

Then came three shining ones. The first said to him, "Thy sins be forgiven thee." The second stripped him of his rags and clothed him with a change of raiment. The third set a seal upon his forehead and gave him a certificate that allowed him to get in the celestial gate. Then Christian gave three leaps for joy and went on singing:

> Thus far did I come, laden with my sin
> Nor could ought ease the grief that I was in,
> Till hither: What a place is this!
> Must here be the beginning of my bliss.
>
> Must here the burden fall from off my back?
> Must here the cords that bound it to me crack?
> Blest cross! blessed sepulchre! blest rather be
> The Man that here was put to shame for me.[3]

In like manner, Paul came to the place called Calvary. Thus, too, he went on his way rejoicing. Thus, too, he sang, "God forbid that I should glory, save in the cross of our Lord Jesus Christ."

The cross represents the greatest *tragedy* in man's dealings with God. For on that cross, man murdered the incarnate Son of God. The human race has gloried in what it has done. As Joseph's brothers stripped him of his coat of many colors, dipped it in blood, and flung it back at their father, so men took the Lord Jesus, God's only begotten and well beloved Son, and flung Him back in God's face. "We will not have this man to reign over us," they said (Luke 19:14). They stood there rejoicing in the cross, in the pain and agony and shame they had inflicted on that Holy One.

The cross likewise represents the greatest *triumph* in God's dealings with man. The cross! Once a symbol of suffering, shame, and death has become the very symbol of God's love and grace. He has actually "made peace through the blood of his cross" (Col. 1:20).

When Adam and Eve were driven out of the Garden of Eden, God placed cherubim at the gate to guard the tree of life along with a flaming sword that turned this way and that way to keep the guilty pair from stealing back and eating of the Tree of Life. Had they done that they would have lived forever in their sins, beyond hope of redemption. The cross was to change all that.

When Moses made the sacred ark of the covenant, he was instructed to fashion a lid for it of solid gold. This cover was called the mercy seat. Out of the same slab of gold, two figures of the cherubim were formed whose wings overshadowed it. Blood was sprinkled there, the blood of atonement (Lev. 16:14–15). The faces of the cherubim were turned inward and downward so that they were forever occupied with the blood (Exod. 25:20–22).

Now, because atonement has been made at Calvary, the cherubim still face inward, contemplating the blood of the atonement at the mercy seat. But it is no longer wrath but mercy that fills the heart of God. More! It is at the mercy seat that God agrees to meet with His own (Exod. 25:22).

All those Old Testament arrangements were types, shadows, pictures of things to come. For us, all now centers on the cross. It was there that the blood of the Lamb was shed. It was there that mercy and truth met together and where righteousness and peace kissed each other. It is there at the cross that God meets with us. No wonder Paul exclaims, "God forbid that I should glory, save in the cross of our Lord Jesus Christ" (Gal. 6:14).

3. A great divide

"The cross of our Lord Jesus Christ, by whom the world is crucified unto me, and I unto the world" (Gal. 6:14), writes Paul. The cross divides us from the world. The cross of Christ divided the two malefactors who were crucified with Christ. One of them went to heaven, the other to hell. The cross drives its wedge between saints and sinners in every group of people. The world is the Devil's lair for sinners and his lure for saints. It may be defined as human life and society with God left out. It is not without its appeal to our fallen natures. Its wares are described as "the lust of the flesh, and the lust of the eyes, and the pride of life" (1 John 2:16).

Again, it is John Bunyan who best depicts for us the atmosphere and attitudes of this evil world. Bunyan's pilgrim, Christian, has met a man called Faithful, and they have become fellow pilgrims on their way to the Celestial City, the beautiful city of God. Bunyan writes:

Presently, they saw a town before them and the name of that town is Vanity and at the town there is a fair kept all the year long. It beareth the name of Vanity Fair because the town where it is kept is lighter than vanity and also because of all that is sold there or that cometh hither is vanity. . . . This fair is no new-erected business, but a thing of ancient standing. . . . Almost five thousand years ago . . . Beelzebub, Apollyon and Legion, with their companions, perceiving that the pilgrims made their way through this town of Vanity, they contrived here to set up a fair wherein should be sold all sorts of vanity, and that it should last all year long. Therefore at this fair are all such merchandise sold as houses, lands, trades, places, honor, preferments, titles, countries, kingdoms, lusts, pleasures, and delights of all sorts as whores, bawds, wives, husbands, children, masters, servants, lives, bodies, souls, silver, gold, pearls, precious stones, and what not. And, moreover, at this fair there are at all times to be seen jugglers, cheats, games, plays, fools, apes, knaves and rogues, and that of every kind. Here are to be seen, too, and that for nothing, thefts, murders, adulteries, false swearers, and that of a blood-red colour. . . . But as in other fairs some one commodity is as the chief of all the fair, so the ware of Rome and her merchandise are greatly promoted in this fair. . . . Now, as I said, the way to the Celestial City lies just through this town where this lust fair is kept; and he that would go to the city, and yet not go through this town "must needs go out of the world." The Prince of Princes Himself went through this town to His own country, and that upon a fair day too; yea, and as I think it was Beelzebub, the chief lord of this fair, that invited Him to buy of his vanities; yea, would have made Him lord of the fair, would He but have done him reverence as He went through the town. Yea, because He was such a person of honor, Beelzebub had Him from street to street, and showed Him all the kingdoms of the world in a little time, that He might, if possible, allure that Blessed One to cheapen and buy some of his vanities; but He had no mind to the merchandise, and therefore left the town without laying out so much as one farthing upon these vanities. This fair, therefore, is an ancient thing of long standing, and a very sweet fair.

Now these pilgrims, as I said, must needs go through this fair. Well, so they did; but behold, even as they entered the fair, all the people in the fair were moved and the town itself, as it were, in a hubbub about them, and that for several reasons. First, the pilgrims were clothed with such kind of raiment as was diverse from the raiment of any that traded in that fair. The people of the fair, therefore, made a great gazing upon them. Some said they were fools; some said they were madmen, and some said they were very odd.

Secondly, just as they wondered at their apparel, so they did likewise at their speech; for few could understand what they said. They naturally spoke the language of Canaan; but they that kept the fair were the men of this world. So that from one end of the fair to the other they seemed barbarians each to the other.

Thirdly, but that which did not a little amuse the merchandisers was that these pilgrims set very light by all their wares. They cared not so much as to look upon them and if they called upon them to buy, they would put their fingers in their ears, and cry, "Turn away mine eyes from beholding vanity. . . ."

At this there was an occasion taken to despise the men the more; some mocking, some taunting, some speaking reproachfully, and some calling on others to smite them. At last things came to a great stir, in so much that all order was confounded. Now word was brought to the great one of the fair, who quickly came down and deputed some of his trusty friends to take these men in for examination. . . . The men told them they were pilgrims and strangers in the world and that they were going to their own country, which was the heavenly Jerusalem. . . . But they that were appointed to examine them did not believe them to be any other than crazy madmen, or else such as would come to put all things into confusion in the fair. Therefore they took them and beat them, and besmeared them with dirt, and then put them into the cage, that they might be made a spectacle to all the men of the fair. . . . Then were these two poor men brought before their examiners again, and there charged as being guilty of the late hubbub that had been in the fair. So they beat them unmercifully and hanged irons upon them and led them in chains up and down the fair for an example to others, lest any should speak in their behalf, or join themselves unto them. But Christian and Faithful behaved themselves yet more wisely. . . .

Then a convenient time being appointed, they brought them forth to their trial, in order to secure their condemnation. When the time was come, they were brought before their enemies and arraigned. The judge's name was Lord Hate-good. . . .

The trial was a mockery. The witnesses, for instance, were Envy, Superstition and Informer. Informer's testimony was particularly damaging, "This fellow (Faithful) I have known for a long time, and have heard him speak things that ought not to be spoken, for he hath railed on our noble Prince Beelzebub, and hath spoken contemptuously of his honorable friends whose names are the Lord Old-man, the Lord Carnal-delight, the Lord Luxurious, the Lord Desire-of-vainglory, my Lord Lechery, my Lord Sir Having Greedy with all the rest of our nobility." Faithful's answer to the judge was to the point. Denying that he had used raillery he said, "the prince of this town, with all the rabblement his attendants, by this gentleman named, are more fit for a being in hell than in this town and country. . . ."

The jury was a remarkable assortment of villains. They numbered in their ranks Mr. No-good, Mr. Malice, Mr. Love-lust, Mr. Liar and Mr. Cruelty. It did not take the jury long to condemn Faithful to death, though Christian was remanded back to prison. The sentence of death was duly carried out, "First they scourged him, then they buffeted him, then they lanced his flesh with knives, after that they stoned him with stones then pricked him with their swords, and last of all, they burned him to ashes at the stake. Thus Faithful came to his end.[4]

Such is the world. It is no wonder it dealt with Faithful the way it did. It did the same to his Lord and ours. It hired false witnesses against

Him who had done them nought but good all the days of His life. The world had Him beaten, blindfolded, buffeted, and scourged to the bone. It pulled the very beard from His cheeks. Then the world took Him out to Calvary's hill and there it nailed Him to a cross of wood and exposed Him to the eyes of the rabble. It mocked Him, and it watched Him die, tortured by cramps and wounds and dislocated joints. Nor was the world satisfied with His death. It thrust a spear home to His great and loving heart, now still in death. Then it sealed Him in a tomb.

Is it any wonder Paul says, "God forbid that I should glory, save in the cross of our Lord Jesus Christ, by whom the world is crucified unto me, and I unto the world" (Gal. 6:14)?

The cross of Christ drives a gorge as wide as eternity between this world and the believer. There is "a great gulf fixed." Between the world and us stands the cross.

The world is never more dangerous than when it offers us its hand in friendship. That was the difference in the Old Testament between Amalek and Moab, the two nations descended from fallen Lot and his daughters, with whom Israel had constant trouble. Amalek represented the world as *a foe.* Moab represented the world as *a friend.* Moab was the more dangerous of the two. It said, "We don't want to fight you. We offer you our daughters for your sons. We would like to share our institutions and our ideals and our inheritance with you. Come and worship on our side of the street. Come and embrace our goals and our girls and our gods."

The cross puts an end to all that. The cross shows up the world for what it is. The cross sets before us *the great divide.* Between the believer and the world stands the bloodstained cross of Christ.

Thus when the world offers us its hand, we reply:

> Nay world, I turn away,
> Though thou seem fair and good,
> That friendly, outstretched hand of thine
> Is stained with Jesus' blood.

Oh my Savior crucified,
Near Thy cross would I abide,
Gazing with adoring eye
On Thy dying agony.

Jesus bruised and put to shame,
Tells me all Jehovah's name;
God is love, I surely know
By the Savior's depths of woe.

In His spotless soul's distress,
I perceive my guiltiness;
Oh how vile my lost estate
Since my ransom was so great!

Yet in sight of Calvary,
Contrite should my spirit be,
Rest and holiness there find,
Fashioned like my Savior's mind.[1]
                    —Robert C. Chapman
                         (1803–1902)

CHAPTER 23

WE PREACH CHRIST CRUCIFIED

1 Corinthians 1:23

1. The man
2. The method
3. The message
4. The mistake
5. The miracle

PUT YOURSELF BACK IN THAT ANCIENT Roman world. Here comes the great apostle to the Gentiles. His voice rings out with authority and power. Merchants in the marketplace look up from their wares. Idlers cock an ear to hear what this Jew has to say, why it is so urgent that he is willing to risk facing charges of breaking the peace. Some Roman soldiers marching through town halt for a moment then go on their way. "Poor fellow!" they say. "He must be mad!" A Greek philosopher bursts into mocking laughter. "The fellow's a fool," he says. Jews standing by the synagogue raise angry fists and throw some stones at him.

No wonder! He is preaching "Christ, and Him crucified." Surely nobody in his right mind would preach any such thing! What! Preach about a man who died a shameful death on a Roman gibbet, accursed by the law, surrounded by a jeering multitude, and overwhelmed by agony and shame? The man must either have taken leave of his senses or else be on to some great hidden secret.

Well, Paul was certainly nobody's fool. He was one of the world's greatest intellectuals and one of the sanest men who ever lived. He combined in his person the attributes of Roman citizenship, Greek sophistication, and Hebrew religious scholarship. Let no one be deceived by his unprepossessing outward appearance. This man was a giant. He was a brilliant intellectual whose books have been studied by millions to this very day. He was a man of unshakable conviction, as bold as a lion, a gifted apostle, a tremendous motivator, and a superlative Christian.

So, since he was no mere crackpot, there must be more to this business of preaching the Cross than lies on the surface. Paul himself later explained to his Corinthian converts. "We preach Christ crucified," he said, "unto the Jews a stumblingblock, and unto the Greeks foolishness; but unto them which are called, both Jews and Greeks, Christ the power of God, and the wisdom of God" (1 Cor. 1:23–24).

1. The man

The man was Paul, the great and gifted apostle. He seems to have had all gifts, and he needed them! Paul was the one who was called by God to evangelize the vast, unsaved Gentile world. The date was some time in August of the year A.D. 51. There he went! He was doing something he rarely did. He was taking in the sights. The city through which he strolled was Athens, the cultural center of the old pagan world. It held plenty to see. Paul was taking in the sights but he was not wasting his time. While awaiting the arrival of some colleagues, he was using his time to study the statues and altars all over the city—hundreds of them, to every conceivable god. Some of the idols were works of art; all of them were an insult to the living God.

Paul was a great walker. During the course of his life, he walked thousands of miles to tell people about Jesus. He walked along fever-haunted coastal plains, across sandy deserts. He walked up through rugged mountain passes that were infested by brigands and wild beasts.

Sometimes he was accompanied by friends, by young disciples, or by colleagues and partners in the gospel. Sometimes he walked alone, communing with God, thinking things through. Sometimes he was hotly pursued by vengeful foes.

His body bore many a scar. He knew what it was like to be molested and mauled, to be beaten unmercifully, to be stoned, to be left for dead. He knew the terror of storms at sea and the horror of shipwreck and peril in the raging deep. He knew the feel of Roman stocks and the stench of Roman prisons. Nothing deterred him.

On and on he walked. Into Antioch, into Ephesus, into Philippi, into Thessalonica. Now we see him walking in Athens, a city that drew him like a magnet draws a needle. As he entered this famous city, he must have been thinking deeply. What should he say? How should he preach in this great university city, the cultural capitol of the world? Perhaps Paul was intimidated by Athens, a place he had heard about ever since he was a little boy at school.

For Athens was like no other city on earth. Corinth, Ephesus, even Rome—they were just cities. Athens was an institution. Athens was the city of Socrates and Plato, the city of Aristotle and Demosthenes, of Pericles and Pythagoras. Athens was a city of poets and philosophers, the place where art and literature, sculpture and architecture had reached their pinnacle. What should he preach to these intellectual Athenians? That would have been the burning question. Surely, here of all places, he should match reason with reason, philosophy with philosophy. Surely, he would need to quote their own great teachers back to them. He would have to establish his own reputation as a scholar if he were to have any chance of reaching scholars.

Establishing himself as a scholar was just what he did. We can go to Mars Hill and hear him for ourselves, for the Holy Spirit has seen fit to record what he said in the book of Acts. Paul reasoned with the Greeks. He talked to them in a direct manner about their superstitions and their idolatry. He spoke to them about the God of nature, talked about the common ties of humanity, and quoted their poets to them. It didn't work.

It never does. God's plan is not to argue with people. The way to the citadel of the soul is not through the intellect but through the conscience. God is not going to bless mere scholarship. He is going to bless Scripture. At the end of his address, Paul turned at last to the gospel. Even at that, he did not talk about the Cross but about the resurrection of Christ. The ridicule he hoped to avoid promptly materialized. As he left, with the ribald jeers of the intellectuals burning in his ears, Paul realized his error. He never repeated the mistake he made on Mars Hill.

He went from Athens to Corinth, another Greek city. Corinth was not without its culture, but Paul ignored it. He had only one message for the Corinthians—Christ crucified. That was the message for him, the message for lost sinners. It is the message that saves. We can take it from the man who knew. Nobody knew better than Paul what it was to preach so as to break through all barriers and bring people to salvation. "We preach Christ crucified," he said (1 Cor. 1:23). That was what he preached—and that is what we preach. So much, then, for the man.

2. The method

"We," he said, "*preach* Christ crucified" (1 Cor. 1:23, italics added). That's the method. Preaching! Many today have a great dislike for preaching. They prefer discussion groups and sharing sessions. Paul's method—God's method!—*was preaching.* Preaching is still God's way to reach the heart, soul, and conscience of an individual or a nation. No substitute for preaching exists.

The history of America is proof enough of that. This nation was born out of decades of revivals that swept up and down the eastern seaboard, from Georgia to New England. The leading figure in those revivals was George Whitfield who made no less than seven preaching trips to America between the years 1738 and 1770.

Then came Charles Finney. He was born in 1792, a first-generation citizen of the United States. When Finney was born, George Washington was still in his first presidency. Finney was a farmer's son, a self-taught lawyer, who was introduced to the Bible by the quotations from the Scripture passages he found in law textbooks. He became a preacher of extraordinary power. Everywhere he went revival broke out. He had no staff and no salary. His equipment amounted to a Bible, a suit of clothes, and a single suitcase. Often he did not know where he would preach next. He would stay in one place weeks or months until revival came. Even in his old age he continued to preach, never ceasing until he died in 1875.

Then there was D. L. Moody (1837–1899). He was followed by Billy Sunday (1862–1935). From the death of Billy Sunday to the time when Billy Graham picked up the heavy mantle of preaching to the conscience of a nation, there were only nine short years. God's method of preaching works.

Think of the impact of John and Charles Wesley on Great Britain. First, however, we must sketch in the condition of England at the time of their birth in that old haunted house at Epworth. The haunting of the parsonage was perhaps a portent reminder to the growing brothers of the haunting of England by many an evil spirit of sin.

The court and the castles of the nobility were licentious in the extreme. The stage was decadent. People were reading Hume and Gibbon, Voltaire and Rousseau. Everywhere, there was open atheism and unbelief.

Drunkenness was widespread. In London, just three years before the first Methodist society was founded, every sixth house was a gin mill. Their signs advertised that they would make a man drunk for a penny and dead drunk for two. From these dark haunts, gangs of thugs sallied forth to commit every sort of crime on peaceful citizens. They would run innocent people through with their swords. Sometimes they would torture them to death.

The universities and colleges were hotbeds of deism and atheism. The priests of the Church of England were mostly worldly men who had nothing to offer as a cure for society's ills. Augustus Toplady (author of the beloved hymn "Rock of Ages") said that, in 1730, a converted Church of England minister was as great a wonder as a comet. The Lord's Day was the Devil's Market Day. The Bishop of Litchfield declared that there were more quarrels, more murders, more drunkenness, and more sin contrived and committed on the Lord's Day than on all the other days of the week combined. Immorality was championed and defended by the media. Bishop Butler, in the preface of one of his books, said that "it was now taken for granted that Christianity was no longer a subject for inquiry but had at length been disclosed as fictitious."

What was God's answer to such a state of affairs? Preaching! God's answer was John Wesley, a man who traveled some 250,000 miles on horseback and who preached to one and all, rich and poor, in the streets and on the highways, in barns and open fields. He is said to have preached some forty thousand sermons, and in so doing brought Britain back to God.

3. The message

Just any kind of preaching will not get the job done. Paul said, "We preach *Christ crucified*" (1 Cor. 1:23, italics added). Preaching "Christ crucified" was what did it in Paul's day and did it again in Wesley's day. "Christ crucified" was and is the message. As soon as we leave that message behind, we leave revival behind as well. The preaching that changes the world is not the kind that is so popular in most pulpits today. The preaching of psychology will never change the world nor will the preaching of "possibility thinking," however appealing they might seem to be.

That kind of preaching often draws the crowds. It often will fill big churches, but it is preaching to the mind, not to the conscience. Moreover, it is addictive. People come with notebooks in hand, eager to learn fourteen ways to deal with teenage depression or seven ways to cope with little Willy's temper tantrums. But then, the next week they want to know how to manage an unsaved husband or how to be a fulfilled single.

When we preach "Christ crucified," we bypass all that. We go to the very heart of the problem. Humanity's problems are problems of sin, guilt, and fear. It is at Calvary alone that we find the cure for those kinds of ills. Paul did not preach a creed—he preached Christ. He did not preach a program—he preached a Person. He did not preach religion—he preached redemption. We can't go wrong if we preach Christ and Him crucified.

Christ is the major theme of all the Scriptures. On the Emmaus road, Christ began with Moses and all the prophets and preached "the things concerning himself" (Luke 24:27) to those discouraged disciples. That's the message—Christ! He is *pictured* in the history books of the Old Testament, *portrayed* in the poetic books, *presented* in the Gospels, *preached* in the book of Acts, *praised* in the Epistles, and *preeminent* in the Apocalypse. We can't go wrong if we preach Christ. In fact, there is nothing else we can preach if we want to touch the mind and heart, conscience and will of people.

That is why the New Testament begins the way it does, with four Gospels each designed to give a different view of Christ. For that is what the faith is all about—Christ, and Him crucified and risen from the dead. "Christ in you, the hope of glory" as Paul puts it (Col. 1:27).

We preach "Christ crucified," Paul said—for that is at the very heart of it all. That is the message that saves. We can preach about the Holy Spirit, and so we should. We can preach about prophecy, and so we should. We can preach about prayer and Bible study and church attendance and consecration and missions, and so we should. But if we want to see people saved, if we want a breath of revival, if we want to make an impact for God upon our generation, then we must get those people to the Cross.

The visitor to London usually passes by Charing Cross. It is located in the heart of the city, and from it road distances to other parts of Britain are measured. It was here, in the year 1290, that King Edward I erected the last of a series of twelve crosses in memory of his beloved Queen Eleanor. The crosses marked the stages of the funeral procession to Westminster Abbey. That cross was destroyed in 1647 during the Civil War. A modern cross now stands in the courtyard of Charing Cross Railway Station. It was raised in 1863. In Britain, history puts down its roots and refuses to let time pass it by. Grim stories cluster around that cross, but there is one that strikes a happier note.

Years ago, a little girl visiting London with her mother became lost.

The rushing crowds had come between them, and there she stood with tearstained face, frightened and alone. A kindly policeman tried to help. "Are you lost, little girl?" he asked. "Where do you live?" The little girl did not know where she lived. It was somewhere in the sprawling city. That was about all she knew. The policeman mentioned various places hoping one of the names would spark a response. "What about Buckingham Palace or St. Paul's Cathedral or the Houses of Parliament or Big Ben? What about Westminster Abbey or the Tower?" All drew a blank.

At last he mentioned Charing Cross. "Suppose, little girl, I were to take you to Charing Cross and to the old stone cross that stands there . . ." At once the little girl responded. She knew she did not live too far from there. "Yes," she said. "That's it! If you take me to the cross, I can find my way home from there."

That, indeed, is it. We must take people to the Cross. They can find their way home from there. As the old hymn puts it:

> I must needs go home
> By the way of the cross,
> There's no other way but this;
> I shall ne'er catch sight
> Of the gates of light,
> If the way of the cross I miss.[2]

4. The mistake

"We preach Christ crucified, unto the Jews a stumblingblock, and unto the Greeks foolishness" (1 Cor. 1:23). That is the mistake—to treat the message of the Cross lightly, to underestimate its importance. Nothing could be more fatal than that. There are two kinds of people most inclined to do that—*religious* people like the Jews and *rationalistic* people like the Greeks.

The Jew was scandalized by the message and by how well Paul knew it. He had been scandalized by it himself for years. The word *stumbling block* he uses here is the word *skandalon* from which we get our

English word "scandalize." It occurs fifteen times in the New Testament. It is often translated "offense" and "offend." It is translated "stumbling block" three times. The Jews were scandalized because the One who claimed to be their Messiah was crucified. They took great offense at that, though they were the very ones who clamored for His murder on the cross.

Religious people want to *do* something for their salvation because that ministers to their pride. They refuse to believe that they are anything like as bad as God says they are, and they are offended by the preaching of the Cross. The Cross reveals how terribly wicked we are. We took God's Son, the incarnate Christ of God, crowned Him with thorns, ploughed His back with a scourge, spat in His face, and nailed Him to a cross. Whatever, in all the annals of time and eternity, could be worse than that?

Yet, God has turned that cross into an instrument of salvation. People want to *do* something; God says it is *done.* The Cross of Christ is God's one and only answer to humanity's guilt and sin. That offends the religious person just as Abel's altar scandalized Cain—especially when he discovered that God accepted Abel's offering and rejected his.

The Greek was scornful of the Cross too. The Greeks of Paul's day knew everything that was knowable, but they did not know God. They did not know what to do with their sins, nor did they want to know. When Paul tried to tell them of the One who had conquered death, their reaction was one of outright scorn. They laughed him out of court.

That, of course, is just where the academic world always sits when it comes to the preaching of Christ crucified. It sits in the seat of the scornful. The idea that a crucified, dead Jew can do for the world what physics and chemistry and biology and psychiatry cannot do strikes them as ridiculous. Tell them that Jesus is not just a crucified, dead Jew but the risen living Son of God, and they will still scoff. The great doctrine of the Christian faith, centered in the Cross and the shed blood of the Lamb, still strikes academics as foolishness. But their mistake is terrible and real.

5. The miracle

"But unto them which are called, both Jews and Greeks, Christ the power of God, and the wisdom of God" (1 Cor. 1:24). As Paul would write to the Romans, "I am not ashamed of the gospel of Christ: for it is the power of God unto salvation to every one that believeth; to the Jew first, and also to the Greek" (Rom. 1:16).

In the gospel, we have the concentrated essence of divine *omnipotence*—the power of God. In the gospel, we have the concentrated essence of divine *omniscience*—the wisdom of God. The Cross may look weak and foolish to people, but we who have been saved by it know that it is, indeed, both the wisdom and the power of God in terms of salvation.

During the Moody-Sankey evangelistic crusades in London in the years 1883–1884, D. L. Moody threw down the gauntlet before atheism and unbelief. He announced he was going to have a special service for atheists, skeptics, and freethinkers. At that time, the champion of atheism in Britain was Charles Bradlaugh. Bradlaugh ordered all of his atheist clubs closed for the night and told his followers to take up the challenge and fill the hall. Five thousand men marched into the hall from all directions and occupied every seat.

D. L. Moody preached from the text, "Their rock is not as our Rock, even our enemies themselves being judges" (Deut. 32:31). He told of the bedsides of atheists he had attended, watching as they died. Then he told of the deaths of believers he had known. He challenged his audience to judge who had had the best of it in the end, whose rock was the best in the swelling of Jordan. Reluctant tears began to flow from the eyes of some, while the majority sat defiant and determined. But as the service wore on, God broke through.

Moody made his appeal for the men to repent, believe, and be born again. One man shouted, "I can't." Another man said, "I won't." Moody, overcome with compassion, burst into tears. "It is 'I will' or 'I won't' for every man in this room tonight. The battle is on the 'will.'" Then, he told the story of the Prodigal Son and renewed his appeal. Five hundred men jumped to their feet. The Holy Spirit broke loose. All over the room men cried out, "I will! I will!" From that night to the end of the week, nearly two thousand men were drawn to Calvary. The atheist clubs never recovered their foothold in his day.

The gospel of Christ crucified was and is and ever will be *the power of God unto salvation.* To those of us who are saved, it is the power of God and the wisdom of God. Not all the power of the enemy can prevail against it.

PART 7

PERENNIAL

Thou art the everlasting Word
The Father's only Son,
God manifestly seen and heard,
And Heaven's beloved One.

In Thee, most perfectly expressed,
The Father's glories shine,
Of the full Deity possessed,
Eternally divine!

True image of the Infinite,
Whose essence is concealed;
Brightness of uncreated light,
The heart of God revealed.

But the high mysteries of His Name
The creature's grasp transcend;
The Father only, glorious claim!
The Son can comprehend.

Throughout the universe of bliss,
The center Thou, and Sun,
The eternal theme of praise is this,
To heaven's beloved One.
Worthy, O Lamb of God, art Thou,
That every knee to Thee should bow![1]
                    —Josiah Conder (1789–1855)

CHAPTER 24

WORTHY IS THE LAMB
THAT WAS SLAIN
Revelation 5:12

When He comes, He is going to:
1. Claim the rule of this world
2. Control the resources of this world
3. Confound the reasoning of this world
4. Crush the rebellion of this world
5. Command the respect of this world
6. Compel the reverence of this world
7. Convert the remnant of this world

KING GEORGE V OF ENGLAND WAS once invited to visit a children's hospital. There was great excitement in the wards as the boys and girls were prepared for the event. About midafternoon of the appointed day the king, polished, articulate, and charming, accompanied by a bevy of officials and their wives, went through the wards. He stopped at every bed to say a word to each child. Later that evening, as the head nurse was making her rounds, she found one little fellow crying. "What's the matter, Jimmy?" she asked. "I thought the king was coming," he said. "Why, Jimmy," said the nurse, "he came. He stopped by your bed and talked to you this afternoon." Jimmy remained unconvinced. "Was *that* the king?" he said, suddenly both enlightened and disappointed. "But he didn't have his crown on!"

Nearly two thousand years ago, the Son of God stepped out of eternity into time. He lived and worked among us for a little over thirty-three years. Then they crucified Him. They didn't know who He was—He did not have on His crown, and He was not on His throne. But He is coming back, and when He comes the next time, there will be no mistaking who He is. He'll have His crown on then, all right! Every knee will bow.

They are looking forward to that in heaven, as they sing His praise: "Worthy is the Lamb that was slain to receive power, and riches, and wisdom, and strength, and honor, and glory, and blessing" (Rev. 5:12). They anticipate with joyful wonder the day when the Lamb of Calvary will be crowned on Planet Earth as King of Kings and Lord of Lords.

When He comes back, the first thing the Lord will do will be to:

1. Claim the rule of this world

"Worthy is the Lamb that was slain to receive *power*" (Rev. 5:12). The original word for power is *dunamis* from which we get our English word *dynamite*. It suggests untrammeled, unhindered, unequalled power. No one is qualified to hold such power because as Lord Acton said, "All power corrupts and absolute power corrupts absolutely."[2] Only Jesus can handle absolute, limitless power.

We are reminded of what Satan offered Jesus in the Temptation. The Devil took Him up into a high mountain and showed Him all the kingdoms of the world in a moment of time. And the Devil said to Him, "All this power will I give thee, and the glory of them" (Luke 4:6). The offer of the *kingdoms,* the *power,* and the *glory* was a parody on the actual claims of Christ as cited in the Lord's Prayer. Jesus said to His Father, "Thine is the kingdom, and the power, and the glory, for ever" (Matt. 6:13).

Beware of the Devil's contracts! Quite apart from the blasphemous conditions attached to this particular contract ("if thou therefore wilt worship me," Luke 4:7), it contained some very fine print indeed. This alone would have rendered it wholly unacceptable to our Lord.

First, the Devil offered Him "the kingdoms," the divided war-torn kingdoms of this world. Jesus had not come into this world to receive "kingdoms" but to receive the kingdom.

Next Satan offered Him "the glory"—the tinsel and tarnished glory of this world along with its empty pomp and pride.

Finally, Satan offered Him "power" but it was not *dunamis* he offered—untrammeled, unhindered, unequalled power. What he offered was *exousia,* power subject to another power, that is, "delegated authority." No wonder Jesus turned it down. The inherent power that Jesus had was enough to make Satan himself tremble and flee.

The story is told of a farmer who was enraged because the highway authorities planned to put a new superhighway right through the center of his favorite field. He fought the decision as long as he could—in vain. Then he received word that the surveyors were coming to mark out the new road. He took his bull out of the barn and turned him loose in the field. The bull went and hid behind a tree. The surveyors arrived to set up their equipment, when out came the bull! They left in a hurry, hotly pursued. Once they had reached the safety of the farmhouse, one of them pulled out a document and showed it to the farmer. "Here is our authority," he said, "to survey this field." The farmer pointed to the bull. "Go and read it to him," he said. The surveyors had the *authority;* the bull had the *power.*

When Jesus comes back He is not only going to have the authority to rule this world; He is going to have the power. They are singing about that in heaven. Those nail-scarred hands will one day hold the scepter.

Then He is going to:

2. Control the resources of this world

"Worthy is the Lamb that was slain to receive . . . *riches*" (Rev. 5:12, italics added). Nobody else is qualified to receive riches. The riches and resources of this world have never been fairly divided. Not capitalism nor colonialism nor communism has given the poor a fair deal. The poor grow poorer, and the rich get richer. Under each system there are the elite, the privileged, the rich, and then there are the poor. When Jesus comes back, however, the wealth of the world will be placed in His hands. It will be different then!

When the Six-Day War erupted between the Arab States and Israel in 1967, the Arabs suddenly discovered they had a powerful weapon in their hands—oil! They formed a cartel and imposed an oil embargo on the world, especially on countries that sided with Israel. As a result, oil prices soared and for a number of years the industrialized nations trod warily, afraid of further blackmail.

The oil crisis passed as the great powers of the West discovered new sources of oil and developed alternate energy resources. Now again, the same scenario casts its shadow across the world. The bitter lesson has been brought home to the world—the resources of this planet are limited.

Ecologists divide the world's resources into two kinds. There are what we call *nonrenewable* resources—things like oil, coal, and uranium of which there are only limited amounts available. When they are gone, they are gone. Some of them are being used up at an alarming rate. There are also *renewable* resources—forests, grasslands, and the great harvests of the sea that, if properly managed, can be replenished. Some of these resources are being consumed faster than they can be replaced. We can liken these resources to capital and interest. Ecologically speaking, in some areas, we have stopped living on our interest and are now consuming our capital. Any businessman knows that kind of thing cannot go on for long.

What a day it will be for this world when all its resources are in our Lord's capable hands! There will be no more fierce competition and no more poverty then. Jesus understands the plight of the poor. He was poor Himself. He was born in a borrowed stable. When He wanted to teach the multitudes and needed a platform, He borrowed Simon Peter's boat. When He wanted to feed those same hungry throngs, He borrowed a little lad's lunch—He did not have one of His own. When

He wanted to fulfill prophecy and ride into Jerusalem, He borrowed a farmer's donkey—He had no means of transportation of His own. When He wanted to keep His last Passover and institute a new feast for a new age, He had to borrow an upper room. He died upon another man's cross, and when the soldiers cast their dice for His material possessions, all they could win were the clothes they had stripped from His back. When He was buried, it was in a borrowed tomb. Yes, Jesus knows what it is like to be poor. "Ye know the grace of our Lord Jesus Christ," says Paul, "that, though he was rich, yet for your sakes he became poor" (2 Cor. 8:9).

The day is coming when all the resources of this world will be in His hands. Then the desert will blossom as the rose, and all people will dwell under their own fig trees and under their own vines. So bountiful and prodigal will be the harvests of this coming age that "the plowman shall overtake the reaper" (Amos 9:13). Moreover, He is going to:

3. Confound the reasoning of this world

"Worthy is the Lamb that was slain to receive . . . *wisdom*" (Rev. 5:12, italics added). Paul reminds us that in Him "are hid all the treasures of wisdom" (Col. 2:3). When Christ lived on earth, He was forever opening His treasure chest to give people glimpses of the riches of His wisdom. His parables were miracles in words just as His miracles were parables in deeds. Even His enemies testified that "never a man spake like this man" (John 7:46). They said one to another, "Whence hath this man this wisdom?" (Matt. 13:54). How could He know anything? He never graduated from our schools. He doesn't have His degree.

On one occasion, He took His listeners back to the glorious days of the Hebrew Empire when Solomon sat upon the throne and when princes came from the ends of the earth to sit at his feet and drink in his wisdom. Said Jesus, with that characteristic honesty of His, "A greater than Solomon is here" (Matt. 12:42).

Today's world has little use for the wisdom of Jesus. People may pay lip service to Him on occasion, but He is ignored in the council chambers of the educators, rulers, and philosophers of this world.

The United States has effectively banned the Bible from its classrooms. Teachers can teach every law known to science except the law of sin and death—the one law that explains human behavior. We do what we do because we are what we are—sinners needing a Savior. How can anyone profess to understand human nature while ignoring *that* basic law? Schools can teach Karl Marx. They can teach the theory of evolution. They can eulogize the pagan philosophers of Greece and Rome. They can teach all that—but they must not teach the Bible.

There never was an age when people had more knowledge than today—and less wisdom. We are living in the midst of a knowledge explosion. So vast is the daily output of information that researchers often find it easier and quicker to repeat an experiment from scratch in their laboratories than to waste time trying to find out if someone has already done it. Knowledge proliferates—but there is no wisdom. We live with a new dread now that international terrorists arm themselves with nuclear weapons and biological and chemical weapons as well. We live in a world where the drug trade and organized crime go hand in hand, mocking all attempts to put a stop to their dreadful activities. Everywhere morality has been replaced by pornography, perversion, and permissiveness. We have plenty of knowledge; it is burgeoning every day, but we have no wisdom. That is our legacy for banning the Bible from our classrooms.

Just before He went to Calvary, Jesus said that in the last days there would be "perplexity" of nations (Luke 21:25). In his monumental work *An Expository Dictionary of New Testament Words,* W. E. Vine tells us that this phrase can be rendered in various ways. He suggests, "no way out" or "at a loss for a way" or "no solution to their embarrassments" or "at their wit's end" or "without resources." It would be nearly impossible to find a collection of phrases that more fittingly describe the dilemma of our day.

When Jesus comes back He will change all that. He will confound the reasoning of this world. Education will be in His hands, the Bible will become the core of the curriculum in every subject in every school, and Spirit-filled, Spirit-anointed men and women will teach the arts and the sciences. In the expressive language of the Old Testament prophet, the earth will be "full of the knowledge of the LORD, as the waters cover the sea" (Isa. 11:9). They are singing about it already in heaven!

But more! He is going to:

4. Crush the rebellion of this world

"Worthy is the Lamb that was slain to receive . . . *strength*" (Rev. 5:12, italics added). One of the great titles of the Lord in the Old Testament is "Lord of Hosts." "The LORD of is a man of war," says Moses (Exod. 15:3). The Old Testament rings with the din and noise of battle, and so does the Apocalypse. There is small need for wonder in that. This world is an armed camp, a planet under siege, in the iron grip of a terrible foe. Jesus is coming back to remove the usurper and to claim His own. The stress and strain of end-times events is already beginning to be felt.

God's plan of redemption includes both the redemption of our *persons* and the redemption of our *property*. This plan is one of the great lessons taught in the book of Ruth. Redemption, in Scripture, is twofold—redemption by *purchase* and redemption by *power*. Redemption by purchase was accomplished at the Lord's first coming. At Calvary He paid the price and secured the title deeds of this planet. Redemption by power will take place at His second coming. It is then that He will put down His foes.

The outstanding feature of our age is rebellion against authority. It begins with rebellion against parental authority in the home and swiftly grows up into a brawling maturity. We see rebellion against school authority and against governmental authority. The main characteristic of the age is lawlessness. This prevailing lawlessness will be headed up eventually by "the man of sin" (2 Thess. 2:3). The Bible calls him "the Wicked One" (1 John 2:13) or "the lawless one," as it can be rendered. He will come to power on the rising tide of widespread lawlessness already evident in our society. Active undercurrents are at work in the world that seek to break down law, order, tradition, the Judeo-Christian ethic, and all that is moral and decent. Its ultimate goal is to break down the establishment itself. These forces are essential to Satan's master plan for the end of the age (2 Thess. 2). When the Antichrist comes, he will seize upon them and direct and motivate them. He will energize them with satanic power and will ride their crest to the throne of the world. Once firmly in control, he will lead the world in one final, mad crusade against God. The focus of the great rebellion will be at Megiddo. Once the anti-God forces of the world have been drawn to that fateful place, the Lord will come and forcefully put down the rebellion of this world. Then He will rule the nations with a rod of iron and establish a thousand-year reign of righteousness (Ps. 2:9). He will also:

5. Command the respect of this world

"Worthy is the Lamb that was slain to receive . . . *honor*" (Rev. 5:12, italics added). This world gives Christ little enough honor today. The printed edition of the *Encyclopedia Britannica,* for instance, devotes five columns to Mussolini and about the same to Henry VIII. It gives two columns to Herod the Great and nearly three columns to H. G. Wells. Yet for Jesus, the most important Person ever to have lived, it gives a bare half column (about the same space it gives to vile Voltaire).

There is very little honor accorded to Jesus now. People use His lovely name as a curse word and link it to the foulest words in human speech. But the day is coming when they will be forced to honor Him.

Come back for a moment to that time in the history of the Persian Empire when the mighty Xerxes, under the influence of his evil prime minister, Haman, decided to exterminate all the Jews in his lands.

Haman was motivated by hatred of Jews in general and of Mordecai in particular. What does God do when a world superpower decides to wipe out a whole segment of the human race? He doesn't need to do very much! When Pharaoh set his hand to the same thing, God simply arranged for a princess of the realm to discover an ark among the bulrushes. In it there lay a handsome baby boy! "And, behold, the babe wept!" (Exod. 2:6). That was all God needed—a tear on the cheek of a babe!

In the days of Xerxes and Haman, all God had to do was give the king a dose of insomnia on a critical night in the story. "That night," we read, "could not the king sleep" (Esther 6:1). Neither could anyone else! The king summoned his librarian and ordered him to read to him. The librarian seized the first book that came to hand and flung it open at a random page. Then he began to read to the king about a man called Mordecai, a Jew, who had saved the king's life! "What has been done for this fellow?" demanded the king. "Nothing, sire," said the librarian.

Who should come along at that very moment but Haman, a powerful man who hated Mordecai and the Jews. The king called Haman to his side and put this question to him: "What shall be done unto the man whom the king delighteth to honour?" (Esther 6:6). Haman thought to himself, "Whom would the king want to honor more than me?" He had his answer ready. "There are three things that should be done for such a man, my lord king," he said. "First you must *prepare* him. You must send down to the royal vaults and bring out your majesty's imperial crown. Send to the royal wardrobe and bring out your majesty's robes of state. Then send to the stables and summon forth your majesty's great warhorse. Use these things, my lord king, to prepare this man. Next, your majesty, you *promote* him. You call for the highest peer of the realm, the greatest noble in the land, the man with the bluest blood, the haughtiest member of your majesty's aristocracy, and you make him this man's slave. And finally, my lord king, you *present* him. The peer of noble blood, having become this man's slave, must crown him with your majesty's royal diadem. He must then dress this favored man in your majesty's royal robes. Then, just like a common groom, he must take bit and bridle, saddle your majesty's warhorse, and lift the honored man into the saddle. Finally, before all the assembled multitudes of your majesty's imperial city, he must run sweating and perspiring down the streets, ahead of this favored individual, proclaiming, 'Thus shall it be done to the man whom the king delighteth to honour'" (Esther 6:9).

"That's very good Haman!" said the king. "Now you go and do all that for Mordecai the Jew."

What shall be done to the Man the king delighteth to honor? "Worthy is the Lamb that was slain to receive . . . honor!" The brow that once was crowned with thorns—bring forth the royal diadem and crown Him Lord of all. Those hands, once stabbed and pierced by cruel nails—bring forth the scepter of universal dominion and place it in those hands. Those feet, once torn and rent by the iron bolts of Rome—bring the world and put it beneath those feet. For "thus shall be done to the Man whom the king delighteth to honor." Moreover He will:

6. Compel the reverence of this world

"Worthy is the Lamb that was slain to receive . . . *glory*" (Rev. 5:12, italics added). That, too, is the endless theme of the redeemed in heaven. They are anticipating the day, with great joy, when heaven's Beloved will receive the glory that belongs to Him. Once, down here on earth, people spat in His face. Once, they blindfolded Him and smote Him and jeered at His claims. Once, they nailed Him to a cross of wood and lifted Him up between heaven and earth, as though He were fit for neither. The angelic hosts and the ranks of the redeemed in heaven eagerly await the day when He will come back with His crown on, indeed. It will be a different story then.

When Christ came to earth the first time, He laid aside the glory that He had with His Father before the worlds began. He was born, of all places, in a cattle shed. He was raised in a despised provincial town and was known as the carpenter's son. As Robert C. Chapman wrote:

> His life of pain and sorrow
> Was like unto His birth,
> It would not glory borrow,
> No majesty from earth.[3]

Our Lord once made a very revealing statement about glory. He picked a small wayside weed, a common hedgerow plant, and held it up before His disciples. Then going back again to the days of Solomon's empire, He said, "Solomon in all his glory was not arrayed like one of these" (Luke 12:27). The difference is evident. Solomon's glory was put on from the outside; the glory of the lily grows from within.

Thus it was with Jesus. His glory is intrinsic glory, inherent glory. When, at last, it is fully revealed, it will compel the reverence of this world. Then—

> The beauty of the Savior
> Will dazzle every eye,
> In the crowning day that's coming
> Bye and bye.[4]

Last of all, He will:

7. Convert the remnant of this world

"Worthy is the Lamb that was slain to receive . . . *blessing*" (Rev. 5:12, italics added). If there is one thing this poor world needs, it is the blessing of God. Today it is under the curse as a direct result of the Fall. All the sounds of nature are pitched in a minor key. As Paul says, "The whole creation groaneth and travaileth" (Rom. 8:22). It is a world of tears and woe. There are wars and rumors of war, famines and pestilences, disasters, persecutions, and holocausts. All that is to be changed.

When Jesus comes back there will be a massive purge of the planet. Millions upon millions of people will already have died under the judgment hand of God in the terrible and successive waves of woe that will mark the apocalyptic age. The surviving remnant will be massed against Him at Megiddo. Those who are still alive after the Battle of Armageddon will be summoned to the Valley of Jehoshaphat to be judged. A terrible weeding out will take place at this judgment. When it is over only a remnant of Jews and Gentiles will be left. These saved and regenerated individuals will be sent to repopulate and renovate the stricken earth.

Then it will be, universally, as it now is in the Psalms. The book of Psalms begins with God blessing us (Ps. 1:1), and it ends with a series of five psalms, each one a doxology of praise, rising higher and higher in ever-increasing crescendo until every tongue and voice is lifted in praise to God.

During the Millennial Age, the converted remnant and their offspring will live under the blessing of God. All the blessings of God will descend from heaven upon Jesus, and He will pass them on to us. In return, a grateful world will bless His holy name, and He will return those blessings to His Father in heaven. "Worthy is the Lamb that was slain to receive . . . blessing!" (Rev. 5:12).

So, Calvary covers it all. Calvary was conceived in the mind of God in a past eternity. Its shadow lies across the entire inspired Old Testament page. Its stark reality is detailed for us in the Gospels. Its blessed results are the themes of the Epistles. In ages yet unborn, Calvary will be the lasting wonder of all God's redeemed. We, who have been saved by the blood of His cross (Col. 1:20) will be the eternal showpiece of His grace to all other orders of creation. "Worthy is the Lamb that was slain!" *That* is the theme of those in heaven above, as it will be one day for those on earth beneath—even of those who are incarcerated in the dark regions of the lost. Every knee shall bow and every tongue confess that Jesus Christ is Lord.

THINGS THAT TOOK PLACE AFTER THE FOUNDATION OF THE WORLD

AS TO EXACTLY *when* THESE THINGS occurred, we are not told. Some of them may have happened very soon after the earth's foundations were laid.

1. For one thing *sin* reared its head, and death followed sin. Sin has left its mark on both heaven and earth. They are tied together in the original creation (Gen. 1:1) and in the catastrophe of sin, judgment, and death. Sin did not begin on earth. It began in heaven; not with Adam and Eve (Gen. 3) but with Lucifer, an angelic being of enormous power. Since sin has defiled both realms, God intends to create a new heaven and a new earth (Rev. 21:1, note the *polysyndeton*).

2. Lucifer was a being of great beauty and power. He was known as "the anointed cherub." Music seems to have been one of his skills. Possibly he was the choirmaster of heaven. In time, pride filled his heart. He aspired to God's throne and became the author of

the mystery of iniquity. Ezekiel 28:12–15 and Isaiah 14:9–14 reveal these things. We infer from Revelation 12:3–4 that one-third of the angelic beings joined Satan in his rebellion against God. The Lord Jesus was an eyewitness of these things (Luke 10:18).

3. It is possible that the original earth of Genesis 1:1 was inhabited by a pre-Adamic race of beings. The Lord Jesus acknowledged Satan to be "the prince of this world" (John 12:31; 14:30). Possibly Satan's original sphere of rule took in earth and the entire solar system. G. H. Pember has suggested that the fossil remains that litter our planet are those of creatures anterior to Adam. He points out they "show evidence of disease, death, and mutual destruction." He says that they "have a sin stained history of their own, a history which ended in ruin both of themselves and their habitation."[1]

4. The angelic beings who joined Satan in his rebellion now rule in "the heavenly places." They are fallen, wicked, and mighty "principalities, . . . powers, . . . rulers of the darkness of this world, . . . spiritual wickedness in high places" (Eph. 6:12).

5. Possibly if a pre-Adamic race of humanoids did once inhabit this planet and if they were involved somehow in Satan's fall, then possibly they were disembodied in the catastrophic overthrow described in Genesis 1:2. Pember thinks so. He says:

> Certainly, one oft-recorded fact seems to confirm such a theory: for we read that the demons are continually seizing upon the bodies of human beings and endeavoring to use them as their own. And may not this propensity indicate a wearisome lack of ease, a wandering unrest, arising from a sense of incompleteness, a longing to escape from the intolerable condition of being unclothed—for which they were not created—so intense that if they can satisfy its cravings in no other way, they will even enter the bodies of swine. We find no such propensity on the part of Satan and his angels. They doubtless still retain their ethereal bodies.[2]

Indeed there is evidence from Scripture that angelic beings can materialize at will and perform physical functions such as eating a meal or cohabiting with women.

6. All this was foreseen by God. Even before Lucifer was created, God decided what His response would be. He would localize sin and bring it to a head at one specific spot in the universe—Planet Earth. No wonder, in describing the original creation, the Holy Spirit makes immediate strategic use of that mighty, little word *and.* So, we have, "In the beginning God created the heaven *and* the earth" (Gen. 1:1).

7. So then sin entered, took hold in heaven, and spread to the pristine earth. A catastrophic judgment followed both in heaven and on earth, and a wrecked and ruined planet spun empty and void in space while fallen Lucifer retired into the shadows to watch and plan. God also made His next move. One member of the Godhead came down to take control of things here on earth. "The spirit of God," we read, "moved upon the face of the waters" (Gen. 1:2). In due time the Holy Spirit took charge of the total renovation of the earth (Gen. 1:3–2:25), restoring it to its original pristine glory. Satan, deposed from his former estates, watched the re-creation of the earth and the creation of Adam and Eve with a malice and rage that defies description.

8. Disguised as a serpent, Satan invaded our planet, not knowing that he was falling into a trap prepared before the foundation of the world. He seduced Eve, subverted Adam, and merged back into the shadows to enjoy their encounter with the living God. What he heard was God pronouncing judgment upon the serpent himself and announcing a glorious plan of salvation for the fallen pair.

9. The apostle Peter drops a hint about these prehistoric matters. He says, "The heavens were of old, and the earth standing out of the water and in the water: Whereby the world that then was, being overflowed with water, perished" (2 Peter 3:5–6). This is apparently a reference to the judgment that overtook the first creation described in Genesis 1:1–2. "But the heavens and the

earth, which are now, by the same word are kept in store, reserved unto fire against the day of judgment and perdition of ungodly men" (2 Peter 3:7). This is a reference to the final judgment of this planet that will result in the creation of a new heaven and a new earth (Rev. 21:1–8). Peter is not concerned here with the flood of Noah's day (though he is fully aware of it, see 1 Peter 3:18–22). As for the final judgment of the heaven and the earth, Peter's description of it is horrific (2 Peter 3:9–13).

Endnotes

Chapter 1

1. Augustus Toplady, "Rock of Ages," in *Sacred Songs and Solos* (London: Morgan and Scott, n.d.), no. 237.
2. For important events that took place after the foundation of the world, see the appendix.
3. G. Campbell Morgan, *The Crisis of the Christ* (London: Revell, 1903–1906), 229, 231.

Chapter 2

1. Fanny Crosby, "Near the Cross," in *Sacred Songs and Solos* (London: Morgan and Scott, n.d.), no. 97.
2. Elizabeth C. Clephane and Ira D. Sankey, "The Ninety and Nine," in *Sacred Songs and Solos* (London: Morgan and Scott, n.d.), no. 154.

Chapter 3

1. Isaac Watts, "Alas, and Did My Savior Bleed," in *Hymns of Worship and Remembrance* (Belle Chasse, La.: Truth and Praise, 1950), no. 143.

Chapter 4

1. James Allen; altered by Walter Shirley, "Sweet the Moments, Rich in Blessing," in *Hymns and Some Spiritual Songs Selected for the Little Flock* (London: G. Morrish, 1881), no. 252.

Chapter 5

1. Isaac Watts, "Not All the Blood of Beasts," in *Hymns of Worship and Remembrance* (Belle Chasse, La.: Truth and Praise, 1950), no. 100.

2. D. M. Panton, "Expiation by Blood," *Present Day Pamphlets* (London: Alfred Holness, 1914), no. 9.

Chapter 6

1. J. Denham Smith, "Rise My Soul! Behold 'Tis Jesus," in *Hymns of Worship and Remembrance* (Belle Chasse, La.: Truth and Praise, 1950), no. 120.

2. Robert Chapman, "No Bone of Thee Was Broken," in *Hymns of Worship and Remembrance* (Belle Chasse, La.: Truth and Praise, 1950), no. 99.

Chapter 7

1. H. Gratton Guinness, "Crowned with Thorns upon the Tree," in *Hymns of Worship and Remembrance* (Belle Chasse, La.: Truth and Praise, 1950), no. 150.

2. Charles Dickens, *Oliver Twist* (Oxford: Oxford University Press, n.d.).

Chapter 8

1. Isaac Watts, "When I Survey the Wondrous Cross," in *Hymns of Worship and Remembrance* (Belle Chasse, La.: Truth and Praise, 1950), no. 188.

Chapter 9

1. Ann Ross Cousin, "O Christ, What Burdens Bowed Thy Head," in *Hymns of Worship and Remembrance* (Belle Chasse, La.: Truth and Praise, 1950), no. 165.

2. This whole question is thoroughly explored in J. B. Phillips, *Your God Is Too Small* (New York: Macmillan, n.d.).

Chapter 10

1. Philip P. Bliss, "Hallelujah! What a Savior," in *Hymns of Worship and Remembrance* (Belle Chasse, La.: Truth and Praise, 1950), no. 96.
2. A. E. Wilder Smith, *The Paradox of Pain* (Wheaton: Harold Shaw, 1971), 46–53.

Chapter 11

1. Elizabeth C. Clephane, "The Ninety and Nine," in *Sacred Songs and Solos* (London: Morgan and Scott, n.d.), no. 97.
2. Ann Ross Cousin, "O Christ, What Burdens Bowed Thy Head," in *Hymns of Worship and Remembrance* (Belle Chasse, La.: Truth and Praise, 1950), no. 165.
3. Katherine A. M. Kelly, "Oh Make Me Understand It," in *Scripture Union Choruses* (London: Scripture Union, 1921), bk. 1, no. 131.
4. Elizabeth C. Clephane, "The Ninety and Nine," in *Sacred Songs and Solos* (London: Morgan and Scott, n.d.), no. 97.

Chapter 12

1. Albert B. Simpson, "What Will You Do with Jesus?" in *Great Hymns of the Faith* (Fort Dodge, Iowa: Gospel Perpetuating Fund, 1952), no. 111.
2. Frederic W. Farrar, *Life of Christ* (New York: World Publishing, n.d.), 2:331.
3. Ibid.
4. Ibid., 2:332.
5. Mary Bowles Peters, "O Blessed Lord, What Hast Thou Done," *Hymns of Worship and Remembrance* (Belle Chasse, La.: Truth and Praise, 1950), no. 101.

Chapter 13

1. Jenny Evelyn Hussey, "Lead Me to Calvary," in *New Songs of Praise and Power* (New York: Hall-Mack, 1921; reprint, Carol Stream, Ill.: Hope Publishing, 1949), no. 176.
2. Robert C. Chapman, "Jesus in His Heavenly Glory," *Hymns of Worship and Remembrance* (Belle Chasse, La.: Truth and Praise, 1950), no. 76.
3. Frederic W. Farrar, *Life of Christ* (New York: World Publishing, n.d.), 2:428.

Chapter 14

1. R. Lowry, "Low in the Grave He Lay," in *Hymns of Worship and Remembrance* (Belle Chasse, La.: Truth and Praise, 1950), no. 257.
2. Joseph Bryant Rotherham, *The Emphasized Bible* (Grand Rapids: Kregel, 1959), 699.
3. Robert Chapman, "Oh My Savior Crucified," in *Hymns of Worship and Remembrance* (Belle Chasse, La.: Truth and Praise, 1950), no. 171.
4. That the only time the Holy Spirit is said to have taken bodily form was at Christ's baptism was no accident (Luke 3:22). Nor was it merely incidental that He took the form of a dove. That takes us right back to the Flood. When the rain stopped, Noah sent forth a dove. The gentle creature found no resting place as it flew above the waters, so it returned to the ark. Just so, ever since the Fall, the Dove of God has found no resting place on earth—until Jesus came. Then the dove descended, and there on Jesus it abode.

Chapter 15

1. Mary Bowles Peters, "The Holiest We Enter," in *Hymns of Worship and Remembrance* (Belle Chasse, La.: Truth and Praise, 1950), no. 123.
2. Henry Barraclough, "Ivory Palaces," in *Great Hymns of the Faith* (Fort Dodge, Iowa : Gospel Perpetuating Fund, 1952), no. 122.
3. T. C. Hammond, *The One Hundred Texts of the Irish Church Missions* (London: Marshal, Morgan & Scott Ltd, 1952), 156.

Chapter 16

1. Thomas Kelly, "Look, Ye Saints! The Sight Is Glorious," in *Hymns of Worship and Remembrance* (Belle Chasse, La.: Truth and Praise, 1950), no. 84.

Chapter 17

1. W. M'K. Darwood, "On Calvary's Brow My Savior Died," in *Hymns of Worship and Remembrance* (Belle Chasse, La.: Truth and Praise, 1950), no. 174.
2. Isaac Watts, "Alas and Did My Savior Bleed," in *Hymns of Worship and Remembrance* (Belle Chasse, La.: Truth and Praise, 1950), no. 143.

Chapter 18

1. Philip B. Bliss, "My Redeemer," in *Great Hymns of the Faith* (Fort Dodge, Iowa: Gospel Perpetuating Fund, 1960), no. 488.

Chapter 19

1. Inglis Fleming, "We Worship Thee," in *Hymns of Worship and Remembrance* (Belle Chasse, La.: Truth and Praise, 1950), 129.

Chapter 20

1. Joseph Hoskins, "Behold! Behold the Lamb of God," in *Hymns of Worship and Remembrance* (Belle Chasse, La.: Truth and Praise, 1950), no. 146.

Chapter 21

1. Mrs. J. A. Trench, "Death and Judgment Are Behind Us, Grace and Glory Are Before," in *Hymns and Some Spiritual Songs Selected for the Little Flock* (London: G. Morrish, 1881), no. 254.

Chapter 22

1. Elizabeth C. Clephane, "Beneath the Cross of Jesus," in *English Hymnal with Tunes,* 2d ed. (London: Oxford University Press, 1933), no. 567.
2. Horatius Bonar, "No Blood, No Altar Now," in *Hymns of Worship and Remembrance* (Belle Chasse, La.: Truth and Praise, 1950), no. 98.
3. John Bunyan, *The Pilgrim's Progress* (Philadelphia: Universal Book and Bible House, 1933), 38–39.
4. Ibid., 65–70.

Chapter 23

1. Robert C. Chapman, "Oh My Savior Crucified," in *Hymns of Worship and Remembrance* (Belle Chasse, La.: Truth and Praise, 1950), no. 171.
2. Jessie B. Pounds, "The Way of the Cross Leads Home," in *Living Praises No. 2* (St. Louis: Christian Publishing Co., 1906), no. 972.

Chapter 24

1. Josiah Conder, "Thou Are the Everlasting Word," in *Hymns of Worship and Remembrance* (Belle Chasse, La.: Truth and Praise, 1950), no. 127.

2. *The Oxford Dictionary of Quotations* (Oxford: Oxford University Press, 1953), 1.

3. Robert C. Chapman, "No Bone of Thee Was Broken," *Hymns of Worship and Remembrance* (Belle Chasse, La.: Truth and Praise, 1950), no. 99.

4. D. H. Whittle, "The Crowning Day," in *The Otterbein Hymnal* (Dayton, Ohio: United Brethren Publishing House, 1892), no. 160.

Appendix

1. G. H. Pember, *Earth's Earliest Ages* (London: Revell, n.d.), 35.

2. Ibid., 72.

Hymn Index

Scripture Index